China's Foreign Investment Legal Regime

China has developed a piecemeal pattern of regulating foreign investment since the end of the 1970s. The latest law is the Foreign Investment Law (FIL), which became effective on 1 January 2020. The groundbreaking new FIL is well acknowledged for its promises and affirmations pledged to investors, signalling China's eagerness to improve its investment environment and regain momentum for investment growth.

This book provides an updated and holistic understanding of the key features of the regulatory regime on foreign investment in China with a critical analysis of laws and their implementation. It also examines sensitive and complex legal issues relevant to foreign investment beyond the 2020 FIL and new developments on foreign-related dispute settlement.

The book uses cases of success and failure to illustrate the nuances and differences between law and practice regarding foreign investment. Considering China's magnitude in the global economy and the weighty role of the regulatory system on foreign investment in China, this book is of great interest to a wide audience including academics in the field of investment law, legal practitioners, policymakers, and master's students in law and in management.

Yuwen Li is a Professor of Chinese law and Director of Erasmus China Law Centre at Erasmus University Rotterdam, the Netherlands.

Cheng Bian is an Academic Researcher at Erasmus China Law Centre and Erasmus School of Law, Erasmus University Rotterdam, the Netherlands.

Routledge Studies in Asian Law

Rethinking South China Sea Disputes
The Untold Dimensions and Great Expectations
Katherine Hui-Yi Tseng

Civil Unrest and Governance in Hong Kong
Law and Order from Historical and Cultural Perspectives
Edited by Michael H.K. Ng and John D. Wong

Writing Chinese Laws
The Form and Function of Legal Statutes Found in the Qin Shuihudi Corpus
Ernest Caldwell

National identity and Japanese revisionism
Abe Shinzō's Vision of a Beautiful Japan and Its Limits
Michal Kolmaš

Constitutional Remedies in Asia
Edited by Po Jen Yap

Chinese Legal Culture and Constitutional Order
Shiping Hua

Land Law and Disputes in Asia
In Search of an Alternative for Development
Edited by Brian Z. Tamanaha, Narufumi Kadomatsu and Yuka Kaneko

China's Foreign Investment Legal Regime
Progress and Limitations
Yuwen Li and Cheng Bian

For more information about this series, please visit: https://www.routledge.com
/asianstudies/series/RSIAL

China's Foreign Investment Legal Regime

Progress and Limitations

Yuwen Li and Cheng Bian

Routledge
Taylor & Francis Group

LONDON AND NEW YORK

First published 2022
by Routledge
2 Park Square, Milton Park, Abingdon, Oxon OX14 4RN

and by Routledge
605 Third Avenue, New York, NY 10158

Routledge is an imprint of the Taylor & Francis Group, an informa business

© 2022 Yuwen Li and Cheng Bian

British Library Cataloguing-in-Publication Data
A catalogue record for this book is available from the British Library

Library of Congress Cataloging-in-Publication Data
A catalog record has been requested for this book

ISBN: 9780367768881 (hbk)
ISBN: 9780367768898 (pbk)
ISBN: 9781003168805 (ebk)

DOI: 10.4324/9781003168805

Typeset in Galliard
by Deanta Global Publishing Services, Chennai, India

Contents

List of figures	vii
List of tables	viii
Abbreviations	ix
Acknowledgements	xiii

Introduction   1

1 The evolving characteristics of the foreign investment legal regime in China   16

   1.1 The five periods of development   16
   1.2 The legal panorama of foreign investment   31
   1.3 Key features of the 2019 FIL   37
   1.4 Conclusion   44

2 Market access and national treatment   46

   2.1 Market access: Relaxation and limitations   46
   2.2 The negative list approach   58
   2.3 National treatment post-establishment in the FIL   65
   2.4 Conclusion   71

3 Foreign mergers and acquisitions of Chinese enterprises   73

   3.1 The status quo *of foreign takeovers in China   73*
   3.2 Foreign takeovers of non-listed companies   75
   3.3 Foreign investment in listed companies   83
   3.4 Foreign complaints about the Chinese M&A market   90
   3.5 Conclusion   100

4 National security review of foreign investment 102

   4.1 *The legal framework relating to national security* 102
   4.2 *The evolutional trajectory of national security*
      review of foreign investment 107
   4.3 *The substantive and procedural review regime* 110
   4.4 *Potential improvement in the national security*
      review of foreign investment 115
   4.5 *Conclusion* 119

5 Protection of foreign investors' intellectual property 120

   5.1 *The legal framework of intellectual property rights* 120
   5.2 *Forced transfer of technology* 136
   5.3 *Protection of commercial secrets* 147
   5.4 *Conclusion* 150

6 Dispute settlement: Foreign-related arbitration 151

   6.1 *The dynamics of law on foreign-related arbitration* 151
   6.2 *Internationalization of arbitration institutions* 154
   6.3 *Ambiguity and trend on foreign arbitration*
      institutions in China 160
   6.4 *Changing policies on foreign arbitration institutions* 167
   6.5 *Experimentation on interim measures by courts* 169
   6.6 *New developments on judicial review* 171
   6.7 *Conclusion* 181

7 Dispute settlement: Investor–state arbitration 182

   7.1 *China as a respondent* 182
   7.2 *Interpretation of 'the amount of compensation*
      for expropriation' 187
   7.3 *Exhaustion of local remedies* 193
   7.4 *Selection of arbitration institutions* 195
   7.5 *Enforcement of arbitral awards* 197
   7.6 *China's position on ISDS reform* 200
   7.7 *Conclusion* 201

   Index 203

Figures

I.1　FDI inflow in China 1979–2019 (billion USD)　　　　　2
I.2　Corporate forms of FIEs in China until 2019　　　　　3
3.1　Value of greenfield and foreign M&A investment
　　　in China 2004–2018 (billion USD)　　　　　74
3.2　Chinese inbound M&A and Chinese outbound
　　　M&A 2004–2018 (billion USD)　　　　　90
6.1　Annual foreign-related commercial arbitration cases
　　　accepted by CIETAC and BAC (2010–2020)　　　　　155

Tables

2.1 The current legal framework of market access for foreign
     greenfield investment   52
2.2 Negative lists in China   60
2.3 Negative Lists for Foreign Investment 2017–2020   63
3.1 Possible approval procedures for foreign takeovers of
     domestic companies   78
3.2 Qualifications of foreign investors on the Chinese
     stock market   84
4.1 China's national security-related laws   107
7.1 China as a respondent in ISA   183
7.2 Interpretation of 'the amount of compensation for
     expropriation' in first-generation Chinese BITs   190

Abbreviations

AI	Artificial Intelligence
AL	Arbitration Law
AML	Anti-Monopoly Law
AMR	Administration for Market Regulation
BAC	Beijing Arbitration Commission
BIT	Bilateral Investment Treaty
CAI	Comprehensive Agreement on Investment
CBIRC	China Banking and Insurance Regulatory Commission
CEPA	Closer Economic Partnership Arrangement
CFIUS	Committee on Foreign Investment in the United States
CICC	China International Commercial Court
CIETAC	China International Economic and Trade Arbitration Commission
CJV	Contractual Joint Venture
CLS	Company Limited by Shares
CNIPA	China National Intellectual Property Administration
CNSC	Central National Security Commission
CPC	Communist Party of China
CPL	Civil Procedure Law
CSRC	China Securities Regulatory Commission
EJV	Equity Joint Venture
EU	European Union
FDI	Foreign Direct Investment
FIE	Foreign-Invested Enterprise
FIL	Foreign Investment Law
FRAND	Fair, Reasonable and Non-Discriminatory
FTA	Free Trade Agreement
FTT	Forced Transfer of Technology
GATT	General Agreement on Tariffs and Trade
GDP	Gross Domestic Product
GDR	Global Depositary Receipt
HFTP	Hainan Free Trade Port
HKIAC	Hong Kong International Arbitration Centre

HPC	High People's Court
ICC	International Chamber of Commerce
ICSID	International Centre for Settlement of Investment Disputes
ICT	Information and Communication Technology
IIA	International Investment Agreement
IMF	International Monetary Fund
IP	Intellectual Property
IPC	Intermediate People's Court
IPO	Initial Public Offering
ISA	Investor–State Arbitration
ISDS	Investor–State Dispute Settlement
IT	Information Technology
JV	Joint Venture
LAC	Local Arbitration Commission
LLC	Limited Liability Company
M&A	Mergers and Acquisitions
MIC	Multilateral Investment Court
MNE	Multinational Enterprise
MOFCOM	Ministry of Commerce
NDRC	National Development and Reform Commission
NEEQ	National Equities Exchange and Quotations
NPC	National People's Congress
NYSE	New York Stock Exchange
OECD	Organisation for Economic Co-operation and Development
PBoC	People's Bank of China
PCA	Permanent Court of Arbitration
PFTZ	Pilot Free Trade Zone
PRC	People's Republic of China
QFII	Qualified Foreign Institutional Investor
QFLP	Qualified Foreign Limited Partner
RMB	Renminbi
SAFE	State Administration of Foreign Exchange
SAIC	State Administration of Industry and Commerce
SAMR	State Administration for Market Regulation
SAR	Special Administrative Region
SASAC	State-Owned Assets Supervision and Administration Commission
SCIA	Shenzhen Court of International Arbitration
SDNY	Southern District of New York
SEP	Standard Essential Patent
SEZ	Special Economic Zone
SGCA	Singapore Court of Appeal
SGHC	Singapore High Court
SHIAC	Shanghai International Arbitration Centre
SIAC	Singapore International Arbitration Centre

SOE	State-Owned Enterprise
SPC	Supreme People's Court
TRIPS	Agreement on Trade-Related Aspects of Intellectual Property Rights
UK	United Kingdom
UNCITRAL	United Nations Commission on International Trade Law
UNCTAD	United Nations Conference on Trade and Development
US	United States
USD	United States Dollar
USTR	United States Trade Representative
VCLT	Vienna Convention on the Law of Treaties
VIE	Variable Interest Entity
WFOE	Wholly Foreign-Owned Enterprise
WIPO	World Intellectual Property Organization
WTO	World Trade Organization

Acknowledgements

In March 2019, the National People's Congress of China promulgated the first unified Foreign Investment Law (FIL). The timing of passing the FIL is interesting as it is in the midst of the US-China Trade War. Recognizing China's intention to use the FIL to show its willingness to address some of the investment-related complaints raised by the United States, questions arose as to whether the FIL could contribute to mitigating the considerable tension in the US-China trade and investment relationship. Furthermore, what are the innovative and substantive features of the FIL? Can these features be implemented in such a way that meets the wide-ranging expectations both from China and abroad? Small wonder the new FIL has generated a lot of professional interest, including ours.

However, writing this book was not on our 2021 agenda. For this our sincere thanks go to Yongling Lam – the book editor for Business Management and Economics at Routledge in Singapore, who has taken the initiative to contact us to write a small book on China's new FIL with a length of approx. 50,000 words. After two anonymous reviews of our book proposal, we were told that we could proceed with writing the book up to a length of 100,000 words in view of the complexity and significance of China's foreign investment legal regime. We appreciate Lam's invitation and the two reviewers' supportive words which inspired us to start this book project.

In the process of writing, we have received valuable comments and suggestions from a number of expert colleagues and friends. Particularly, we would like to express our sincere gratitude to: Manjiao Chi, Professor of international law at China University of International Business and Economics in Beijing; Tianxiang He, Assistant Professor at the School of Law of City University of Hong Kong; Richard Wagner, lawyer at Allen & Overy in Hong Kong; Melody Wang, lawyer at Allen & Overy in Beijing; and Teng Wang, lawyer, China representative at Taylor Wessing in London. We enjoyed our discussions with each of them on those issues which gave rise to different opinions. Their views have stimulated us to rethink certain matters and to provide critical, yet objective analysis as much as we could. Of course, in its last analysis, we are responsible for all views and errors in this book.

Needless to say, the year of 2021 has been difficult for all, as the COVID-19 continued to spread. We would like to express our deepest gratitude to Cheng Bian's family in China and Yuwen Li's family in the Netherlands, for their patience and resilience that empower us in writing this book despite all the disturbance and sadness associated with the pandemic.

Yuwen Li
Cheng Bian
Rotterdam, December 2021

Introduction

In just three decades, from 1979 when China commenced the 'reform and opening up' policy to 2010, China became the world's second-largest economy after the United States (US) and has successfully maintained this position since then.[1] This meteoric growth in China's gross domestic product (GDP) is accompanied by other significant achievements and improvements. For instance, China ranks 31st out of 190 economics on the Ease of Doing Business 2019, an index devised by the World Bank to evaluate the level of conduciveness of the regulatory environment of a state for a foreign investor to start and operate a business.[2] China also performs considerably well in its innovation capabilities, as it ranks 14th among 131 economies in the Global Innovation Index 2020 compiled by World Intellectual Property Organization (WIPO).[3] However, according to the Corruption Perceptions Index 2020, China ranks 78th out of 179 economies at the level of government cleanness, transparency and integrity.[4]

The most impressive indicator of China's economic success is its allure to foreign direct investment (FDI). From 2017 to 2020, China was the world's second-biggest FDI recipient for four consecutive years, second only to the US.[5] Amid the looming Covid-19 pandemic in 2020, although global FDI inflow decreased by 35% from the previous year, China was still able to maintain a slight increase, attracting an FDI inflow of 149 billion United States dollars (USD).[6] In 2020, FDI in China alone accounted for 14.9% of global FDI inflow.[7] FDI

---

1 In 2010, the US had a GDP of 14.9 trillion USD, and China 6 trillion USD. In 2020, the US had a GDP of 20.9 trillion USD, and China 14.7 trillion USD. World Bank, Data GDP – China, United States, https://data.worldbank.org/indicator/NY.GDP.MKTP.CD?locations =CN-US, last accessed on 1 July 2021.
2 World Bank, Ease of Doing Business Rankings, https://www.doingbusiness.org/en/rankings, last accessed on 1 July 2021.
3 Soumitra Dutta, Bruno Lanvin and Sacha Wunsch-Vincent (eds.), *Global Innovation Index 2020* (Geneva: WIPO, 2020), p. 239.
4 Transparency International, Corruption Perceptions Index 2020, https://www.transparency .org/en/cpi/2020/index/chn, last accessed on 1 July 2021.
5 UNCTAD, *World Investment Reports 2018–2021* (New York: UN Publications, 2018–2021).
6 UNCTAD, *World Investment Report 2021* (New York: UN Publications, 2021), p. 5.
7 Global FDI inflow in 2020 recorded 1 trillion USD. Ibid, p. 2.

DOI: 10.4324/9781003168805-1

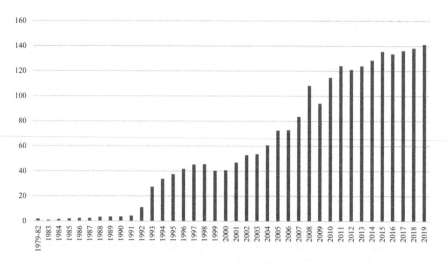

Figure I.1 FDI inflow in China 1979–2019 (billion USD) (Source: MOFCOM, 中国外资统计公报2020 (Statistical Bulletin of FDI in China 2020), http://images.mofcom.gov.cn/wzs/202011/20201111182920243 .pdf, last accessed on 1 July 2021, p. 26. UNCTAD sources show a high level of conformity with MOFCOM sources. For example, UNCTAD shows that FDI inflow in China in 2019 recorded 141 billion USD, which was almost identical to 141.23 billion USD as provided by MOFCOM. This book adopts sources from MOFCOM to maintain statistical consistency. UNCTAD, *World Investment Report 2020* (New York: UN Publications, 2020), p. 12.)

in China has witnessed a steady and robust growth since 1979 (see Figure I.1). From 1983 to 2019, FDI in China recorded an average annual growth rate of 15%,[8] while during the same period global FDI inflow was at an average annual growth rate of 10.1%.[9] This means that Chinese FDI inflow grew at a faster pace than the global average and was thus a major propeller of global FDI growth in the past four decades. In terms of corporate forms of foreign-invested enterprises (FIEs) in China, more than one million FIEs had been established by the end of 2019, and wholly foreign-owned enterprises (WFOEs) remained the most prevalent entry model (see Figure I.2).

8 Calculated by the authors, source obtained from MOFCOM, *Statistical Bulletin of FDI in China 2020*, http://images.mofcom.gov.cn/wzs/202011/20201111182920243.pdf, last accessed on 1 July 2021, p. 26.
9 Global FDI inflow was 53.073 billion USD in 1983, and 1744 billion USD in 2019. World Bank, Foreign Direct Investment, World Net Inflows 1970–2019, https://data.worldbank .org/indicator/BX.KLT.DINV.CD.WD, last accessed on 1 July 2021.

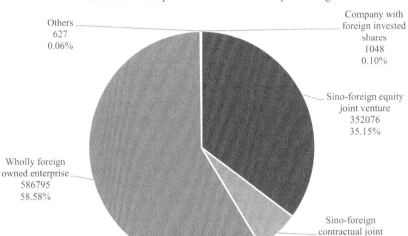

Number of enterprises established and percentage

Others
627
0.06%

Company with
foreign invested
shares
1048
0.10%

Sino-foreign equity
joint venture
352076
35.15%

Wholly foreign
owned enterprise
586795
58.58%

Sino-foreign
contractual joint
venture
61089
6.10%

Figure I.2 Corporate forms of FIEs in China until 2019 (Source: MOFCOM, 中国外资统计公报2020 (Statistical Bulletin of FDI in China 2020), http://images.mofcom.gov.cn/wzs/202011/20201111182920243 .pdf, last accessed on 1 July 2021, p. 2.)

It is widely acknowledged that FDI has contributed significantly to China's economic and social development over the past four decades. One study found that FDI has contributed 33% of China's total GDP and 27% of China's employment in 2013.[10] Local statistics demonstrate similar results. For example, it was reported that in 2019 FIEs in Shanghai only accounted for 2% of registered enterprises, but made up 20% of employment, 27% of GDP, 33% of tax revenue, 60% of industrial production value, and 65% of import and export.[11] Many factors contribute to China's appeal to foreign investment. The sheer size of the Chinese market alone is an advantage that is hardly replicable anywhere else. This is accompanied by a relatively cheap and educated workforce, state-of-the-art infrastructure, a stable political regime, and accessibility to production resources.[12]

10 Michael J. Enright, *Developing China: The Remarkable Impact of Foreign Direct Investment* (Abingdon and New York: Routledge, 2017).
11 Juan Zou and Sisi Chen, '上海高质量发展调研行 外企以约2%的数量贡献20%的就业' (Shanghai High-Quality Development Survey: FIEs Take 2% of Registered Enterprises but 20% of Employment), *The Paper*, 10 April 2019, https://www.thepaper.cn/newsDetail _forward_3278199, last accessed on 1 July 2021.
12 Andrew Bloomenthal, 'Six Factors Driving Investment in China', *Investopedia*, 30 April 2020, https://www.investopedia.com/articles/economics/09/factors-drive-investment-in -china.asp, last accessed on 11 August 2021.

Foreign companies remain attracted to investing in China for two principal reasons. First and foremost, multinational enterprises (MNEs) in China gain relatively high investment returns in general. One study found that between 2002 and 2012, FDI in China generated a profit of 9.4%, compared to 5.8% for FDI in the US.[13] It is reported that 490 of the top 500 Fortune Global companies invested in China in 2019.[14] A second reason is MNEs' global strategy of locating themselves in China to achieve low production costs and high production efficiency. MNEs' operation in China not only contributes to China's economic development by bringing in capital, advanced technology and managerial expertise but also plays an integral and sometimes irreplaceable role in the MNEs' global production and value chain. For example, it is reported that Apple assembles the majority of its products in China because only Chinese factories have the capacity to support Apple's high global demand, and producing an iPhone in China costs an estimated 65 USD less than producing one in the US.[15] Tesla China, the first WFOE in automobile manufacturing in China, set up its Shanghai Gigafactory and began production in December 2019. According to Tesla, its Shanghai factory had an installed annual capacity of 450,000 cars in 2020, which accounted for more than 40% of its global production capacity.[16] The cost of production in Shanghai is estimated to be 20% to 28% less than in the US factory.[17]

In the context of China's outstanding performance in attracting FDI and availing foreign businesses, China's foreign investment regulatory regime has become the focus of both positive and negative attention among scholars, practitioners, foreign investors and other stakeholders.[18] Since the inception of its economic

---

13 Ryan Rutkowski, 'China Maintains Its Allure for Foreign Firms', *PIIE*, 28 January 2014, https://www.piie.com/blogs/china-economic-watch/china-maintains-its-allure-foreign-firms, last accessed on 1 July 2021.

14 'China Attracts Investment from 98% of Fortune Global 500 Companies', *People's Daily*, 22 August 2019, http://en.people.cn/n3/2019/0822/c90000-9608286.html, last accessed on 1 July 2021.

15 Charles Duhigg and Keith Bradsher, 'How the U.S. Lost Out on iPhone Work', *The New York Times*, 21 January 2012, https://www.nytimes.com/2012/01/22/business/apple-america-and-a-squeezed-middle-class.html?_r=1&ref=charlesduhigg&pagewanted=all, last accessed on 1 July 2021.

16 The total installed annual capacity in 2020 is 1,050,000 cars. Tesla, Q4 and FY2020 Update, https://tesla-cdn.thron.com/static/1LRLZK_2020_Q4_Quarterly_Update_Deck_-_Searchable_LVA2GL.pdf?xseo=&response-content-disposition=inline%3Bfilename%3D%22TSLA-Q4-2020-Update.pdf%22, last accessed on 15 June 2021, p. 8.

17 Michelle Toh, 'Tesla's China Factory Is About to Play an Even Bigger Role in Its Global Ambitions', *CNN Business*, 21 October 2020, https://edition.cnn.com/2020/10/21/business/tesla-model-3-china-europe-intl-hnk/index.html, last accessed on 1 July 2021.

18 For a critical analysis on the legal environment and legal risks for FIEs in China, see Shoushuang Li, *The Legal Environment and Risks for Foreign Investment in China* (Berlin: Springer, 2007). For an overview of Chinese FDI inflow and outflow by country and region, see Xiuping Zhang and Bruce P. Corrie, *Investing in China and Chinese Investment Abroad* (Singapore: Springer, 2018). For a historical and comprehensive overview of China's FDI regulatory regime, see Tarrant Mahony, *Foreign Investment Law in China: Regulation, Practice and Con-*

reform and opening-up in 1979, China's foreign investment policy has been characterized by a dichotomy of incentives and control.[19] A dual-track system has been applied which separates the laws and regulations applying to FIEs from those applying to domestic enterprises in regard to establishment and business operation,[20] although the dual-track system has gradually become less distinct over time. In terms of incentives, FIEs enjoyed exclusive preferential treatment, such as lower income tax, tax reduction and exemptions, local government's discretion in charging lower land use right fees, and favourable regional treatment policies such as special economic zones (SEZs) and Western region development. In terms of control, FIEs were only allowed to establish three exclusive business vehicles, namely an equity joint venture (EJV) since 1979, a WFOE since 1986, and a contractual joint venture (CJV) since 1988.[21] Since 1995 China has periodically issued the *Catalogue of Industries Guiding Foreign Investment*, categorizing foreign investment into the encouraged, restricted and prohibited catalogues, and the rest of the sectors not enumerated in the Catalogue were regarded as a tacitly permitted catalogue.[22] Above all, foreign investment in China, including both greenfield and mergers and acquisitions (M&A), required a case-by-case approval procedure for market entry.[23]

While over the past nearly four decades China has improved its foreign investment law in a piecemeal manner, it is the US–China Trade War that has resulted in a substantial overhaul. The US–China Trade War erupted in January 2018 when the Trump administration accused China of unfair trade practices that distorted the global trade market and created a huge US–China trade deficit. When the

---

text (Beijing: Tsinghua University Press, 2015).

19 Pitman B. Potter, 'Foreign Investment Law in the People's Republic of China: Dilemmas of State Control', *The China Quarterly*, No. 141 (1995), pp. 155–185.

20 Yasheng Huang, 'One Country, Two Systems: Foreign-Invested Enterprises and Domestic Firms in China', *China Economic Review*, Vol. 14 Issue 4 (2003), pp. 404–416.

21 中华人民共和国中外合资经营企业法 (Law on Chinese-Foreign Equity Joint Ventures) (Promulgated by the Standing Committee of the National People's Congress on 8 July 1979, 1st revision on 4 April 1990, 2nd revision on 15 March 2001, 3rd revision on 3 September 2016). 中华人民共和国外资企业法 (Law on Foreign-Capital Enterprises) (Promulgated by the NPC on 12 April 1986, 1st revision on 31 October 2000, 2nd revision on 3 September 2016). 中华人民共和国中外合作经营企业法 (Law on Chinese-Foreign Contractual Joint Ventures) (Promulgated by the NPC on 13 April 1988, 1st revision on 31 October 2000, 2nd revision on 3 September 2016, 3rd revision on 11 July 2016, 4th revision on 11 April 2017).

22 外商投资产业指导目录 (Catalogue of Industries Guiding Foreign Investment) (Promulgated by State Development & Planning Commission (predecessor of NDRC), State Economic & Trade Commission (repealed), and Ministry of Foreign Trade & Economic Cooperation (predecessor of MOFCOM) on 14 July 1995, 1st revision on 31 December 1997, 2nd revision on 11 March 2002, 3rd revision on 30 November 2004, 4th revision on 31 October 2007, 5th revision on 24 December 2011, 6th revision on 10 March 2015, 7th revision on 28 June 2017).

23 For a detailed discussion on market access of foreign investment, see Chapter 2 on greenfield investment, and Chapter 3 on M&A.

US started to impose tariffs and other trade barriers on Chinese imports, China retaliated by levying tariffs on US imports. The US also made a series of allegations on non-trade related issues, *inter alia*, China's insufficient market access in the service sector and especially the financial sector, lack of intellectual property (IP) rights protection, theft of commercial secrets and confidential information, and practices of forced transfer of technology (FTT). As a reaction to US pressure and a grand gesture of compromise, in 2019 China promulgated its unified *Foreign Investment Law* (FIL)[24] and its Implementing Regulation,[25] which have addressed some of the non-trade-related complaints, albeit in declaratory promises and pledges rather than substance. The US and China managed to reach a temporary truce in January 2020 by signing the Phase I Agreement.[26]

The FIL has introduced some unprecedented provisions in China's FDI regulatory regime to satisfy US demands. For example, market access for FDI has been liberalized by granting foreign investors pre-establishment national treatment with a negative list approach, which repeals the previous case-by-case approval for foreign investment and the *Catalogue of Industries Guiding Foreign Investment*. The FIL also declares to protect foreign investors' IP rights, to prohibit the divulgation of investors' commercial secrets and to eliminate practices of FTT. Other innovative aspects of the FIL also include post-establishment equal treatment to foreign investors, protection of investors, an information reporting system, and the unification of corporate governance between domestic and foreign enterprises. The FIL abolished the three basic laws on equity and contractual joint ventures and wholly foreign-owned enterprises, thus transforming the foreign investment legal regime from subject supervision (主体监管) to conduct inspection (行为监管).[27]

These new elements in the FIL, on the one hand, make laudable promises to investors and signal China's inclination to achieve investment liberalization and high-quality regulation; on the other hand, however, they are questioned for their ambiguity and vagueness, and possible lax implementation. According to the

---

24 中华人民共和国外商投资法 (Foreign Investment Law of China) (Promulgated by the National People's Congress on 15 March 2019, effective on 1 January 2020).

25 中华人民共和国外商投资法实施条例 (Implementing Regulation of the Foreign Investment Law) (Promulgated by the State Council on 26 December 2019, effective on 1 January 2020).

26 Economic and Trade Agreement Between the Government of the United States of America and the Government of the People's Republic of China (Signed on 15 January 2020, effective on 14 February 2020).

27 For an overview of the key features of the FIL, see Chapter 1, Section 1.3. For a comprehensive discussion on the provisions of the 2019 FIL, see Qingjiang Kong, 《中华人民共和国外商投资法》解读 (*An Interpretation of the Foreign Investment Law of the People's Republic of China*) (Beijing: Law Press, 2019). Mo Zhang, 'Change of Regulatory Scheme: China's New Foreign Investment Law and Reshaped Legal Landscape', *UCLA Pacific Basin Law Journal*, Vol. 37 Issue 1 (2020), pp. 179–238. For a practical guide to the 2019 FIL and FIEs doing business in China, see Robert Lewis, *The Dawn of a New Era for FDI in China* (Beijing: Law Press, 2020).

Organisation for Economic Co-operation and Development (OECD) Regulatory Restrictiveness Index, China is ranked as the 11th most restricted country in terms of openness to FDI out of 84 mapped countries in 2020, and came 9th in the 2019 Index (the closer a host state comes to the top of the list, the more restrictive it is).[28] This appears to suggest that since the FIL came into force in January 2020, China's FDI regulatory regime has witnessed a marginal improvement towards openness. The mixed perception of the FIL begs the question of whether and to what extent China's new foreign investment legal regime might actually achieve its acclaimed goals and eventually lead to the regeneration of FDI growth as desired.

Since 2020, the global breakout of the Covid-19 pandemic has created a trend toward deglobalization, which is an ideology that advocates the reduction of economic dependence on foreign trade and investment and emphasizes domestic sourcing based on national security concerns.[29] This trend has added fuel to the US–China Trade War and provided new rationales for protectionist and anti-China policies by the US government, resulting in fast-deteriorating US–China bilateral relations not just in trade, but also in investment, citizen mobility, technology and diplomacy, to list a few. Consequently, the Trade War has evolved into a Tech War,[30] and a duelling lawfare: a tit-for-tat retribution of restrictive measures and sanctions against each other.[31] The US has adopted a series of restrictive measures and sanctions against Chinese companies and individuals. In May 2019, the US Department of Commerce included the Chinese company Huawei and its foreign subsidiaries, and later more Chinese companies, on its Entity List under the Export Administration Regulations,[32] which prohibited US companies from engaging in any business with these listed Chinese companies without a government licence.[33] In July and August 2020, sanctions were

---

28 OECD, FDI Restrictiveness Index, https://data.oecd.org/fdi/fdi-restrictiveness.htm, last accessed on 2 July 2021.

29 Douglas A. Irwin, 'The Pandemic Adds Momentum to the Deglobalization Trend', *PIIE*, 23 April 2020, https://www.piie.com/blogs/realtime-economic-issues-watch/pandemic-adds-momentum-deglobalization-trend, last accessed on 5 August 2021.

30 The Tech War between the US and China is a competition for global technological leadership that is perhaps more significant than the Trade War, whereby the US tries to maintain its innovative and technological supremacy, and China faces an innovation imperative to catch up and close the technological gap between itself and the US. For a more detailed discussion, see Anthea Roberts, Henrique Choer Moraes and Victor Ferguson, 'The U.S.-China Trade War is a Competition for Technological Leadership', *Lawfare*, 21 May 2019, https://www.lawfareblog.com/us-china-trade-war-competition-technological-leadership, last accessed on 5 August 2021.

31 The term 'lawfare' was developed from 'legal warfare'. For a detailed discussion on the term in general, see Orde F. Kittrie, *Lawfare: Law as a Weapon of War* (Oxford: OUP, 2016).

32 Bureau of Industry and Security of the US Department of Commerce, Supplement No. 4 to Part 744 – Entity List, 19 July 2021, Export Administration Regulations, 15 C.F.R. § 730 *et seq.*

33 David Shepardson and Karen Freifeld, 'China's Huawei, 70 Affiliates Placed on U.S. Trade Blacklist', *Reuters*, 16 May 2019, https://www.reuters.com/article/us-usa-china-huaweitech/chinas-huawei-70-affiliates-placed-on-u-s-trade-blacklist-idUSKCN1SL2W4, last accessed on 29 July 2021.

imposed on a number of Chinese officials according to the Specially Designated Nationals and Blocked Persons List[34] for their connections to the alleged human rights violations in Xinjiang and the alleged erosion of Hong Kong's autonomy.[35]

China, for its part, has adopted a series of laws on anti-foreign restrictive measures and anti-foreign sanctions as countermeasures. The *Provisions on the Unreliable Entity List*, adopted in September 2020, are a countermeasure to the US Department of Commerce's Entity List and prohibit sanctioned foreign entities and individuals from engaging in trade, investment and citizen mobility with China.[36] The *Export Control Law*, promulgated in December 2020, imposes state control over the export of certain items, technologies and services with relevance to national security and national interests;[37] it is considered an emulation of the US Export Administration Regulations in many regards.[38] The *Rules on Counteracting Unjustified Extra-Territorial Application of Foreign Legislation and Measures*, adopted in January 2021, are designed primarily to block the extra-territorial applicability of the US Export Administration Regulations that preclude non-US companies in third countries from exporting components to Chinese companies such as Huawei.[39] Lastly, the *Anti-Foreign Sanctions Law*, promulgated in June 2021, allows China to adopt corresponding countermeasures against foreign individuals and entities who have engaged in discriminatory and restrictive measures against Chinese citizens and entities, and acts as a direct response to sanctions implemented by the US, the European Union (EU), the United Kingdom (UK) and Canada which target Chinese individuals and entities.[40] In contrast to the principled liberal stance to foreign investment advocated

---

34 Office of Foreign Assets Control of US Department of Treasury, 'Specially Designated Nationals and Blocked Persons List', 16 July 2021, https://www.treasury.gov/ofac/downloads/sdnlist.pdf, last accessed on 21 July 2021.

35 US Department of Treasury, 'Treasury Sanctions Chinese Entity and Officials Pursuant to Global Magnitsky Human Rights Accountability Act', 9 July 2020, https://home.treasury.gov/news/press-releases/sm1055, last accessed on 29 July 2021. US Department of Treasury, 'Treasury Sanctions Individuals for Undermining Hong Kong's Autonomy', 7 August 2020, https://home.treasury.gov/news/press-releases/sm1088, last accessed on 29 July 2021.

36 不可靠实体清单规定 (Provisions on the Unreliable Entity List) (Promulgated by MOFCOM on 19 September 2020, effective on promulgation).

37 中华人民共和国出口管制法 (Export Control Law of China) (Promulgated by the NPC on 17 October 2020, effective on 1 December 2020).

38 Lianzhong Pan and Jonathan R. Todd, 'China's New Export Control Law: A Fact Sheet with Practical Applications', *Benesch Friedlander Coplan & Aronoff*, 25 November 2020, https://www.beneschlaw.com/resources/chinas-new-export-control-law-a-fact-sheet-with-practical-applications.html?utm_source=Mondaq&utm_medium=syndication&utm_campaign=LinkedIn-integration, last accessed on 18 March 2021.

39 阻断外国法律与措施不当域外适用办法 (The Rules on Counteracting Unjustified Extra-Territorial Application of Foreign Legislation and Measures) (Promulgated by MOFCOM on 9 January 2021, effective on promulgation).

40 中华人民共和国反外国制裁法 (Anti-Foreign Sanctions Law) (Promulgated by the Standing Committee of the NPC on 10 June 2021, effective on promulgation).

in the FIL, these four newly adopted laws post-FIL avail China of 'a comprehensive toolbox to defend its interests against foreign restrictive measures', but also 'add to the risk of facing conflicting compliance requirements relating to sanctions, export controls and potentially other restrictive measures' for foreign investors doing business in China.[41] Consequently, they may cast a shadow over the path towards an efficient and effective implementation of the FIL.

Against this background, this book aims to provide an up-to-date, holistic and insightful understanding of the foreign investment legal regime in China with a critical analysis of law and practice. This book has three objectives. First, the evolving character of China's foreign investment legal regime is presented in order to illustrate the radical overhaul of the previous system, which had developed during the four decades between 1979 and 2019, into the 'new' regime, marked by the FIL took effect in 2020. Second, this book focuses on a detailed analysis of the key innovations as well as the controversies of foreign investment laws, so as to demonstrate the multiformity, complexity, and sometimes inconsistency of legal statutes, their implementation, and the various institutions that promulgate and enforce them. Third, this book examines laws and regulations that go beyond the framework set forth in the FIL, such as the *Negative List for Market Access*, the *Trademark Law*, the *Arbitration Law*, the *Anti-Monopoly Law*, and the recently adopted laws on anti-foreign restrictive measures and anti-foreign sanctions such as the *Export Control Law*. Although they do not specifically govern foreign investors and their investment *per se*, they have a profound significance for FIEs' compliance programs in China.

Apart from this Introduction, this book contains seven chapters.

Chapter 1 provides a panoramic landscape and the evolving characteristics of China's foreign investment legal regime during the period 1979–2021. China's economic development and success coincide with its experience in attracting FDI, which can be divided into five periods. From the outset, foreign investment was welcomed with extreme caution, featured by a mixed policy of incentives and control. Later, piecemeal reform took place which guided the regime towards more investment liberalization, while at its core a dual-track system was maintained to separate the governance of domestic and foreign businesses. The promulgation of the FIL marks a complete overhaul of China's FDI regulatory regime, whilst external factors, especially relations with the US, propelled China to adopt a series of legal tools to counter foreign restrictive measures and sanctions against China's security and interest. As a whole, China's foreign investment legal regime is exceedingly complicated: it is a system with hierarchical sources of law, adopted by different agencies at both central and local levels, and enforced by multiple

---

41 Marnix Somsen *et al.*, 'China's New Blocking Rules – More Conflicting Requirements for International Business', *De Brauw*, 16 March 2021, https://www.debrauw.com/articles/chinas-new-blocking-rules-more-conflicting-requirements-for-international-business #experts, last accessed on 3 July 2021.

institutions independently or collectively. Therefore, this chapter aims to navigate through the complexity of a foreign investment legal regime by giving a holistic picture of the sources of law and the available options for foreign investors to enter the Chinese market. In addition, this chapter also provides a brief inventory of the key and innovative features of the FIL.

Chapter 2 discusses the most revolutionary aspect of the FIL, namely its national treatment commitment. At the pre-establishment phase, national treatment is achieved by the adoption of the *Negative List for Foreign Investment*, an approach first found in US bilateral investment treaties (BITs). Due both to internal impetus, namely slowing FDI growth in the last decade, and to external factors, *inter alia*, foreign complaints about China's market access regime and the rising tension from US–China trade friction, the FIL inaugurates a pre-establishment national treatment with a negative list approach. Although the *Negative List for Foreign Investment* witnessed a substantial abridgment from 2017 to 2020, the market access regime for foreign investment is still characterized by multi-layered review procedures, including national security review, sectoral approval and licencing, land use rights approval, and environmental assessment. This chapter provides a critical appraisal of the newly adopted pre-establishment national treatment in the FIL, which acknowledges the progress and commitment in market access, on the one hand, and recognizes the potential challenges and remaining procedural burden for foreign investors to establish a presence in China, on the other. Furthermore, post-establishment national treatment is achieved by a plethora of pledges and guarantees for equal treatment between foreign and domestic investors in areas such as national preferential policies, government procurement and product standards. This chapter reveals that these laudable promises on equal treatment may encounter setbacks in enforcement, because of the monopolistic and favourable position of state-owned enterprises (SOEs) in the Chinese economy.

Chapter 3 explicates the regulatory regime of foreign M&A. Compared with the prosperity of greenfield investment in China, foreign M&A have been relatively inactive. The FIL is extremely brief on M&A, simply mentioning in the definition that foreign investment includes 'a foreign investor acquiring shares, equities, property rights, or any other similar rights of a domestic company'.[42] This inclusion indicates that foreign M&A should enjoy national treatment in the same way as greenfield investment. By examining pertinent laws and regulations on the possible approval procedures and qualifications for a foreign investor to participate in China's takeover market, this chapter demonstrates that foreign takeovers of non-listed companies are subject to significant market entry barriers. Furthermore, for foreign takeovers of public Chinese companies, there is a huge discrepancy between foreign and domestic investors in terms of their accessibility to China's stock market. There are still mounting concerns over the lack of a level playing field between foreign acquirers in China vis-à-vis Chinese buyers abroad.

---

42 FIL (2019), Art. 2.

Targeted law enforcement to the advantage of domestic acquirers and to the detriment of foreign ones in a cross-border takeover may hinder the principled liberal objective of the FIL. And more prominently, the variable interest entity (VIE) structure adopted by some Chinese companies to circumvent Chinese law and seek overseas listing still remains in a regulatory grey zone, as their existence appears to be neither encouraged nor prohibited in law and judicial practice. Consequently, foreign investors involved in the Chinese VIE structures face unpredictability now and in the near future.

Chapter 4 elucidates the national security review of foreign investment. In 2011 the State Council and Ministry of Commerce (MOFCOM) issued two rules that established the original system of national security review for foreign investment. China's national security conceptualization was formulated in 2014 as the 'holistic national security outlook' and was codified in *National Security Law* in 2015.[43] The Law also mandates that subsequent legislation should be promulgated to enforce national security review in a specific field, including foreign investment. Art. 35 of the FIL reiterates this legislative envisagement, calling for the establishment of a review system to protect national security. As a result, the *Measures for the National Security Review of Foreign Investment* promulgated in 2020 supersede the original 2011 rules and execute Art. 35 of the FIL.[44] The 2020 Measures provide a detailed and workable system for foreign investors, including substantive standards, procedural guidelines and a newly established review body, namely the Working Mechanism Office under the administration of the National Development and Reform Commission (NDRC). This is considered to be a positive legislative development, because China is protecting its national security and legitimate interests by adopting a legal instrument that has been widely taken in other developed economies. Be that as it may, this chapter also points out the room for legal improvement, such as incorporating legal principles of proportionality, predictability, transparency and accountability.

Chapter 5 expounds on the protection of foreign investors' IP rights. The FIL allocates three designated provisions regarding IP: better protection of IP rights of foreign investors and FIEs and the prohibition of FTT (Art. 22), prohibition of the divulgation of commercial secrets (Art. 23), and the legal liability for the divulgation of commercial secrets (Art. 39). This chapter demonstrates that, while these provisions are considered a best effort in protecting IP rights and China's determination in battling IP infringement, and more importantly, a grand gesture to meet US demands and alleviate foreign investors' concerns, the FIL is likely to play a limited role. China's IP lawmaking and enforcement has witnessed a constant improvement, envisaged in the interval amendments of *Patent*

---

43 中华人民共和国国家安全法 (National Security Law of China) (Promulgated by the NPC on 1 July 2015, effective on promulgation).
44 外商投资安全审查办法 (Measures for the National Security Review of Foreign Investment) (Promulgated by the NDRC and MOFCOM on 19 December 2020, effective on 18 January 2021).

Law,[45] *Trademark Law*,[46] and *Copyright Law*,[47] establishment of designated IP Courts, more efficient and effective IP litigation, and better judicial quality supported by empirical evidence. However, the IP legal regime is still stymied by high quantity but low quality of patents, trademark squatting, counterfeiting and piracy, and allegations of judicial bias against foreign investors. Although China has adamantly denied, and promised to terminate, the practice of FTT, foreign investors continue to complain about its persistence. It was alleged that FTT practice was prevalent as a precondition for market access for foreign investors, indulged by discriminatory laws and regulations and conducted by forced disclosure of commercial secrets and sensitive technical information during government approval procedures. China appears to have adopted a paradoxical narrative over time in rebutting these foreign allegations on FTT practice. Whether and to what extent the succinct provisions on the prohibition of FTT in the FIL and the Implementing Regulation will effectively eradicate FTT practice and alleviate investors' concerns eventually depends on a vigorous law enforcement.

Chapter 6 focuses on arbitration in the settlement of foreign-related commercial disputes in China. While crediting the fact that the 1994 *Arbitration Law* and other relevant laws have distinguished foreign-related arbitration from domestic arbitration by applying more internationally recognized principles and standards to the former, this chapter demonstrates that arbitration practices have advanced swiftly, rendering legislative products either outdated or impossible to enforce. Consequently, one can observe a dynamic change in the landscape of foreign-related arbitration. The leading arbitration commissions have issued and amended their arbitration rules constantly by integrating the most cutting-edge international practice, so as to magnetize disputants to use Chinese domestic arbitration commissions, and subsequently to mitigate the situation that most foreign-related disputes are settled by international arbitration institutions. In addition, the recent government policy has 'legitimized' foreign arbitration institutions to administer arbitration in China, which is labelled as an 'invite-in' trend to open the arbitration market with a twofold purpose: to bring in best international practice to China and to stimulate competition. These goals contribute to an upsurge in the credibility of arbitration in China in the long run. Although arbitration is a system to be distinguished from litigation, Chinese courts play an important role in recognizing and enforcing arbitral awards. Thus, this chapter also examines the new developments of judicial review proactively headed by the

---

45 中华人民共和国专利法 (Patent Law of China) (Promulgated by the NPC on 12 March 1984, 1st revision on 4 September 1992, 2nd revision on 25 August 2000, 3rd revision on 27 December 2008, 4th revision on 17 October 2020, effective on 1 June 2021).

46 中华人民共和国商标法 (Trademark Law of China) (Promulgated by the NPC on 23 August 1982, 1st revision on 22 February 1993, 2nd revision on 27 October 2001, 3rd revision on 30 August 2013, 4th revision on 23 April 2019, effective on 1 November 2019).

47 中华人民共和国著作权法 (Copyright Law of China) (Promulgated by the NPC on 7 September 1990, 1st revision on 27 October 2001, 2nd revision on 26 February 2010, 3rd revision on 11 November 2020, effective on 1 June 2021).

Supreme People's Court aiming to create an arbitration-friendly judicial system. This effort can be understood as part and parcel of prioritizing judicial work in the context of serving China's 'Belt and Road' strategy.

Chapter 7 examines investor–state arbitration by mainly focusing on the situation of China as a respondent. Statistics show a relatively low number of cases against China; however, the trend is increasing. The fact that four investor–state arbitration (ISA) cases involve China as a respondent from 2020 to 2021 signifies that foreign investors are increasingly using investor–state dispute settlement (ISDS) to protect their rights and interests. The key issues exposed in cases concerning China are examined in this chapter, such as the controversial interpretation of the treaty clause on the 'amount of compensation for expropriation' and exhaustion of local remedies. As three Chinese arbitration commissions have expanded their jurisdiction to manage ISA cases, questions of whether and what legal complications may involve in selecting them to arbitrate are also examined in this chapter. In addition, so far there is not yet one arbitral award which imposes compensation to be paid to investors by China. However, in light of the growing number of cases, such a state of affairs may occur. China's reservations to the Convention on the Settlement of Investment Disputes Between States and Nationals of Other States (ICSID Convention) and the Convention on the Recognition and Enforcement of Foreign Arbitral Awards (New York Convention), as well as the lack of domestic legal provisions, raise serious questions on the enforcement of ISA awards. These questions are explored in this chapter. Finally, treaty-based arbitration has been heavily criticized at the global level over the past years. Options for systemic reform,[48] incremental reform,[49] or substituting ISA with domestic remedies, have been put forward by influential states as well as the European Union. China's stance on this fundamental issue is also examined in this chapter, not only because this will have a direct practical bearing on foreign investors in China, but also in view of China's rising weight in reshaping the ISDS regime. Some even forecast China to become 'a global ISDS power'.[50]

In conclusion, China's foreign investment regulatory regime is characterized by its adaptive, complex and fast-changing nature. The FIL and its subsequent implementing regulations come as a timely rejoinder to perennial and novel demands, complaints and challenges towards China's investment climate based

---

48 Systemic reformers 'view investor-state arbitration as a seriously flawed system' and advocate 'more significant, systemic reforms, such as replacing investor-state arbitration with a multilateral investment court and an appellate body.' For a comprehensive discussion on the incremental, systemic and paradigmatic reform of ISDS, see Anthea Roberts, 'Incremental, Systemic, and Paradigmatic Reform of Investor-State Arbitration', *American Journal of International Law*, Vol. 112, Issue 3 (2018), pp. 410–432.

49 Incrementalists 'favour retaining the existing dispute resolution system but instituting modest reforms that would redress specific concerns'. Ibid.

50 Diane A. Desierto, 'China as a Global ISDS Power', *Investment Claims*, 24 August 2018, https://oxia.ouplaw.com/page/715, last accessed on 3 August 2021.

on both domestic and international circumstances. Some unprecedented provisions are introduced in the new regime. For market access, the FIL introduced pre-establishment national treatment with a negative list approach. In the post-establishment phase, the FIL pledges multiple equal treatment commitments in business operations between domestic and foreign investors. For foreign takeovers, the FIL claims to grant M&A activities pre- and post-national treatment in the same ways that greenfield investment would enjoy. The FIL updates China's national security review system, which was originally adopted nearly a decade ago. For IP, the FIL allocates three provisions on strengthened protection of foreign investors' IP rights, prohibition on forced transfer of technology and prohibition on divulgation of commercial secrets. In terms of dispute settlement relating to foreign investors, leading Chinese arbitration commissions have made various efforts to adopt cutting-edge international practices to attract foreign disputants to settle disputes in China, and are 'going out' by participating in dispute settlements abroad. The Chinese government has also gradually opened up the arbitration market with the 'invite-in' policy to foreign arbitration institutions to arbitrate in China. China has become more actively engaged in ISDS reform in the international realm.

While recognizing the FIL and its subsequent implementing laws and regulations as a positive step in the right direction, one can also hardly ignore its obviously flawed limitations: the mere 42 provisions of the FIL cannot substitute in one moment the entire foreign investment legal regime that has been incrementally formed over the past four decades. In the market access phase, foreign investment is still subject to multi-layered review procedures by different central or local agencies, and the realization of equal treatment post-establishment can be seriously hindered by the monopolistic and favoured SOEs in the Chinese economy. Foreign takeovers of Chinese companies are still subject to significant market entry barriers, and foreign investors only have marginal access to China's securities market compared with domestic investors. Foreign investors also suffer from a troubled takeover market which is not yet fully fledged. For national security review, the regime could not yet bring the level of clarity and certainty that a system of good governance should have, and there is still much to be desired for further improvement. For IP protection, many have worried that the FIL may only pay lip service by giving policy-like commitments, and China's IP system is still stymied by some perennial complaints and new venues of opportunity for forced transfer of technology and divulgation of commercial secrets. For foreign-related commercial arbitration, practices have advanced swiftly, which render substantive and procedural laws either outdated or impossible to enforce, at least until the new amendment of the *Arbitration Law* is formally promulgated. For ISA, several pressing issues are still left unanswered, which may impede foreign investors' access to ISA, *inter alia*, the inconsistent interpretation of certain Chinese BITs, Chinese institutions' awkward position in administering ISA cases and the lack of an enforcement mechanism for ISA awards.

Moreover, the lack of conformity between the 'new' regime envisaged in the FIL and the regime prior to the FIL needs to be fully considered and adequately addressed in the future. This problem is perhaps best emblemed by the example of the still effective *2009 Provisions on Mergers and Acquisitions of Domestic Enterprises by Foreign Investors*, which introduce a case-by-case approval for foreign M&As but are in contradiction with the pre-establishment national treatment commitment in the FIL. In addition to the issue of non-conformity in written law, a most critical next step in deciding the success or failure of the 'new' regime in stimulating China's FDI growth and protecting foreign investors' legitimate interests is whether and how an effective and efficient enforcement program would be followed, especially at local levels.

1 The evolving characteristics of the foreign investment legal regime in China

1.1 The five periods of development

1.1.1 The initial stage from 1979 to 1991

China's journey of economic development began in 1978, when the 'reform and opening-up' policy was initiated at the Third Plenary Session of the 11th Central Committee of the Communist Party of China (CPC).[1] Attracting foreign direct investment (FDI) was one of the pivotal decisions made at the time that was 'ideologically inconsistent with the accepted communist ideas', which had rejected the notion of private property rights and foreign involvement in the domestic economy from 1949 to 1978.[2] In 1979 China promulgated the first foreign investment law, namely the *Law on Sino-Foreign Equity Joint Ventures* (EJV Law).[3] This was followed by the promulgation of the *Implementing Regulation of the EJV Law* in 1983.[4] In 1986, the *Law on Wholly Foreign-Owned Enterprises*

---

1 It is commonly acknowledged in literature that China's foreign investment legal regime began in 1979, but it can be divided into different stages prior to the FIL. For example, Mahony divides the regime into the first period (1979–1991), the second period (1992–2000), the third period (2001–2008) and the fourth period (2008 onwards). Tarrant Mahony, *Foreign Investment Law in China: Regulation, Practice and Context* (Beijing: Tsinghua University Press, 2015), pp. 1–94. Zhang and Corrie divide the regime into stage one (1979–1982), stage two (1983–1991), stage three (1992–2000) and stage four (2001 onwards). Xiuping Zhang and Bruce P. Corrie, *Investing in China and Chinese Investment Abroad* (Singapore: Springer, 2018), pp. 3–5. Gallagher and Shan divide the system into the nationalization and exclusion stage (1949–1978), the gradual resumption stage (1979–1991), the first surge stage (1992–2000), and the second surge stage (2001 onwards). Norah Gallagher and Wenhua Shan, *Chinese Investment Treaties: Policies and Practice* (Oxford: OUP, 2009), pp. 4–10. In this book, we divide the system into five periods: the initial period (1979–1991), the rapid development period (1992–2000), the post-WTO period (2001–2012), the transitional period (2013–2019) and the post-FIL period (2020–present).
2 Norah Gallagher and Wenhua Shan, *supra* note 1, p. 6.
3 中华人民共和国中外合资经营企业法 (Law on Sino-Foreign Equity Joint Ventures) (Promulgated by the National People's Congress (NPC) on 8 July 1979, 1st revision on 4 April 1990, 2nd revision on 15 March 2001, 3rd revision on 3 September 2016).
4 中华人民共和国中外合资经营企业法实施条例 (Implementing Regulation for Law on Sino-Foreign Equity Joint Ventures) (Promulgated on 20 September 1983, 1st revision on 22 July 2001, 2nd revision on 8 January 2011, 3rd revision on 19 February 2014).

DOI: 10.4324/9781003168805-2

(WFOE Law) was adopted,[5] accompanied by its Implementing Regulation adopted in 1990.[6] And in 1988, the *Law on Sino-Foreign Contractual Joint Ventures* (CJV Law) was promulgated.[7] In the same vein, its Implementing Regulation was promulgated in 1995.[8] The aforementioned laws constituted China's 'three primary foreign investment laws', which established the rudimentary legal framework for foreign-invested enterprises (FIEs) in China. The most significant feature of these laws was case-by-case approval for the establishment and termination of an FIE, which existed for nearly four decades until 2017. It is notable that the three foreign investment laws were adopted even before China's first *Company Law* was formally introduced in 1993.[9] This suggests that China at the time regarded the regulation and protection of FIEs as a top priority and was able to first establish a legal framework for FIEs akin to the modern corporate governance and pursuant to prevailing international practice, and only after that did China consider a *Company Law* for the governance of domestic enterprises.[10]

In addition to the foundational three foreign investment laws and their implementing regulations, other regulatory means were also devised on contracts, taxation and foreign exchange. All these regulatory regimes adhered to the dual-track system, meaning that FIEs and domestic enterprises were governed under separate sets of rules. For contracts, until China adopted its first unified *Contract Law* in 1999, domestic contracts and foreign-related contracts were governed, respectively, by the *Economic Contract Law* promulgated in 1981 and the *Foreign-Related Economic Contract Law* promulgated in 1985.[11] For taxation,

---

5 中华人民共和国外资企业法 (Law on Wholly Foreign-Owned Enterprises) (Promulgated by the NPC on 12 April 1986, 1st revision on 31 October 2000, 2nd revision on 3 September 2016).

6 中华人民共和国外资企业法实施细则 (Implementing Regulation for Law on Wholly Foreign-Owned Enterprises) (Promulgated on 12 December 1990, 1st revision on 12 April 2001, 2nd revision on 19 February 2014).

7 中华人民共和国中外合作经营企业法 (The Law on Sino-Foreign Contractual Joint Ventures) (Promulgated by the NPC on 13 April 1988, 1st revision on 31 October 2000, 2nd revision on 3 September 2016, 3rd (partial) revision on 7 November 2016, 4th revision on 4 November 2017).

8 中华人民共和国中外合作经营企业法实施细则 (Implementing Regulation for Law on Sino-Foreign Contractual Joint Ventures) (Promulgated on 4 September 1995, 1st revision on 19 February 2014, 2nd revision on 1 March 2017, 3rd revision on 17 November 2017).

9 公司法 (Company Law) (Promulgated by the Standing Committee of the NPC on 29 December 1993, 1st revision on 25 December 1999, 2nd revision on 28 August 2004, 3rd revision on 27 October 2005, 4th revision on 28 December 2013, 5th revision on 26 October 2018).

10 Tarrant Mahony, *supra* note 1, pp. 4–5.

11 中华人民共和国经济合同法 (Economic Contract Law) (Promulgated by the NPC on 13 December 1981, 1st revision on 2 September 1993). 中华人民共和国涉外经济合同法 (Foreign-Related Economic Contract Law) (Promulgated by the Standing Committee of the NPC on 21 March 1985, effective on 1 July 1985).

FIEs were taxed under the *Equity Joint Venture Income Tax Law* of 1980[12] or the *Foreign Enterprise Income Tax Law* of 1982.[13] These two laws were superseded by the *Income Tax Law for Foreign Invested Enterprises and Foreign Enterprises* of 1991, which unified taxation for FIEs.[14] Notably, this was even before an enterprise income tax law for domestic enterprises was promulgated in 1993. For foreign exchange, China had a dual currency system where an FIE must maintain a Renminbi (RMB) account and a Foreign Exchange Certificate at the Bank of China; all foreign exchange transactions were required to comply with national plans for its quota and purpose, and all foreign exchange accounts required close monitoring and government approval, *inter alia*, a case-by-case approval for the remittance of profits to a foreign country.[15]

In 1980, the State Council approved the establishment of the first four special economic zones (SEZs): Shenzhen, for its proximity to Hong Kong; Zhuhai, for its proximity to Macao; Shantou, which was the hometown of many entrepreneurs overseas with a Chinese heritage; and Xiamen, for its proximity to Taiwan. In 1988, Hainan Province also became an SEZ. SEZs enjoy preferential and exclusive trade and investment policies. Preferential treatment, such as special tax incentives and use of lands, is given to attract foreign investments in the SEZs. In the Shenzhen SEZ, for example, foreign corporate income tax was 15% as opposed to 33% in the rest of China, and qualified export-oriented and high-tech foreign enterprises only needed to pay half of the market-price fees for industrial land-use rights in the first five years.[16] SEZs have been testing grounds for

12 中华人民共和国中外合资经营企业所得税法 (Income Tax Law on Sino-Foreign EJVs) (Promulgated by the Standing Committee of the NPC on 10 September 1980, 1st revision on 2 September 1983).

13 中华人民共和国外国企业所得税法 (Income Tax Law for Foreign Enterprises) (Promulgated by the NPC on 13 December 1981, effective on 1 January 1982).

14 中华人民共和国外商投资企业和外国企业所得税法 (Income Tax Law for Foreign-Invested Enterprises and Foreign Enterprises) (Promulgated by the NPC on 9 April 1991, effective on 1 July 1991).

15 The major governing laws for foreign exchange control were 中华人民共和国外汇管理暂行条例 (Provisional Regulation for Foreign Exchange Control) (Promulgated by the State Council on 18 December 1980, effective on 1 March 1981); 对侨资企业、外资企业、中外合资经营企业外汇管理施行细则 (Implementing Rules on Foreign Exchange Control Relating to Overseas Chinese Enterprises, Foreign Enterprises and Sino-Foreign Equity Joint Ventures) (Promulgated by the State Administration of Foreign Exchange on 1 August 1983, effective on promulgation). For a comprehensive overview of taxation of FIEs in the 1980s, see Jinyan Li, 'Taxation of Foreign Investment in the People's Republic of China', *Loyola of Los Angeles International and Comparative Law Journal*, Vol. 12 No. 1 (1989), pp. 35–50. Paul D. McKenzie, 'Foreign Exchange and Joint Ventures with China: Short-Term Strategies and Long-Term Prospects', *Canadian Business Law Journal*, Vol. 17 Issue 1 (1990), pp. 114–149.

16 Yiming Yuan *et al.*, 'China's First Special Economic Zone: The Case of Shenzhen', in Douglas Zhihua Zeng (ed.), *Building Engines for Growth and Competitiveness in China: Experience with Special Economic Zones and Industrial Clusters* (Washington D.C.: World Bank, 2010), pp. 55–86.

China's reform and opening-up policy and have served as an emblematic example of China's economic success. They have proven that market mechanisms rather than state planning should be the decisive factor in the course of China's economic reform, and SEZs 'contributed significantly to national gross domestic product (GDP), employment, exports, and attraction of foreign investment and new technologies, as well as the adoption of modern management practices, among others'.[17] As a result, FDI inflow in China from 1983 to 1991 witnessed an annual growth rate of 21.5%.[18]

1.1.2 The rapid development from 1992 to 2000

In 1992, Deng Xiaoping made an impromptu trip to several cities in Guangdong Province and other inland cities, and delivered a simple but clear message: China would continuously and adamantly implement the reform and opening-up policy, in which FDI played a central role. This trip, commonly known as Deng's Southern Tour, marked the beginning of a new phase of development. The State Council decided to open up 6 more cities, 13 inland border cities and 18 provincial capital cities which enjoyed similar policy benefits as the SEZs.[19] In 1993, the Third Plenary Session of the CPC 14th Central Committee officially adopted a 'socialist market economy' as China's fundamental economic system, and paved the way for later fiscal, financial, foreign trade and investment, and state-owned enterprise (SOE) reform. The Constitution was revised accordingly to include the development of a socialist market economy as a fundamental national goal.[20] FDI inflow from 1992 to 2000 saw an annual increase rate at about 17.8%.[21]

Relating to foreign investment, several landmark legislations were introduced or revised. Both the WFOE Law and the CJV Law were revised in 2000. The 2000 WFOE Law abrogated the local content requirement in terms of purchase of production resources for an FIE, whereas the 1986 WFOE Law required that an FIE must first consider domestic sourcing in purchasing production materials if available.[22] The same abolition of the local content requirement was observed

17 Douglas Zhihua Zeng, 'How Do Special Economic Zones and Industrial Clusters Drive China's Rapid Development?' in Douglas Zhihua Zeng (ed.), *Building Engines for Growth and Competitiveness in China Experience with Special Economic Zones and Industrial Clusters* (Washington D.C.: World Bank, 2010), pp. 1–54, at 12–24.

18 Calculated by the authors. Source obtained from MOFCOM, 中国外资统计公报2020 (Statistical Bulletin of FDI in China 2020), http://images.mofcom.gov.cn/wzs/202011/20201111182920243.pdf, last accessed on 1 July 2021, p. 26.

19 For a detailed discussion on these regional policies attracting foreign investment, see Xiuping Zhang and Bruce P. Corrie, *supra* note 1, pp. 13–17.

20 中华人民共和国宪法 (1993修正) (Constitutional Law 1993 Amendment) (Promulgated by the NPC on 29 March 1993, effective on promulgated), Art. 15.

21 Calculated by the authors. Source obtained from MOFCOM, *supra* note 18.

22 Law on Wholly Foreign-Owned Enterprises (2000), Art. 15.

in the 2000 CJV Law.[23] The first *Contract Law* was adopted in 1999, which unified the governance of contracts without distinguishing between domestic and foreign-related contracts, thus eliminating the dual-track system for contracts that existed in the initial period.[24] In taxation, domestic enterprises were taxed under the *Provisional Regulation on Enterprise Income Tax* of 1993,[25] while FIEs continued to be taxed under the *Income Tax Law for Foreign Invested Enterprises and Foreign Enterprises* of 1991. Domestic enterprises were subject to a 33% income tax, while FIEs enjoyed an exclusive package of lower tax base, tax exemption and tax deduction schemes. For instance, all FIEs in the SEZs, alongside FIEs in the energy, transportation, seaports or other state-encouraged sectors in cities designated by the State Council, enjoyed a 15% income tax.[26] This dual-track system for taxation was long debated for its rationale. Opponents of the system argued that favourable tax incentives for FIEs would force domestic enterprises out of competition because of the latter's cumbersome tax burdens, whereas proponents of the system feared that 'prematurely eliminating tax advantages enjoyed by FIEs' would discourage foreign investors and wane China's appeal as a recipient for FDI.[27]

Another significant liberalization in FDI governance took place in foreign exchange control. Since 1993, RMB convertibility for current account transactions was formally announced by the Chinese government as leverage to negotiate China's entry into the General Agreement on Tariffs and Trade (GATT).[28] In November 1996, China announced in a letter to the International Monetary Fund (IMF) that it would officially accept the obligations under Art. VIII of the IMF Articles of Agreement for current account convertibility.[29] In 1996, the *Regulation on the Management of Foreign Exchanges* was promulgated and revised in 1997 to include the provision on the free convertibility of international current account transactions.[30]

In 1995, a landmark foreign investment legislation was the promulgation of the *Catalogue of Industries Guiding Foreign Investment*, which was later revised

---

23 Law on Sino-Foreign Contractual Joint Ventures (2000), Art. 19.
24 中华人民共和国合同法 (Contract Law of China) (Promulgated by the NPC on 15 March 1999, effective on 1 October 1999).
25 中华人民共和国企业所得税暂行条例 (Provisional Regulation on Enterprises Income Tax) (Promulgated by the State Council on 13 December 1993, effective on 1 January 1994).
26 Income Tax Law for Foreign-Invested Enterprises and Foreign Enterprises (1991), Art. 7.
27 Xiaoyang Zhang, 'Eliminating Privileges Enjoyed by Foreign Investors in China: Rationality and Ramifications under a Unified Tax Code', *Deakin Law Review*, Vol. 12 No. 2 (2007), pp. 79–104, at 87–89.
28 For a comprehensive review of China's foreign exchange policies from 1979 to 2003, see Guijin Lin and Ronald M. Schramm, 'China's Foreign Exchange Policies since 1979: A Review of Developments and an Assessment', *China Economic Review*, Vol. 14 (2003), pp. 246–280.
29 Ibid, at 260–261.
30 中华人民共和国外汇管理条例 (Regulation on the Management of Foreign Exchanges) (Promulgated by the State Council on 29 January 1996, 1st revision on 14 January 1997), Art. 5.

at intervals until 2017.[31] The Catalogues were aimed at giving the government the maneuverer to 'adjust the guidance direction of the foreign invested enterprises according to the needs of China's economic development' at different times.[32] However, its existence was questioned by foreign investors for its lack of clear boundaries and vagueness of rules, as foreign investors had to constantly seek clarification from the authorities interpreting the Catalogues, which created opportunities of rent-seeking and control of foreign investment.[33] The mixture of FDI policies in both inducement and control was a result of China's dichotomic mindset: attracting foreign investment was perennially treated as a top priority for central and local governments, and a pivotal barometer for assessing governmental performance of a particular term. Meanwhile, the Chinese government intended to retain heavy administrative intervention over FDI in general, and a large number of restricted and prohibited sectors were kept away from the market entry of FDI in order to protect infant domestic companies in those strategic and vital industries from fierce market rivalry with foreign firms in China.[34]

1.1.3 The post-World Trade Organization (WTO) time from 2001 to 2012

China's accession into the WTO in 2001 marked a new era for foreign trade and investment. From 2001 to 2012, FDI inflow in China witnessed an annual increase of 9%.[35] In order to comply with WTO requirements, China modified a massive number of laws and regulations.

For a start, the EJV Law was revised in 2001, along with the revisions of the Implementing Regulation of the EJV Law and the Implementing Regulation of the WFOE Law.[36] The Implementing Regulation of the EJV Law underwent the most significant revision, *inter alia*, the deletion of export performance requirements and domestic sales restrictions, the deletion of reporting requirements on the EJV's production and operation plans, and the deletion of local contents requirements (priority in domestic sourcing).[37] In the field of foreign exchange control, the *Regulation on the Management of Foreign Exchanges* was revised in 2008 and remains effective today. According to the Regulation, capital account

---

31 外商投资产业指导目录 (Catalogue of Industries Guiding Foreign Investment) (1995) (1997) (2002) (2004) (2007) (2011) (2015) (2017) (All repealed).

32 Xiuping Zhang and Bruce P. Corrie, *supra* note 1, p. 18.

33 Shoushuang Li, *The Legal Environment and Risks for Foreign Investment in China* (Berlin: Springer, 2007), pp. 314–315.

34 Lu Yuan and Terence Tsai, 'Foreign Direct Investment Policy in China', *China Review* (2000), pp. 223-247, at 237.

35 Calculated by the authors. Source obtained from MOFCOM, *supra* note 18.

36 For a comprehensive discussion of these revisions, see Wenhua Shan, 'Towards a Level Playing Field of Foreign Investment in China', *Journal of World Investment & Trade*, Vol. 3 Issue 2 (2002), pp. 327–343.

37 Ibid, at 333–334.

transactions in China still require approval from the State Administration of Foreign Exchange (SAFE). In the field of taxation, a unified *Enterprise Income Tax Law* was adopted in 2007, which governed the taxation of all forms of enterprises in China without a distinction between their domestic or foreign ownership.[38] Pursuant to the *Enterprise Income Tax Law*, FIEs and domestic enterprises are taxed under the same 25% income tax rate, which means that domestic and foreign enterprise taxpayers now compete on an equal footing. In 2007, China's first Anti-Monopoly Law (AML) was adopted and remains effective today.[39] The AML applies to both domestic and foreign business operators in China, emanating a legislative trend that integrates the governance of domestic and foreign market participants into a unified code in a specific field.

Since China's accession to the WTO, foreign takeovers of Chinese companies began to emerge. Mergers and acquisitions (M&A) has been a predominant form of FDI at the global level since the 1980s but was nevertheless negligible in China. According to the Organisation for Economic Co-operation and Development (OECD), in 2003 China was the largest recipient of FDI globally and represented 9.6% of global FDI inflow that year, but cross-border M&A deals in China only represented 1.3% of global M&A transactions; from 2000 to 2003, foreign M&As in China varied between 5% and 7% of the total FDI inflow in China annually.[40] This sluggish proportion of M&As to total FDI inflow in China did not rapidly change until 2015. According to the Ministry of Commerce (MOFCOM), foreign M&A activities still remained less than 7% of total inward FDI in China from 2004 to 2014, but suddenly soared to 11%–16% from 2015 to 2018.[41] The possibility for foreign investors to acquire Chinese companies began with the reform of SOEs in state-asset privatization and restructuring since the late 1990s, envisaged in the *Provisional Regulation on the Use of Foreign Investment for the Asset Restructuring of SOEs* of 1998.[42] The *Notice on Transfer to Foreign Investors of State-Owned Shares and Legal Person Shares*

---

38 中华人民共和国企业所得税法 (Enterprise Income Tax Law) (Promulgated by the NPC on 16 March 2007, 1st revision on 24 February 2017, 2nd revision on 29 December 2018).

39 反垄断法 (Anti-Monopoly Law) (Promulgated by the NPC Standing Committee on 30 August 2007, effective on 1 August 2008).

40 OECD, *China: Open Policies towards Mergers and Acquisitions* (Paris: OECD Publishing, 2006), p. 19.

41 MOFCOM, *Report on Foreign Investment in China 2019*, http://images.mofcom.gov.cn/wzs/202008/20200819101923422.pdf, p. 62. MOFCOM, *Report on Foreign Investment in China 2018*, http://images.mofcom.gov.cn/wzs/201810/20181009090547996.pdf, p. 101. MOFCOM, *Report on Foreign Investment in China 2017*, http://images.mofcom.gov.cn/wzs/201804/20180416161221341.pdf, p. 101. Statistics from 2004 to 2015 are retrieved from MOFCOM, *Report on Foreign Investment in China 2016*, http://images.mofcom.gov.cn/wzs/201612/20161230131233768.pdf, pp. 7–8. All links are accessed on 3 July 2021.

42 关于国有企业利用外商投资进行资产重组的暂行规定 (Provisional Regulation on the Use of Foreign Investment for the Asset Restructuring of SOEs) (Promulgated by State Economic & Trade Commission on 14 September 1998, effective on promulgation).

of Listed Companies of 2002 in principle allowed foreign investors to acquire state-owned shares of listed companies, which nevertheless was subject to rigorous approval procedures.[43] A landmark legislation was promulgated in 2003 and established the overall framework of foreign M&A in China, namely the *Interim Provisions on Mergers and Acquisitions of Domestic Enterprises by Foreign Investors*, which was revised in 2006 and 2009, and remains effective today.[44] Since 2003, foreign takeovers in China have been subject to rigid and multiple approval procedures, *inter alia*, a case-by-case approval by MOFCOM until 2017.[45]

An eminent policy adjustment during this period was a shift from emphasizing only the quantity of FDI to also considering its quality.[46] Continuously attracting FDI was no longer the Chinese government's sole concern; they moved instead towards attracting FDI that upgrades China's industrial structure. This policy shift was epitomized in a number of documents, *inter alia*, the *11th Five-Year Plan on the Utilization of Foreign Investment* of 2006[47] and the *Catalogue of Industries Guiding Foreign Investment* of 2007. From 2006 to 2010, China endeavoured to attract FDI that could bring advanced technologies, managerial expertise and highly skilled personnel; emphasized ecological preservation, environmental protection, resource saving and energy conservation instead of only economic growth; and shifted the focus of FDI from basic processing, assembly and low-level manufacturing to research and development, high-end design, high value-added production, and the service sector.[48]

1.1.4 The transitional move from 2013 to 2019

In 2013 during the negotiation of a prospective China–United States (US) bilateral investment treaty (BIT), China for the first time in history made a commitment with the US to negotiate a pre-establishment national treatment clause with a negative list approach.[49] This commitment, however, never materialized

---

43 关于向外商转让上市公司国有股和法人股有关问题的通知 (Notice on Transfer to Foreign Investors of State-Owned Shares and Legal Person Shares of Listed Companies) (Promulgated by the China Securities Regulatory Commission, Ministry of Finance and State Economic & Trade Commission on 1 November 2002, effective on promulgation).
44 外国投资者并购境内企业暂行规定 (Interim Provisions on Mergers and Acquisitions of Domestic Enterprises by Foreign Investors) (Promulgated by Ministry of Foreign Trade & Economic Cooperation, State Taxation Administration, State Administration for Industry & Commerce, and State Administration of Foreign Exchange on 7 March 2003, 1st revision on 8 August 2006, 2nd revision on 22 June 2009).
45 For a detailed discussion, see Chapter 3.
46 Norah Gallagher and Wenhua Shan, *supra* note 1, p. 9.
47 利用外资"十一五"规划 (11th Five-Year Plan on the Utilization of Foreign Investment) (Published by MOFCOM on 13 November 2006, effective on promulgation).
48 Ibid.
49 Norah Gallagher, 'China's BIT's and Arbitration Practice: Progress and Problems', in Wenhua Shan and Jinyuan Su (eds.), *China and International Investment Law: Twenty Years of ICSID* Membership (Leiden: Brill, 2014), pp. 180–214, at 186–187.

because of the fallout of the China–US BIT. Instead, radical reform took place indigenously. FDI in China from 2013 to 2019 experienced feeble growth, at an annual growth rate of 2.2%, which was the lowest among previous periods of development. China's economy at the time was losing competitiveness: wages and production costs had significantly risen; China was in danger of falling into the middle-income trap; and bureaucratic hurdles, lax intellectual property (IP) protection and a cosseted service sector in China were driving foreign investors away.[50] In this context, the launch of the Shanghai Pilot Free Trade Zone (PFTZ) in 2013 aimed at deepened economic reform, trade facilitation and investment liberalization. In the area of FDI, the Shanghai PFTZ explored a number of unprecedented and pioneering measures that were later promoted to other PFTZs and finally nationwide. They include integrated law enforcement by the Shanghai PFTZ Management Committee on multiple administrative affairs; the opening-up of service sectors such as finance, culture and education that were prohibited or restricted by the Catalogue at the time; the abolition of the case-by-case approval system and the adoption of the recordation system for the establishment and operation of FIEs; the introduction of pre-establishment national treatment with a negative list; free convertibility of the capital account; and government transparency.[51] Similar policies were implemented in 20 other PFTZs established from 2013 to 2020.

A draft *Foreign Investment Law* was published by MOFCOM in January 2015, containing 170 elaborative articles that proposed a radical reform of China's FDI regulatory regime, including pre- and post-establishment national treatment and a negative list approach, national security review, information reporting, investment promotion and protection, and a unified corporate governance for FIEs under *Company Law*, among others.[52] Nonetheless, it never went through a formal legislative procedure. The reason for the failure of the 2015 draft law was allegedly because of bureaucratic power grabbing and competition among different government agencies at both central and local levels, in particular MOFCOM, the State Administration for Market Regulation (SAMR), the National Development and Reform Commission (NDRC), and various industrial regulators.[53] Because

---

50 Wei Shen and Matthias Vanhullebusch, 'Where Is the Alchemy? The Experiment of the Shanghai Free Trade Zone in Freeing the Foreign Investment Regime in China', *European Business Organization Law Review*, Vol. 16 (2015), pp. 321–352, at 323.

51 中国（上海）自由贸易试验区管理办法 (Measures for the Administration of the China (Shanghai) Pilot Free Trade Zone) (Promulgated by Shanghai Municipality on 29 September 2013, effective on 1 October 2013). See also Gladie Lui, 'Shanghai Pilot Free Trade Zone: Shaping of China's Future Foreign Investment Environment', *International Tax Journal*, Vol 40 Issue 4 (2014), pp. 31–44.

52 中华人民共和国外国投资法（草案征求意见稿）(Draft Foreign Investment Law of China) (Published by MOFCOM on 19 January 2015). For an overview of this draft law, see Meichen Liu, 'The New Chinese Foreign Investment Law and Its Implication on Foreign Investors', *Northwestern Journal of International Law & Business*, Vol. 38 Issue 2 (2018), pp. 285–306.

53 Xiaojun Li, 'The Durability of China's Lawmaking Process under Xi Jinping: A Tale of Two Foreign Investment Laws', *Issues & Studies: A Social Science Quarterly on China, Taiwan, and East Asian Affairs*, Vol. 57 No. 1 (2021), pp. 1–22, at 9.

each of these agencies and departments wanted to ensure that their interests and power were preserved in the draft law, there were wide-ranging disagreements in the inter-agency review process, which eventually led to a standstill.[54]

In 2016 and 2017, the three primary foreign investment laws underwent partial modification, which for the first time in history, repealed the case-by-case approval for the establishment of an FIE that was imposed for more than three decades in China.[55] The case-by-case approval was temporarily replaced by a transitional *ex post* recordation system,[56] until the *Foreign Investment Law* (FIL) came into force in 2020 and formally introduced the information reporting system. These modifications were a bellwether of China's attempt at exploring new ways to restructuring its FDI regulatory regime.

China in late 2018 and early 2019 expedited the legislative process for the FIL that had been shelved since 2015. From December 2018, when the National People's Congress (NPC) published a draft FIL for public comments, it took less than four months for the law to be formally adopted in March 2019. While various factors may have contributed to the fast-track promulgation of the FIL, the most decisive one may be that China, in an attempt to reconcile with the US and reach a truce as promptly as possible, intended to assuage the accusations regarding China's unfair trade and investment practices in the still ongoing US–China Trade War that had commenced in January 2018.[57] The FIL received mixed reactions. The American Chamber of Commerce in China commented that, though seen as a step in the right direction, the FIL in its current form is light on substance and the next critical development would be to monitor whether law enforcement could be strengthened.[58] The vagueness of the FIL is also suspected to be intentional, to leave room for creative interpretation for the local governments in enforcement, which will make the law less consistent and

---

54 Ibid.
55 全国人民代表大会常务委员会关于修改《中华人民共和国外资企业法》等四部法律的决定 (Decision of the Standing Committee of the National People's Congress on the Revision of Four Laws Such as the Law on Wholly Foreign-Owned Enterprises) (Promulgated on 3 September 2016, effective on 1 October 2016). Law on Wholly Foreign-Owned Enterprises (2016), Art. 23. Law on Sino-Foreign Cooperative Joint Ventures (2017), Art. 25. Law on Sino-Foreign Equity Joint Ventures (2016), Art. 15.
56 外商投资企业设立及变更备案管理暂行办法 (Provisional Measures on the Administration of Recordation for Establishment and Modification of Foreign-Invested Enterprises) (Promulgated by MOFCOM on 8 October 2016, effective on promulgation).
57 Xiaojun Li, *supra* note 53, at 2, 14, 17. The European Union Chamber of Commerce in China opined that the FIL 'is being squeezed between the normal legislative process and the negotiation table with the US, in part to address the trade conflict', and due consultation period was not adequately respected, especially consultation with foreign businesses who are supposed to have the most ramifications by this legislation. European Union Chamber of Commerce in China, 'European Chamber's Stance on the (Draft) Foreign Investment Law', 25 February 2019, https://www.europeanchamber.com.cn/en/press-releases/2902/european_chamber_s_stance_on_the_draft_foreign_investment_law, last accessed on 22 June 2021.
58 Alexander Chipman Koty, 'China's New Foreign Investment Law', *American Chamber of Commerce in China*, 26 March 2019, https://www.amcham-shanghai.org/en/article/chinas-new-foreign-investment-law, last accessed on 1 July 2020.

transparent than it claims to be.[59] The European Union (EU) shares similar concerns, commenting on 'the use of broad terms and vague language throughout the FIL and its Implementation Regulation, as many of its articles read more like policy commitments than binding legal clauses, which leaves room for discretionary implementation'.[60] In view of China's long-standing lax law enforcement,[61] some Western concerns at the moment are understandable. That being said, one must also acknowledge that any legal reform is an incremental process and can only be realistically achieved step by step in China.

In April 2018, the Hainan Free Trade Port (HFTP) was established. PFTZs elsewhere in China were questioned for being too small, geographically, to 'provide a meaningful trialling ground' for China's future deepened reform.[62] Against this background, the HFTP includes the whole island of Hainan, which is slightly larger in size than Belgium, is the biggest PFTZ in China and represents the highest level of openness and liberalization. The central government has supported the HFTP development with a number of fundamental policy documents and legislation,[63] which enabled the central and Hainan governments to adopt various departmental rules and local regulations on a series of matters such as one-stop customs, construction of infrastructure, trade facilitation such as zero tariffs on import, investment liberalization, immigration, people mobility and talent attraction, finance, taxation, education, and big data on governance. In the field of foreign investment, the HFTP grants more freedom of market access to foreign investors than other PFTZs. For instance, the *Negative List for Foreign Investment in the HFTP* includes 17 prohibited areas and 10 restricted ones,[64] compared to 19 prohibited areas and 11 restricted ones in the *2020 Negative List for Foreign Investment in the PFTZs*, and 21 prohibited areas and 12 restricted ones in the *2020 Negative List for Foreign Investment* applicable nationwide.

59 Ibid.
60 European Union Chamber of Commerce in China, *supra* note 57.
61 See for example, Donald C. Clarke, 'Power and Politics in the Chinese Court System: The Enforcement of Civil Judgments', *Columbia Journal of Asian Law*, Vol. 10 Issue 1 (1996), pp. 1–92.
62 Matthew Harrison *et al.*, 'The Promise of China's Free Trade Zones – The Case of Hainan', *Asian Education and Development*, Vol. 9 No. 3 (2020), pp. 297–308, at 300.
63 海南自由贸易港建设总体方案 (Overall Plan for the Construction of Hainan Free Trade Port) (Issued by Central Committee of the CPC and State Council on 1 June 2020, effective on promulgation). 中共中央、国务院关于支持海南全面深化改革开放的指导意见 (Guiding Opinions of the CPC Central Committee and the State Council on Supporting Hainan in Comprehensively Deepening Reform and Opening Up) (Issued on 11 April 2018, effective on promulgation). 中华人民共和国海南自由贸易港法 (Law of Hainan Free trade Port) (Promulgated by the Standing Committee of the NPC on 10 June 2021, effective on promulgation).
64 海南自由贸易港外商投资准入特别管理措施（负面清单）(Special Administrative Measures for Market Access of Foreign Investment in the Hainan Free Trade Port (Negative List)) (Promulgated by NDRC and MOFCOM on 31 December 2020, effective on 1 February 2021).

1.1.5 *The post-FIL phase since 2020*

After the promulgation of the FIL in March 2019, a number of implementing laws and regulations have been adopted to substantiate the succinct provisions in the FIL. The *Implementing Regulation of the FIL* was promulgated in December 2019 and became effective on 1 January 2020.[65] The *Measures for Information Reporting of Foreign Investment* was also promulgated in December 2019, implementing Art. 34 (information reporting) of the FIL.[66] In August 2020, the *Working Measures for Complaints of FIEs* were adopted to enforce Art. 26 (complaint system) of the FIL.[67] In December 2020, the *Measures for National Security Review of Foreign Investment* were adopted to implement Art. 35 (national security review) of the FIL.[68] More implementing rules can be anticipated in the coming years to the repletion of the FIL.

However, with the global breakout of the Covid-19 pandemic in 2020 and the ongoing pervading anti-China policy adopted by the US government, US–China bilateral relations witnessed serious deterioration. The US has adopted a series of restrictive measures and sanctions against Chinese companies and individuals. As a result, China has adopted a series of laws on anti-foreign restrictive measures and anti-foreign sanctions as countermeasures. In contrast to the principled liberal stance to foreign investment in the FIL, these newly adopted laws post-FIL avail China of a comprehensive legal toolbox to protect its national security and interests, and to defend itself against undue foreign interference, restrictions and sanctions.

The *Provisions on the Unreliable Entity List*[69] is a counterpart to the US Department of Commerce's Entity List which prohibits a number of Chinese companies, such as Huawei, from accessing US products.[70] Foreign individuals and entities on China's Unreliable Entity List are those who (1) endanger China's sovereignty, security and development interest; (2) violate 'normal market transaction principles' and suspend normal transactions with Chinese companies, organizations and individuals; or (3) take discriminatory measures against

---

65 中华人民共和国外商投资法实施条例 (Implementing Regulation of the Foreign Investment Law) (Promulgated by the State Council on 26 December 2019, effective on 1 January 2020).

66 外商投资信息报告办法 (Measures for Information Reporting of Foreign Investment) (Promulgated by MOFCOM and SAMR on 30 December 2019, effective on 1 January 2020).

67 外商投资企业投诉工作办法 (Working Measures for Complaints of FIEs) (Promulgated by MOFCOM on 25 August 2020, effective on 1 October 2020).

68 外商投资安全审查办法 (National Security Review of Foreign Investment) (Promulgated by the NDRC and MOFCOM on 19 December 2020, effective on 18 January 2021).

69 不可靠实体清单规定 (Provisions on the Unreliable Entity List) (Promulgated by MOFCOM on 19 September 2020, effective on promulgation).

70 Bureau of Industry and Security of the US Department of Commerce, Supplement No. 4 to Part 744 – Entity List, 19 July 2021, Export Administration Regulations, 15 C.F.R. § 730 *et seq.*

Chinese companies, organizations, and individuals, and seriously impair their legitimate rights.[71] If blacklisted on the Unreliable Entity List, foreign corporations, organizations and individuals are restricted or prohibited from conducting import and export with China or making an investment in China, among other sanctions.[72] To date, the List itself has not been published. One comment points out that China's Unreliable Entity List may not pose any substantial threat to US companies, because US companies don't rely on China's supply chain to survive in the way that Huawei relies on the US supply of components for production. On the contrary, it may be counterproductive and harmful to China's long-term interests because foreign companies being blacklisted in China could simply diversify their supply chains to outside of China, thus debilitating China's position as a recipient in international trade and investment.[73]

The *Export Control Law* aims to protect national security and interests, fulfil the international obligations of non-proliferation and strengthen export control.[74] The Law imposes state control over the export of dual-use items;[75] military products; nuclear items; and other items, technologies and services with relevance to national security and national interests.[76] The export of controlled items, which are listed and published in separate catalogues,[77] is subject to licencing requirements.[78] The jurisdiction of the *Export Control Law* is considered extremely broad: it holds exporters and intermediary service providers, as well as importers and end users of controlled items, liable and publishable. And the Law has an extra-territorial effect: violators of the *Export Control Law* outside of the territory of China will also be held accountable. Some have observed the similarity between China's *Export Control Law* and the US Export Administration Regulations, as both systems include the elements of commodity lists, licensing requirements,

---

71 Provisions on the Unreliable Entity List (2020), Art. 2.

72 Ibid, Art. 10.

73 Qingxiu Bu, 'China's Blocking Mechanism: The Unreliable Entity List', *Journal of International Trade Law and Policy*, Vol. 19 No. 3 (2020), pp. 159–180, at 171.

74 中华人民共和国出口管制法 (Export Control Law of China) (Promulgated by the NPC on 17 October 2020, effective on 1 December 2020), Art. 1. The meaning of non-proliferation is not clearly provided in the law.

75 Dual-use items refer to goods and technologies that can be applied to the design, development, production, or usage for both civil and military purposes. Ibid, Art. 2.

76 Ibid, Arts. 1 and 2.

77 两用物项和技术进出口许可证管理目录 (Catalogue of Licensed Dual-Use Items and Technology for Import and Export) (Promulgated by MOFCOM and General Administration of Customs on 31 December 2020, effective on 1 January 2021). 中国禁止出口限制出口技术目录 (Catalogue of Technologies Prohibited or Restricted from Export) (Promulgated by MOFCOM and Ministry of Science and Technology on 28 August 2020, effective on promulgation). 关于发布商用密码进口许可清单、出口管制清单和相关管理措施的公告 (Catalogue of Commercial Cryptography for Import Licensing, Export Control and Relevant Administrative Measures) (Promulgated by MOFCOM, State Cryptography Administration and General Administration of Customs on 26 November 2020, effective on 1 January 2021).

78 Export Control Law (2020), Art. 12.

deemed export and re-export restrictions, extra-territoriality, national security impetus, and criminal liabilities, to name a few.[79]

The *Rules on Counteracting Unjustified Extra-Territorial Application of Foreign Legislation and Measures* (Blocking Rules) intend to block the extra-territorial application of foreign laws that prohibit or restrict business between China and a third country, when the application of those foreign laws is deemed detrimental to China's 'national sovereignty, security, development, and the legitimate interests of Chinese individuals and companies'.[80] The Blocking Rules are promulgated as a countermeasure to the US export and sanction measures against Chinese companies, *inter alia*, Huawei and its overseas affiliates. The US *Export Administration Regulations* not only prohibit US companies from exporting goods to Huawei but also preclude non-US companies in third countries from exporting to Huawei if their products comprise at least 25% US-made components.[81] Even if the 25% threshold is not met, the US government may adopt diplomatic ways to prevent foreign governments selling critical products to China. For example, the Trump administration commenced an intensive campaign to the Dutch government in 2020, which successfully blocked ASML, a Dutch semiconductor equipment company, from selling its advanced lithography machine to the Chinese Semiconductor Manufacturing International Corp. in order to prohibit sensitive technology leaks to China on grounds of national security.[82] It is against this background that China contemplated adopting legal tools of its own to block the extra-territorial application of foreign laws that harm its interests. The existence of unjustified extra-territorial application of foreign laws is determined by an inter-departmental working mechanism led by MOFCOM, based on several vaguely worded considerations.[83] China's Blocking Rules, after the existence of unjustified extra-territorial application of a foreign law is confirmed, delegate MOFCOM to issue a 'prohibition order' which will render the

---

79 Lianzhong Pan and Jonathan R. Todd, 'China's New Export Control Law: A Fact Sheet with Practical Applications', *Benesch Friedlander Coplan & Aronoff*, 25 November 2020, https://www.beneschlaw.com/resources/chinas-new-export-control-law-a-fact-sheet-with -practical-applications.html?utm_source=Mondaq&utm_medium=syndication&utm_cam- paign=LinkedIn-integration, last accessed on 18 March 2021.

80 阻断外国法律与措施不当域外适用办法 (Rules on Counteracting Unjustified Extra-Terri- torial Application of Foreign Legislation and Measures) (Promulgated by MOFCOM on 9 January 2021, effective on promulgation), Art. 1.

81 Export Administration Regulations, 15 C.F.R. § 734.4 - De minimis U.S. content.

82 Alexandra Alper, Toby Sterling and Stephen Nellis, 'Trump Administration Pressed Dutch Hard to Cancel China Chip-Equipment Sale: Sources', *Reuters*, 6 January 2020, https://www .reuters.com/article/us-asml-holding-usa-china-insight-idUSKBN1Z50HN, last accessed on 21 July 2021.

83 These considerations include (1) whether international law or principles of international relations are violated; (2) whether there is a potential impact on China's sovereignty, secu- rity, and development; (3) whether there is a potential impact on the legitimate rights and interests of Chinese parties; and (4) other factors deemed necessary. Rules on Counteract- ing Unjustified Extra-Territorial Application of Foreign Legislation and Measures (2021), Art. 6.

foreign legislation or measure in question 'not recognized, not executed, or not obeyed'.[84] The prohibition order creates confusion on whether it is applicable to any third-country parties: if yes, the Blocking Rules create a jurisprudential paradox as it seeks to block and deny the extra-territorial applicability of a foreign legislation by bestowing and enforcing the extra-territorial application of Chinese domestic law; if no, the Blocking Rules then lose their teeth as third-country parties will have no ramifications in continuing to comply with the foreign legislations or measures harming China's interest.[85]

The *Anti-Foreign Sanctions Law* allows the State Council to adopt corresponding countermeasures against foreign individuals and entities that have imposed discriminatory restrictive measures against Chinese citizens and entities.[86] The *Anti-Foreign Sanctions Law* is promulgated in response to sanctions implemented by the US, the EU, the United Kingdom (UK) and Canada targeting Chinese individuals and entities, based on allegations of human rights violations in Xinjiang and erosion of Hong Kong autonomy, both of which are deemed by the Chinese government as malicious foreign interference with China's internal affairs.[87] The objective of the Law is to defend state sovereignty, national security, development interests, and the legitimate rights of Chinese individuals and entities.[88] When foreign states violate international law and basic international relations, restrict or suppress China according to their national laws, meddle with China's internal affairs, and impose discriminatory restrictive measures on Chinese individuals and entities, the State Council may add individuals and entities who directly or indirectly formulate, determine, or implement those discriminatory restrictive measures to China's Countermeasure List.[89] Individuals and entities on the Countermeasure List will be subject to deportation, confiscation of assets, and prohibition to conduct transactions or cooperation with Chinese individuals and companies.[90]

It remains uncertain what economic and legal implications the aforementioned four post-FIL legislations may bring to foreign businesses in China and abroad, and how actively the Chinese government would apply them in practice. Certainly, these post-FIL legislations will significantly affect the direction of the implementation of the FIL.

---

84 Ibid, Art. 7.
85 Marnix Somsen, 'China's New Blocking Rules – More Conflicting Requirements for International Business', *De Brauw*, 16 March 2021, https://www.debrauw.com/legalarticles/chinas-new-blocking-rules-more-conflicting-requirements-for-international-business/, last accessed on 19 March 2021.
86 中华人民共和国反外国制裁法 (Anti-Foreign Sanctions Law) (Promulgated by the Standing Committee of the NPC on 10 June 2021, effective on promulgation).
87 B. Chen Zhu *et al.*, 'China's New Anti-Foreign Sanctions Law: Understanding Its Scope and Potential Liabilities', *Morrison Foerster*, 30 June 2021, https://www.mofo.com/resources/insights/210630-chinas-new-anti-foreign-sanctions-law.html, last accessed on 21 July 2021.
88 Anti-Foreign Sanctions Law (2021), Art. 1.
89 Ibid, Arts. 3 and 4.
90 Ibid, Art. 6.

1.2 The legal panorama of foreign investment

1.2.1 The sources of foreign investment law

It can be a formidable task to navigate through China's foreign investment laws and regulations which have been adopted and updated for more than four decades.[91] China's foreign investment legal regime is characterized by three distinctive features. First, it is a multi-level system with hierarchical sources of law, comprising, at the central level, law promulgated by the NPC and its Standing Committee,[92] administrative regulations promulgated by the State Council,[93] departmental rules adopted by departments of the State Council,[94] and judicial interpretations issued by the Supreme People's Court (SPC);[95] and local laws and regulations, including local regulations promulgated by local People's Congresses and their Standing Committees, local rules adopted by provincial and certain municipal people's governments, autonomous ordinances issued by local autonomous governments, and economic provisions adopted by special economic zones.[96] Due to the different levels of sources of foreign investment law, their titles can be rather disparate, such as 'law', 'regulations', 'rules', 'provisions', 'measures', 'decisions', 'notices', 'guidance', 'opinions' and 'interpretations'.

Second, China's foreign investment legal regime has a central–local dualist function. Laws and regulations adopted by the central organs apply nationwide, and local legislations are only effective within the local jurisdiction. This central–local dualist function creates two problems. To begin with, local governments ran the risk of abusing their legislative competence and stipulating local regulations that were usually more restrictive than, or in contradiction with, laws and regulations of the central government, in order to create rent-seeking

---

91 A keywork search in the ChinaLawInfo database demonstrates the complexity and perplexity of China's foreign investment legal regime. A search for the keyword '外商' (foreign investors) only in the titles of legislations reveals 928 pieces of central and local legislations, including both obsolete and effective ones. In the same vein, a search for '外资' (foreign capital) reveals 294 pieces of legislations, and a search for '外国投资' (foreign investment) reveals 32 results. Altogether these three keyword searches add up to 1,254 pieces of legislations. And this does not count laws and regulations that do not include the keywords in their titles, but includes provisions relating to foreign investment, foreign capital or foreign investors. The database can be retrieved from https://www.pkulaw.com/english.

92 For example, the Foreign Investment Law promulgated by the NPC on 15 March 2019.

93 For example, 国务院办公厅关于进一步做好稳外贸稳外资工作的意见 (Opinions of the General Office of the State Council on Further Stabilizing Foreign Trade and Foreign Investment) (Promulgated on 5 August 2020, effective on promulgation).

94 For example, 外商投资安全审查办法 (Measures for National Security Review of Foreign Investment) (Promulgated by NDRC and MOFCOM on 19 December 2020, effective on 18 January 2021).

95 For example, 最高人民法院关于适用〈中华人民共和国外商投资法〉若干问题的解释 (Interpretation of the SPC on Several Issues concerning the Application of the Foreign Investment Law) (Issued on 26 December 2019, effective on 1 January 2020).

96 Due to the limited scope, local legislations are not elaborated in this book.

opportunities or to execute a local protectionism agenda.[97] For instance, some local governments in the past implemented a more restrictive FDI market access regime within their jurisdictions than the nationwide *Catalogue of Industries Guiding Foreign Investment*, in order to shield local SOEs from the competition of FIEs. To alleviate this problem, the FIL stipulates that local governments are prohibited from derogating foreign investors' lawful rights granted by central legislations or burdening foreign investors with additional obligations that are not prescribed by central legislations.[98] The State Council adopted the *Regulation on Optimizing the Business Environment* in October 2019, which specifically stipulates that local governments or departments are prohibited from developing any market access rules.[99] Furthermore, in order to attract more FDI, some local governments also conducted destructive competition with other local governments by promising foreign investors preferential treatment, which brought more harm than good to the local economy. For instance, local governments created local economic development zones that granted various favourable taxation policies, lowered utility prices, discounted land use fees, concessional financing conditions and so on to foreign investors. However, some of these economic development zones never received any investment although the local governments had already spent enormous sums of their fiscal revenue to build state-of-the-art infrastructure in advance, and agricultural lands witnessed a rapid reduction as they were transformed into industrial lands to make room for these local economic development zones.[100]

Third, China's foreign investment legal regime is a multi-institutional system at both central and local levels, with each institution mandated independently or combined with others to a certain regulatory purpose, depending on their distinctive expertise. At the central level, the State Council and its departments in principle own the legislative and policy competence over foreign investment. The two most important departments responsible for foreign investment are NDRC and MOFCOM, which have broad power on market access approval for the restricted catalogue of the *Negative List for Foreign Investment*, national security review, anti-monopoly review, approval for fixed-asset investment, the Unreliable Entity List, and the Countermeasure List, blocking unjustified extra-territorial application of foreign laws. As one scholar indicates, there has been a long-existing jurisdiction duelling over foreign investment between NDRC and MOFCOM, which leads to, in many cases, an equal and dual leadership in a regulatory area

---

97 Qingjiang Kong, 《中华人民共和国外商投资法》解读 (*An Interpretation of the Foreign Investment Law of the People's Republic of China*) (Beijing: Law Press, 2019), p. 79.

98 FIL (2019), Arts. 18 and 24.

99 优化营商环境条例 (Regulation on Optimizing the Business Environment) (Issued by the State Council on 22 October 2019, effective on 1 January 2020), Art. 20.

100 Junfu Zhang, 'Interjurisdictional Competition for FDI: The Case of China's "Development Zone Fever"', *Regional Science and Urban Economics*, Vol. 41 (2011), pp. 145–159.

as a result of political bargaining and compromise.[101] Other important institutions at the central level responsible for foreign investment include the SAMR in charge of FIE registration and information reporting, the State-Owned Assets Supervision and Administration Commission (SASAC) in charge of state-asset transfer of SOEs, the SAFE and the People's Bank of China (PBoC) responsible for foreign exchange control, the State Taxation Administration for the taxation of enterprises, and the China Securities Regulatory Commission (CSRC) responsible for stock market regulation. In addition, sectoral regulators will be involved if the investment takes place in a sector that requires approval, licensing, qualification or review processes according to the *Negative List for Market Access*.[102] For example, the production of weapons and ammunitions was eliminated from the *Negative List for Foreign Investment* since 2018, but this doesn't mean that foreign investors could make an investment with no market access preconditions. According to the *Negative List for Market Access*, the development, production, configuration, sale, purchase and transportation of weaponry and any other relevant production of items concerning public safety require the approval from multiple departments of the State Council, *inter alia*, the Ministry of Public Security, applicable to both domestic and foreign investors.[103]

1.2.2 *The corporate forms of FIEs*

1.2.2.1 *Legal persons*

Pursuant to the entry into force of the FIL on 1 January 2020, the three primary foreign investment laws were repealed. The EJVs, CJVs and WFOEs already established before 1 January 2020 can either remain in a five-year grace period from 1 January 2020 to 31 December 2024 or adjust their corporate forms according to *Company Law* and *Partnership Enterprise Law*. After the expiry of the grace period, still existing EJVs, CJVs and WFOEs will no longer be able to register with the SAMR, and their inconformity with the FIL will be publicly announced.[104] New establishments of FIEs pursuant to the EJV Law, CJV Law and WFOE Law are not allowed as of 1 January 2020.

    Limited liability companies (LLCs) or companies limited by shares (CLSs) under the *Company Law* will become the dominant corporate forms of FIEs. An LLC is a legal person that is formed by a minimum of one and a maximum of 50 shareholders (either natural or legal persons); and a CLS, also known as a

---

101 Xingxing Li, 'An Economic Analysis of Regulatory Overlap and Regulatory Competition: The Experience of Interagency Regulatory Competition in China's Regulation of Inbound Foreign Investment', *Administrative Law Review*, Vol. 67, No. 4 (2015), pp. 685–750, at 700–708.
102 市场准入负面清单 (Negative List for Market Access) (Promulgated by MOFCOM and NDRC on 10 December 2020, effective on promulgation).
103 Ibid, Item 27.
104 Implementing Regulation of the FIL (2019), Art. 44.

stock company, is a legal person that is established either by means of promotion (发起设立) or through public offering (募集设立), and in both cases the number of promoters varies from 2 to 200 natural or legal persons.[105] The *Company Law* doesn't impose restrictions on the qualification of shareholders that initially establish an LLC, while the promoters of a CLS are subject to residency requirements. According to the *Company Law*, more than half of the promoters of a CLS must have a domicile in China.[106] This would infer that to establish a CLS, foreign natural or legal persons as promoters must not exceed half of the total number of promoters and the CLS needs to be established under a Chinese-foreign mixed ownership structure.

1.2.2.2 Non-legal persons

Foreign investors can also choose to form a non-legal person entity in China. According to the *Partnership Enterprise Law*, a partnership enterprise can be adopted as a general partnership enterprise or a limited liability partnership enterprise, and both can be established by domestic and foreign natural persons, legal persons, or other organizations.[107] If an investment is made in the restricted catalogue of the *Negative List for Foreign Investment* that has shareholding ratio restrictions, a partnership enterprise is not allowed to be established.[108]

Other non-legal entities for a foreign investor to make its market entry in China include representative offices or branches of a foreign company. According to Chinese law, a representative office is 'a working organization established by a foreign enterprise within the territory of China … to conduct non-profit activities related to the business of foreign enterprises.'[109] Representative offices provide an option for foreign investors who 'simply want to better understand the market and potential opportunities' of doing business in China and assist the overseas foreign company in developing a long-term investment strategy, nevertheless cannot engage in any form of profit-making businesses.[110] Representative offices were a popular first choice for market entry historically, as they were 'the simplest and least expensive entity for foreign investors to establish'.[111] But they

---

105 公司法 (Company Law) (Promulgated by the Standing Committee of the NPC on 26 October 2018, effective on promulgation), Arts. 3, 24, 77, 78.

106 Ibid, Art. 78.

107 中华人民共和国合伙企业法 (Partnership Enterprise Law) (Promulgated by the Standing Committee of the NPC on 27 August 2006, effective on 1 June 2007). For a comprehensive understanding of foreign invested limited partnership enterprise in China, see Stephan Kuntner, *China's Foreign-Invested Limited Partnership Enterprise* (Cham: Springer, 2020).

108 Negative List for Foreign Investment (2020), Art. 4.

109 外国企业常驻代表机构登记管理条例 (Regulation on the Administration of Registration of Resident Representative Offices of Foreign Enterprises) (Promulgated by the State Council on 18 September 2018, effective on promulgation), Art. 2.

110 For a detailed discussion on the representative office in China, see Tarrant Mahony, *supra* note 1, pp. 155–173.

111 Ibid, p. 156.

have become very scarce nowadays, because of their significant restrictions. A branch of a foreign company is a non-legal entity registered in China by a foreign company based outside of China; its establishment is subject to a case-by-case approval and governed by the *Company Law* (Chapter 11).[112] Compared with a representative office, a branch of a foreign company can conduct business for profit in China.[113] For example, foreign banks or foreign insurance companies can set up a branch in China and conduct business, but the overseas foreign company and its branch in China undertake joint liability as the Chinese branch is not a legal entity.

Other more temporary types of investment involve Chinese-foreign cooperation, such as build–operate–transfer (BOT), cooperative exploration and exploitation of natural resources, and contract construction projects. Foreign enterprises do not need to establish any organizational presence in China as a legal or non-legal entity to engage in these businesses, but their business activities are governed by *Administrative Measures for the Registration of Production and Operation of Enterprises of Foreign Countries (Regions) in China*.[114] Foreign enterprises are required to register with the SAMR and obtain a business licence in order to conduct production or operation activities. For certain activities such as exploration and exploitation of oil and mineral resources, additional *ex ante* approval is required.[115]

1.2.2.3 Foreign-invested investment vehicles

Foreign investors can also choose to establish a company for the sole purpose of investment in China. An FIE as an investment company is not a separate type of corporate form in China, but it is distinctive from traditional FIEs as it does not produce any products or provide any services. In practice, an FIE that solely conducts investment business is commonly referred to as a holding company.[116] There are three types of foreign-invested investment vehicles according to law, namely an investment FIE (外商投资性公司), a foreign-invested start-up investment company (外商投资创业投资企业) and a Qualified Foreign Limited Partner (QFLP) private equity investment fund (境外有限合伙人私募股权投资基金).

First, according to the *Provisions on the Establishment of Investment Companies by Foreign Investors*, an investment FIE can adopt the form of an LLC or a CLS, which is either wholly foreign owned or takes a mixed ownership with Chinese

---

112 Company Law (2018), Arts. 192, 195.

113 For a detailed discussion on foreign branches, see Danling Yu, *Chinese Business Law* (Singapore: Palgrave Macmillan, 2019), pp. 54–55.

114 外国（地区）企业在中国境内从事生产经营活动登记管理办法 (Administrative Measures for the Registration of Production and Operation of Enterprises of Foreign Countries (Regions) in China) (Promulgated by SAMR on 23 October 2020, effective on promulgation).

115 Ibid, Arts. 3, 4, and 7.

116 Tarrant Mahony, *supra* note 1, p. 206.

investors, and conducts direct investment in China.[117] To establish an investment FIE requires rigorous qualification requirements on its global value, registered capital in China, assets under management and reputation, in addition to a case-by-case approval by MOFCOM.[118]

Second, a foreign investor may independently, or together with a Chinese investor, establish a foreign-invested start-up investment company in China, according to *Provisions Concerning the Administration of Foreign-Invested Start-up Investment Company*.[119] The foreign investor first establishes a company or a partnership enterprise, which then makes equity investment in other non-listed Chinese companies in the new and high-tech sector and at its initial phase of development, in order to obtain prospective capital gains.[120] To establish this type of FIE also includes a number of qualification requirements and approval from MOFCOM, which are much less stringent compared with that of an investment FIE.[121]

Third, a foreign investor can act as a QFLP and establish a foreign-invested private equity investment fund in China, most commonly in the corporate form of a limited liability partnership enterprise, together with a qualified Chinese partner who acts as a general partner. A limited partnership is a favourable form for QFLPs because, among other benefits, no enterprise income tax is required for a partnership enterprise in China.[122] The foreign-invested private equity investment fund may raise private financing overseas and domestically, and then acquire shares of Chinese non-listed companies. The QFLP scheme has only been available in several trial cities since 2010, and its establishment is subject to different local requirements and approval processes.[123]

117 商务部关于外商投资举办投资性公司的规定 (Provisions on the Establishment of Investment Companies by Foreign Investors) (Promulgated by MOFCOM on 28 October 2015, effective on promulgation), Art. 2.
118 Ibid, Art. 6.
119 外商投资创业投资企业管理规定 (Provisions Concerning the Administration of Foreign-Invested Start-up Investment Company) (Promulgated by MOFCOM on 28 October 2015, effective on promulgation), Art. 2.
120 Ibid, Arts. 3 and 4.
121 Ibid, Arts. 6–8.
122 Robbie Chen, 'Expanded Implementation of Qualified Foreign Limited Partnership Heats Up Foreign Equity Investments in China', *Winston & Strawn LLP*, 15 January 2021, https://www.lexology.com/library/detail.aspx?g=65a2ef79-f9be-46c1-85d1-70c8191c06b7, last accessed on 13 July 2021.
123 At the moment, the QFLP scheme is available in Shanghai (2010); Beijing, Chongqing, Tianjin (2011); Qingdao (2015); Shenzhen, Guizhou (2017); Fujian (Province), Zhuhai (2018); Guangzhou (2019); Suzhou, and Hainan (Province) (2020). See, e.g., 海南省关于开展合格境外有限合伙人(QFLP)境内股权投资暂行办法 (Interim Measures on Equity Investment in China by QFLPs in Hainan Province) (Promulgated by Hainan Financial Supervision and Administration Bureau *et al.* on 10 October 2020, effective on promulgation).

Fourth, according to Chinese law, to establish a new enterprise, including an FIE, there must be a registered scope of business on its business licence.[124] An enterprise cannot conduct business operations that are outside the registered scope of business. This means that for an FIE to conduct equity investment in China, its business scope must be registered as 'investment', using one of the aforementioned three investment vehicles. However, some leeway in recent years has been given for an FIE to conduct equity investment, even though investment is not registered as its scope of business. This is realized by the Notice issued by the SAFE in 2019, commonly referred to as Order No. 28, which in theory, permits any FIEs in China to utilize their own capital in making equity investments in other companies in China, under the condition that the equity investment complies with the *Negative List for Foreign Investment* and that projects to be invested are authentic and legitimate.[125] Nevertheless, how Order No. 28 is implemented in practice remains to be clarified. Note that all the aforementioned investment vehicles are only allowed to conduct equity investment in non-listed companies. For foreign investors to conduct stock investment in China, a different set of qualification and approval procedures applies.[126]

1.3 Key features of the 2019 FIL

The FIL includes 6 chapters and 42 provisions, and its content is divided into five categories – definition and scope, investment facilitation, investment protection, investment management, and legal liabilities.[127] Chapter 1 (General Provisions) explicates the objective of the law, the definition of 'foreign investment' and FIEs, and the principle of pre-establishment national treatment, among others. Chapter 2 (Investment Facilitation) provides guarantees on equal treatment between foreign investors and domestic ones in areas of national industrial policies, transparency of legislation, the development and application of national compulsory standards, and participation in public procurement. Chapter 3 (Investment Protection) pledges not to expropriate foreign investment unless under specified lawful circumstances, free remitting of foreign exchanges, protection of investors'

---

124 企业法人登记管理条例 (Regulation on the Administration of Registration of Enterprise Legal Persons) (Promulgated by the State Council on 2 March 2019, effective on promulgation), Art. 9.

125 国家外汇管理局关于进一步促进跨境贸易投资便利化的通知 (Notice of the SAFE on Further Facilitating Cross-Border Trade and Investment) (Promulgated by SAFE on 23 October 2019, effective on promulgation), Art. 2.

126 For a detailed discussion on investment on the stock market by foreign investors, see Chapter 3, Section 3.3.

127 For a comprehensive discussion on the provisions of the FIL, see Qingjiang Kong, *supra* note 97. Mo Zhang, 'Change of Regulatory Scheme: China's New Foreign Investment Law and Reshaped Legal Landscape', *UCLA Pacific Basin Law Journal*, Vol. 37 Issue 1 (2020), pp. 179–238. Yawen Zheng, 'China's New Foreign Investment Law and Its Contribution Towards the Country's Development Goals', *Journal of World Investment & Trade*, Vol. 22 Issue 3 (2021), pp. 388–428.

IP rights, prohibition of forced transfer of technology, protection of commercial secrets, consistency between central and local foreign investment legislation, stability of government contracts, and the complaint system. Chapter 4 (Investment Management) stipulates the negative list for foreign investment, the corporate forms of FIEs, anti-monopoly compliance, information reporting system, and national security review. Chapter 5 (Legal Liabilities) prescribes investors' liability in violation of the negative list; liability in violation of the information reporting system; and reiterates state functionaries' administrative and criminal liability in cases of abusing power, neglecting duties, embezzlement, and divulgation of investors' commercial secrets. The following section discusses in some detail the innovative aspects of the FIL that are of particular interest and significance to foreign investors.

1.3.1 Pre-establishment national treatment

One of the most striking breakthroughs of the FIL is the introduction of pre-establishment national treatment with a negative list approach. Due to the fact that uneven market access and lack of reciprocity have become a constant complaint from foreign investors and foreign governments, and that some pressure was imposed by the US amid the US–China Trade War, China for the first time in codified national law committed itself to granting pre-establishment national treatment to foreign investors, with the only exception of the *Negative List for Foreign Investment.* As a result, foreign investors and their investment are accorded treatment no less favourable than that accorded to domestic investors in the market access phase, except that investment to be made in the *Negative List for Foreign Investment* is either prohibited or restricted with additional conditions.[128] Chapter 2, Sections 2.1 and 2.2 of this book provide a comprehensive understanding and a critical appraisal of the pre-establishment national treatment with a negative list approach.

1.3.2 Post-establishment national treatment

The FIL and its Implementing Regulation emphasize equal treatment for foreign and domestic investors post-establishment. As a general rule of thumb, foreign investment made outside of the *Negative List for Foreign Investment* shall be governed under the principle of equal treatment vis-à-vis domestic investment.[129] Specifically, the FIL promises equal treatment in the field of national preferential policies in support of the development of enterprises; participation in the formulation of standards; application of compulsory state standards; government

---

128 FIL (2019), Art. 4.
129 FIL (2019), Art. 28.

procurement; and sectoral approval and licencing.[130] Chapter 2, Section 2.3 explicates these post-establishment national treatment provisions in the FIL.

1.3.3 National security review

Because the FIL is intended to serve as a constitutional-like law in regard to China's foreign investment regulatory regime, its implementation is dependent on the specific departmental rules and regulations to be subsequently promulgated. Now that China's FDI market access has been largely liberalized, a national security review system becomes imperative and acts as a last line of defence to address security-related implications. Art. 35 of the FIL stipulates that 'the state shall establish national security review of foreign investment that impacts or may impact national security'. This stipulation apparently is not enforceable in practice without a further workable framework. In addition, Art. 40 of the FIL Implementing Regulation duplicates Art. 35 of the FIL, resulting in two identical provisions in the law. As both provisions are not in the least practical, NDRC and MOFCOM adopted the *Measures for the National Security Review of Foreign Investment* in December 2020 that substantiate the national security provision in the FIL.[131] Chapter 4 compendiously analyzes China's national security concept and the system of national security review of foreign investment.

1.3.4 Information reporting system

Both the FIL and its Implementing Regulation call for the establishment of an information reporting system, which consists of information reporting upon the occurrence of statutory events and an annual report.[132] The Online Enterprise Registration System was reformed in 2017 by the State Administration of Industry and Commerce (SAIC; predecessor of SAMR) to digitize and streamline the registration process for both domestic and foreign businesses under one unified online platform.[133] The National Enterprise Credit Information Publicity System was launched in 2014 by the SAIC to mandate the submission of annual reports, also applicable to both domestic and foreign enterprises, in order to render certain corporate information publicly accessible and transparent.[134]

---

130 FIL (2019), Arts. 9, 15, 16, 30.
131 外商投资安全审查办法 (Measures for the National Security Review of Foreign Investment) (Promulgated by NDRC and MOFCOM on 19 December 2021, effective on 18 January 2021).
132 FIL (2019), Art. 34; Implementing Regulation of the FIL (2019), Arts. 38 and 39.
133 企业登记网上注册系统 (Online Enterprise Registration System), accessible at http://wsdj.samr.gov.cn/saicmcdjweb/, last accessed on 8 August 2021.
134 国家企业信用信息公示系统 (National Enterprise Credit Information Publicity System), accessible at http://www.gsxt.gov.cn/index.html, last accessed on 13 July 2021. For a detailed discussion on the Online Enterprise Registration System and the National Enterprise Credit Information Publicity System, see Mo Zhang, *supra* note 127, at 226–229.

Since December 2019, MOFCOM, SAMR and SAFE have issued multiple measures on information reporting and annual reporting to implement the information reporting provision in the FIL.[135] According to *Measures on Information Reporting of Foreign Investment*, foreign investors and FIEs are required to submit initial reports, modification reports and deregistration reports on the Online Enterprise Registration System, and annual reports on the National Enterprise Credit Information Publicity System.[136] An initial report should be filed when a foreign investor establishes a new FIE or acquires shares of a wholly domestic-owned enterprise, and a modification report should be submitted when certain changes to the original information in the initial report take place.[137] In the event that an FIE ceases to exist, the foreign investor is only obliged to undertake the enterprise deregistration procedure with the relevant local Administration for Market Regulation, which will be deemed as having submitted the deregistration report simultaneously.[138] An annual report is to be submitted between January and June regarding basic information of the FIE, information of the investors and their actual controllers, information on business operation, assets and liabilities, and the like.[139]

The information reporting system implies positive significance for foreign investors. It replaces the previous *ex ante* case-by-case approval system with *ex post*, signifying a shift from prior administrative approval to post-supervision to foreign investment.[140] While seen as a leap forward in alleviating the administrative burden for foreign businesses, the information reporting system raises concerns on the scope of business information required to be submitted and disclosed, and the confidentiality of the contents, especially in the context of China's alleged practice of forced transfer of technology (FTT) against FIEs.[141] One may speculate that the information reporting system could become a new avenue for the Chinese government to request and obtain technology, know-how and commercial secrets from FIEs. Further, the enforcement of information reporting at the local levels may contradict the original intention of the central government

---

135 市场监管总局　商务部　外汇局关于做好年报'多报合一'改革有关工作的通知　(Notice by the SAMR, MOFCOM, and SAFE on Effectively Completing the Reform of 'Integrating Multiple Reports into One') (Issued on 16 December 2019, effective on promulgation). 外商投资信息报告办法 (Measures on Information Reporting of Foreign Investment) (Promulgated by MOFCOM and SAMR on 30 December 2019, effective on 1 January 2020). 商务部关于外商投资信息报告有关事项的公告 (Notice of MOFCOM Concerning Matters on Information Reporting of Foreign Investment) (Issued on 31 December 2019, effective on 1 January 2020). 商务部　市场监管总局　外汇局关于开展2019年度外商投资信息报告年度报告的公告 (Announcement of MOFCOM, SAMR and SAFE on the 2019 Annual Report of Foreign Investment) (Issued on 31 December 2019, effective on 1 January 2020).

136 Measures on Information Reporting of Foreign Investment (2019), Art. 8.

137 Ibid, Arts. 9–11.

138 Ibid, Art. 13.

139 Ibid, Arts. 14 and 15.

140 FIL (2019), Art. 34; Implementing Regulation of the FIL (2019), Art. 38.

141 For a detailed discussion on FTT, see Chapter 5, Section 5.2.

in establishing such a system. It is reported that some local Administrations for Market Regulation, for instance in Shanghai, have required foreign investors to submit an initial report as a prerequisite before they can proceed to the enterprise registration procedure, which is the very first step to establish any business in China.[142] In this case, information reporting appends an additional procedural hurdle to foreign investors when establishing an FIE in China. Considering the fact that information reporting is administered by local governments, which are notorious for their creative interpretation of national laws and for their adoption of self-interested local regulations in order to achieve local protectionism or rent-seeking opportunities,[143] it remains to be seen whether the information reporting system will be implemented to the benefit or detriment of foreign investors in practice.

1.3.5 Investors' protection

In general, the Chinese government asserts the protection of foreign investors and their investment, profits, and other lawful rights and interests.[144] The government shall not expropriate foreign investment unless expropriation is under extraordinary circumstances, for a public interest purpose, according to laws and regulations, under lawful procedures and in an indiscriminatory manner, and compensated in a fair, reasonable and timely manner and per market value.[145] Chapter 2, Section 2.3 discusses in detail the expropriation clause.

Foreign investors are allowed to remit freely into or outside of China, in RMB or any foreign currency, its capital subscription, profit and any other monetary gains made within China.[146] It is emphasized in particular that no individuals or entities may impose restrictions on the type of currency, amount and frequency of the remittance.[147] However, China's rigorous and complex foreign exchange control raises considerable doubt regarding the applicability of this provision in practice.[148] Pursuant to the *Regulation on the Management of Foreign Exchange*, foreign exchange regarding foreign direct or indirect investment is regulated under the capital account, which is subject to registration, restrictive conditions or approval by the SAFE depending on the matters of transaction.[149] It remains

---

142 Yu Zheng, Guanqiao Chen and Yiru Liu, 'Navigating the New Foreign Investment Information Reporting System', *JunHe*, 31 March 2020, http://www.junhe.com/legal-updates/1131?locale=en, last accessed on 5 July 2021.
143 Yawen Zheng, *supra* note 127, at 417.
144 FIL (2019), Art. 5.
145 FIL (2019), Art. 20; Implementing Regulation of the FIL (2019), Art. 21.
146 FIL (2019), Art. 21.
147 Implementing Regulation of the FIL (2019), Art. 22.
148 Mo Zhang, *supra* note 127, at 234–235.
149 中华人民共和国外汇管理条例 (Regulation on the Management of Foreign Exchange) (Promulgated by the State Council on 8 May 2008, effective on promulgation), Arts. 16 and 22.

to be seen how the 'free' remittance of foreign exchange as promised in the FIL can be reconciled with existing foreign exchange control measures in practice.

China in the FIL pledges to protect foreign investors' IP rights.[150] Any infringement on IP rights will be austerely held legally accountable.[151] The transfer of technology shall only be based on a fair and consensual basis, and no administrative coercion on the transfer of technology is permitted.[152] The Implementing Regulation reiterates that administrative agencies shall not explicitly force, or force in a disguised form, the transfer of technology by administrative means, such as licensing, inspection, penalty or compulsion.[153] Administrative agencies and officials are subject to confidentiality obligations when they acquire commercial secrets of foreign investors.[154] Chapter 5 provides a comprehensive analysis of law and practice on China's IP legal regime, forced transfer of technology and protection of commercial secrets.

1.3.6 The complaint system

The complaint system is not a novel invention in the FIL. MOFCOM released the *Interim Working Measures for the Complaint System of FIEs* as early as 2006;[155] it has now been superseded by the *2020 Working Measures for the Complaint System of FIEs*.[156]

In the event that an FIE or a foreign investor deems their legitimate rights and interests infringed by an administrative agency or its functionaries, or when an FIE or an investor proposes general complaints or suggestions to the business environment, the FIE or the investor may initiate a procedure with a competent agency to mediate and reconcile the complaints or disputes. The competent agency responsible for the hearing of complaints are pertinent departments at local governments designated by MOFCOM or local governments above the county level. Foreign-related commercial and civil disputes are explicitly excluded from the purview of the complaint system.[157] At the central level, MOFCOM establishes an inter-ministerial joint meeting system (部际联席会议制度) to coordinate, command and supervise local governments in administering complaints,

---

150 FIL (2019), Art. 22; Implementing Regulation of the FIL (2019), Art. 23.
151 FIL (2019), Art. 22.
152 FIL (2019), Art. 22.
153 Implementing Regulation of the FIL (2019), Art. 24.
154 FIL (2019), Art. 23.
155 外商投资企业投诉工作暂行办法 (Interim Working Measures for the Complaint System of FIEs) (Promulgated by MOFCOM on 1 September 2006, effective on 1 October 2006). For a detailed discussion on this Interim Working Measures and other relevant regulations, see Zhang Demiao and Zhao Jianya, 'The Practical Difficulties and Solutions of the Mechanism for Coordinating and Handling Foreign Complaints in View of the Business Environment under the Rule of Law', *China Legal Science*, Vol. 8 Issue 4 (2020), pp. 48–72.
156 外商投资企业投诉工作办法 (Working Measures for the Complaint System of FIEs) (Promulgated by MOFCOM on 25 August 2020, effective on 1 October 2020).
157 Ibid, Art. 2.

and also establishes a National FIE Complaint Centre to hear complaints against departments of the State Council or provincial governments.[158] The complaint system is independent of other administrative remedies; it is neither a precondition to nor an exclusion of foreign investors' rights of access to administrative reconsideration or litigation.[159] The competent agency has 7 working days to make a decision on whether the complaint is accepted upon receiving the full set of required documents, and should conclude the review within 60 working days in principle, but is subject to extension in complicated cases.[160] The dispute can be resolved by reaching a reconciliation or a settlement agreement between disputants.[161]

The complaint system gives foreign investors the opportunity to inform and challenge all levels of government up to the ministerial and provincial level, and gives the governments 'the opportunity to take appropriate actions to make further improvements'.[162] Its success, however, will significantly depend on whether foreign complaints will be handled efficiently and effectively, and to what extent the settlement agreement will be respected, recognized and enforced in practice.

1.3.7 Corporate governance of FIEs

From 1 January 2020, the FIL officially repealed the three primary foreign investment laws, and newly established FIEs ought to conform with China's *Company Law* or the *Partnership Enterprise Law*.[163] This terminates the dual-track regime of corporate governance of FIEs and domestic enterprises for newly established FIEs. Existing CJVs, EJVs and WFOEs may maintain their original corporate forms for another five years.[164] These existing three types of FIEs are not mandated, but only advised, to adjust their corporate structures to be in line with China's *Company Law* or the *Partnership Enterprise Law* within the five-year grace period. Failure to do so after 1 January 2025 does not result in a nullification, but their nonconformity with the FIL will be publicly disclosed.[165]

Since the corporate structure of a WFOE has already been governed in principle by *Company Law*, the transformation in corporate governance brings significant

158 Ibid, Arts. 5 and 6. The National FIE Complaint Centre is administered under the Investment Promotion Agency of MOFCOM, accessible at http://www.cipainvest.org.cn/article/guanywm/200908/20090806464229.shtml, last accessed on 13 July 2021.
159 Ibid, Art. 8.
160 Ibid, Arts. 15 and 19.
161 Ibid, Art. 18.
162 Sofia Baruzzi, 'China's New Mechanism to Handle Complaints by Foreign-Invested Entities', *China Briefing*, 9 October 2020, https://www.china-briefing.com/news/china-new-mechanism-to-handle-complaints-by-foreign-invested-entities/, last accessed on 28 June 2021.
163 FIL (2019), Art. 31.
164 FIL (2019), Art. 42.
165 Implementing Regulation of the FIL (2019), Art. 44.

implications, mostly to joint ventures.[166] Under the obsolete EJV Law and CJV Law, the highest authority in a joint venture was the board of directors (in an EJV) or the Joint Management Committee (in a CJV); in contrast, the Shareholders Meeting shall be the highest authority in an LLC or the Shareholders' Assembly in a CLS under the *Company Law*.[167] Other distinctions in corporate governance between the JV Laws and the *Company law* include different voting rules in the highest authority for major issues, different number of directors on the board, different terms for directors and different eligible personnel as legal representatives of the company.[168] Undoubtedly, the transformation from EJVs, CJVs and WFOEs to an LLC or a CLS will pose unchartered challenges to existing FIEs in terms of corporate governance, documentations, compliance, contracts, shareholder agreements and articles of associations.[169]

1.4 Conclusion

The evolution of China's FDI regulatory regime reflects the dynamic nature of lawmaking which corresponds to the country's economic development. There is no doubt that FDI is tremendously beneficial to China's economic growth and modernization. China's foreign investment laws serve the primary purpose of protecting China's economic interests and security, but also have always been conscious of catering to foreign investors' needs and expectations. A perennial theme in the legislative history and in the *status quo* is a blend of incentives that attract FDI and various control mechanisms over FDI. This mixed character cannot be more pronounced, for instance, in the FIL that introduces pre- and post-establishment national treatment on the one hand, and the negative list approach and national security review regime on the other. Another lingering theme in the course of FDI governance in China is the oscillation between flexibility and principality. China's reform and opening-up over more than 40 years are a testament to the adaptiveness of its foreign investment law and policy, and the incremental

---

166 Unlike the CJV Law and the EJV Law, the WFOE Law does not stipulate the corporate governance of a WFOE, only that a WFOE can acquire legal person status according to Chinese law. Since 2006, it has become clear that the corporate governance of a WFOE should comply with Company Law. 关于外商投资的公司审批登记管理法律适用若干问题的执行意见 (Implementing Opinions on Issues Relating to the Application of Law for Approval, Registration and Administration of Foreign-Invested Enterprises) (Promulgated by General Administration of Customs, MOFCOM, State Administration for Industry and Commerce, and SAFE on 24 April 2006, effective on promulgation), Art. 3.

167 Mark Schaub *et al.*, 'China Foreign Investment Law: How Will It Impact the Existing FIEs?' *King & Wood China Law Insights*, 3 June 2019, https://www.chinalawinsight.com/2019/06/articles/foreign-investment/china-foreign-investment-law-how-will-it-impact-the-existing-fies/, last accessed on 30 June 2020.

168 Ibid.

169 For a comprehensive discussion and a practical guide on FIE contract templates in the five-year transition period, see Robert Lewis, *The Dawn of a New Era for FDI in China* (Beijing: Law Press, 2020).

liberalization process emanates flexible rule-making that responds to external demands and challenges. Nonetheless, there are also bottom lines that will not be crossed. China maintains that the Party-state polity, its socialist market economy, state control in critical sectors, and state sovereignty and economic security are deemed uncompromisable.

With the entry into effect of the FIL, novel challenges abroad and at home also come to the fore. As the world's second-largest economy, the world's biggest FDI recipient and the world's biggest exporter of goods, China's demographic and economic size might be seen as a concern or, in many cases, a blatant threat to other comparable Western economies. The US has labelled China as a global trade extorter and a predatory worldwide investor for years, and anti-China sentiment hit its climax during the Trump administration and amid the US–China Trade War. The EU now follows suit and regards China as 'an economic competitor in the pursuit of technological leadership, and a systemic rival promoting alternative models of governance'.[170] These external circumstances suggest that foreign governments will likely be more critical of China's domestic FDI governance and that foreign investors will likely be more discreet when investing in China. Internally, China is witnessing a slowing economy; rising costs in production resources, land and labour; and potent SOEs that continue to enjoy unparallel competitive advantages at the expense of squeezing out private and foreign businesses, to name a few. Future success or failure will largely depend on whether and how well the FIL and China's FDI regulatory regime thereafter can keep pace with new external and internal developments and tackle new challenges.

---

170 European Commission, 'Joint Communication to the European Parliament, the European Council and the Council: EU-China – A Strategic Outlook', JOIN(2019) 5 final, 12 March 2019, https://ec.europa.eu/info/sites/default/files/communication-eu-china-a-strategic-outlook.pdf, last accessed on 28 June 2021, p. 1.

2 Market access and national treatment

2.1 Market access: Relaxation and limitations

2.1.1 The evolution of China's market access for foreign investment

From 1979 to 2013, China adopted a rigorous control style of governance for foreign investors entering the Chinese market, epitomized by three main elements: the control of sectors to be invested, restrictions on corporate forms of a foreign-invested enterprise (FIE), and a multi-government level and multi-institutional case-by-case approval system for the establishment of FIEs.

First, in terms of control of sectors, from 1995 onwards China periodically issued the *Catalogue of Industries Guiding Foreign Investment* (the Catalogue), categorizing foreign investment into three explicit clusters and one tacit cluster.[1] The Catalogue included encouraged sectors, in principle tertiary and high-tech industries, where foreign investment was desired and might receive preferential policy support; restricted sectors, where foreign investors were only allowed for market entry on specific conditions such as joint venture requirements, shareholding caps in the joint venture and a ban on the foreign investors acting as high-level management personnel in the joint venture; prohibited sectors, where foreign investors were denied market entry in the most strategic and sensitive sectors; and tacitly permitted sectors, which included all the rest of the sectors not covered in the Catalogue.

Second, in terms of corporate forms, the 'three primary foreign investment laws' provided three exclusive business vehicles for FIEs: an equity joint venture (EJV) from 1979, a wholly foreign-owned enterprise (WFOE) from 1986 and a contractual joint venture (CJV) from 1988. The control of corporate forms of FIEs was achieved in tandem with the Catalogue, *inter alia*, the mandatory EJV or CJV requirements in the majority of restricted sectors in the Catalogue.

---

1 外商投资产业指导目录 (Catalogue of Industries for Guiding Foreign Investment) (1995) (1997) (2002) (2004) (2007) (2011) (2015) (2017) (All repealed). For a historical overview of the three primary foreign investment laws and the Catalogue, see Introduction and Chapter 1, Section 1.1.

DOI: 10.4324/9781003168805-3

Third, to establish new FIEs, in addition to conformity with the Catalogue and the corporate form requirement, foreign investors needed to gain government approval on a case-by-case basis.[2] To begin with, project approval from either the National Development and Reform Commission (NDRC) or local DRCs was required, depending on the size of the proposed investment, for investment planning examination and verification.[3] This was followed by the approval from the Ministry of Commerce (MOFCOM) or local Bureaus of Commerce, also based on the size of the proposed investment, for the contracts of joint ventures, articles of association of the FIE and corporate forms of the FIE, to list a few.[4] Also, the State Administration for Industry and Commerce (SAIC) or local AICs had to approve the name of the FIE and the registration of the establishment of the FIE, and had to conduct the administrative oversight of the operation of the FIE.[5] Further, if an investment was made in specific sectors, for example, banking, insurances, securities, education or medicine, a foreign investor needed to obtain additional approvals or licences from the industry regulators such as the China Banking and Insurance Regulatory Commission (CBIRC), the China Securities Regulatory Commission (CSRC), Ministry of Education or National Medical Products Administration, according to relevant provisions scattered in miscellaneous laws and regulations. In the event of a foreign takeover of a domestic company, the transaction is subject to a different set of approval procedures.[6]

Since the establishment of the Shanghai Pilot Free Trade Zone (PFTZ) in 2013, China's foreign direct investment (FDI) regulatory regime has embarked

---

2 For a detailed discussion on China's case-by-case approval for foreign investment, see Tarrant Mahony, *Foreign Investment Law in China: Regulation, Practice and Context* (Beijing: Tsinghua University Press, 2015), pp. 118–145. US Chamber of Commerce, *China's Approval Process for Inbound Foreign Direct Investment: Impact on Market Access, National Treatment and Transparency* (2012), https://www.uschamber.com/sites/default/files/documents/files/020021_China_InboundInvestment_Cvr.pdf, last accessed on 7 June 2021, pp. 10–20.

3 外商投资项目核准暂行管理办法 (Interim Administrative Measures for the Verification and Approval of Foreign Investment Projects) (Promulgated by the NDRC on 9 October 2004, effective on promulgation). In order to submit a request for NDRC or local DRC approval, foreign investors needed to obtain several Letters of Approval from different central and/or local governments as essential documents, including the approval of land use rights from the Land and Resources Department, an environmental impact assessment from the Environmental Protection Departments, a zoning approval on the planned location from the Planning Department, and, if applicable, approval from the State-Asset Supervision and Administration Commission (SASAC) if state assets or state-owned land use rights were involved. US Chamber of Commerce, *supra* note 2, p. 13.

4 The legal basis for MOFCOM's or local Bureaus of Commerce's approval was the three primary foreign investment laws.

5 中华人民共和国企业法人登记管理条例 (Regulation on the Registration and Administration of Legal Persons) (Promulgated by the State Council on 3 June 1988, effective on 1 July 1988), Art. 2.

6 For a detailed discussion on the market access scheme for foreign mergers and acquisitions (M&A), see Chapter 3.

on a gradual yet radical reform.[7] This piecemeal reform eventually led to a full transformation, namely the promulgation of the *Foreign Investment Law* (FIL) in 2019.[8] In terms of market access, Art. 4 of the FIL grants pre-establishment national treatment to foreign investors with a negative list approach. The *Negative List for Foreign Investment* includes a prohibited catalogue and a restricted catalogue. Foreign investment in the prohibited catalogue is not allowed, and foreign investment in the restricted catalogue is subject to restrictive conditions such as joint venture requirements and approval procedures according to pertinent laws and regulations.[9] For foreign investors and their investment outside of the *Negative List for Foreign Investment*, they should be treated no less favourably than domestic investors in the market entry phase, i.e., national treatment.

As a result, the current FDI legal regime introduces three major transformations in terms of market access. First, the control of sectors in the Catalogue is replaced by the *Negative List for Foreign Investment*. Second, the corporate form restrictions on FIEs in three primary foreign investment laws are repealed, and corporate governance for FIEs and domestic enterprises is unified according to the *Company Law* and the *Partnership Enterprise Law*. And lastly, the case-by-case approval *ex ante* for the establishment of FIEs is replaced by the pre-establishment national treatment commitment and an information reporting obligation *ex post*.[10]

2.1.2 The rationale for pre-establishment national treatment in the FIL

The stipulation of the pre-establishment national treatment with a negative list approach in the FIL may be a result of both internal impetus and external pressure, underlined by three significant factors: the internal impetus to regain rapid and steady FDI growth, external pressure for China to address its lack of reciprocity and the mounting pressure for deepened domestic reform from foreign countries.

First, China's FDI inflow has demonstrated feeble growth in the last decade. Although FDI in China has maintained over 40 years of growth at a remarkable speed, a watershed year was 2008 when the global financial crisis erupted, which led to the biggest decline of FDI inflow in history: it shrank by 13.2% in 2009 compared to 2008.[11] Although the pace of growth has quickly picked up

---

7 For a detailed discussion on China's foreign investment law reform from 2013 to 2019, see Chapter 1, Section 1.1.
8 中华人民共和国外商投资法 (Foreign Investment Law of China) (Promulgated by the National People's Congress on 15 March 2019, effective on 1 January 2020).
9 外商投资准入特别管理措施 (负面清单) (2020) (Special Administrative Measures for Market Access of Foreign Investment – Negative List for Foreign Investment 2020) (Promulgated by NDRC and MOFCOM on 23 June 2020, effective on 23 July 2020).
10 For a detailed discussion on the information reporting system, see Chapter 1, Section 1.3.4.
11 Inward FDI in China in 2008 recorded 108.3 billion USD, and 94 billion USD in 2009. MOFCOM, '中国外资统计公报' (Statistical Bulletin of FDI in China 2020), http://images

again since 2010, the average growth rate of FDI in China between 2009 and 2019 was merely 4.62%, which is significantly lower than the average growth rate of 21.98% from 1983 to 2008.[12] FDI is an important contributor to China's gross domestic product (GDP), which is the most crucial indicator for determining the success or failure of China's economy. Therefore, China has adopted a progressive agenda for FDI liberalization in the hope of revamping foreign investment that would sustain China's much-desired high-speed GDP growth.

Second, an externalized factor that originated as an internal problem is the perennial compliant about China's market access scheme for foreign investment, which was considered by foreign governments and investors as cumbersome, complex, bureaucratic and non-transparent.[13] For instance, there were 180 prohibited and restricted sectors in the *2011 Catalogue of Industries Guiding Foreign Investment*.[14] Even if foreign investors were allowed to enter the Chinese market in sectors other than the prohibited ones, their investment was subject to case-by-case approval, which was a multi-layered process conducted by different government agencies at different levels of government. China's market access for foreign investment was deemed far less problematic in the past, when China was still a major capital importing economy, than it is today. The narrative dramatically changed when China transformed from a net capital importing country to an equally powerful capital exporting country and launched high-profile national campaigns such as the Belt and Road Initiative in 2013. China's outbound FDI is massive in size, and some consider it aggressive, driven by strategic-asset-seeking motives, and backed by state endorsement such as cheap financing and state subsidies.[15] In the meantime, when it comes to inbound FDI, the policy priority shifts to the localization of high-tech value chains and self-sufficiency within China in core industries, and 'achieving global dominance in key technologies' as envisaged in the Made in China 2025 strategy, which 'fueled concerns that

---

.mofcom.gov.cn/wzs/202011/20201111182920243.pdf, last accessed on 22 December 2020, p. 26.

12 Calculated by the authors. Source obtained from ibid.

13 See, in general, US Chamber of Commerce, *supra* note 2. Covington & Burling LLP, *Measures and Practices Restraining Foreign Investment in China, Prepared for the European Commission Directorate-General for Trade*, 10 August 2014, http://www.iberchina.org/files /2017/restrictions_investment_china.pdf, last accessed on 7 June 2021.

14 外商投资产业指导目录 (2011) (Catalogue of Industries Guiding Foreign Investment (2011 Revision) (Promulgated by NDRC and MOFCOM on 24 December 2011, effective on 30 January 2012).

15 For example, Chinese outbound FDI in Europe is considered to be problematic for its technology-seeking and strategic infrastructure-seeking motives, the political nature of Beijing's policy initiatives in shaping Chinese investment overseas, national security concerns, a lack of reciprocity and fair competition, the permissive role of the state in China's economy, and as a source and a tool of political and geopolitical influence in Europe and divisions within Europe. John Seaman, Mikko Huotari and Miguel Otero-Iglesias (eds.), *Chinese Investment in Europe: A Country-Level Approach*, A Report by the European Think-Tank Network on China (ETNC), December 2017, pp. 10–13.

foreign competitors would be pushed out' of the Chinese market in these strategic sectors.[16] Because of this contradictory narrative whereby China is able to invest abundantly and relatively free of restrictions abroad, but foreign investors are subject to heavy restrictions when attempting to enter the Chinese market, concerns about the lack of reciprocity and the lack of a level playing field become rampant.[17] As the lack of reciprocity has become an imminent problem harming the interests of Chinese outbound investment, China now has both the incentive and the necessity to liberalize its market access regime at home for foreign investment in exchange for fair and reciprocal treatment of Chinese investment abroad.

It was perhaps the third and decisive factor, namely the external call for more drastic reform from foreign countries, and especially from the trade friction between the United States (US) and China, that resulted in the liberalization of market access in the FIL. Although China's piecemeal FDI reform since 2013 was in general recognized and welcomed as a positive endeavour and a 'best effort' from the Chinese government, such reform was considered insufficient and ineffective in addressing some of the fundamental and perennial problems, and foreign investors begin to show a 'promise fatigue' in anticipating that China would eventually develop into a market economy based on Western terms, especially considering many signs of a turn towards a more state-led economy as of late.[18] Believing that China's business environment was deteriorating for

---

16 Max J. Zenglein and Anna Holzmann, 'Evolving Made in China 2025: China's Industrial Policy in the Quest for Global Tech Leadership', *Merics Papers on China No. 8*, July 2019, pp. 8 and 19.

17 For a lack of reciprocity of FDI in the China–US and China–EU contexts, see Adam Chilton, Helen Milner and Dustin Tingley, 'Reciprocity and Public Opposition to Foreign Direct Investment', *British Journal of Political Science*, Vol. 50, Issue 1 (2020), pp. 129–153, at 131–132. Thilo Hanemann and Mikko Huotari, 'EU-China FDI: Working towards Reciprocity in Investment Relations', *Rhodium Group and Merics Papers on China No. 3*, May 2018, https://merics.org/sites/default/files/2020-04/180723_MERICS-COFDI-Update_final_0.pdf, last accessed on 30 June 2020, pp. 11–14. John Seaman, Mikko Huotari and Miguel Otero-Iglesias, *supra* note 15, pp. 12, 60, 65–67. David Dollar, 'China as a Global Investor', in Ligang Song *et al.* (eds.), *China's New Sources of Economic Growth: Reform, Resources, and Climate Change* (Canberra: Australian National University Press, 2016), pp. 197–214, at 207–210.

18 Since 2016, there is 'an intensifying chorus of German and European business complaints about a deterioration of the business climate in China and "promise fatigue" about Chinese announcements to liberalize inbound FDI'. John Seaman, Mikko Huotari and Miguel Otero-Iglesias, *supra* note 15, p. 65. The 2019 business climate survey conducted by the American Chamber of Commerce in China revealed that the biggest challenges US companies face in China included inconsistent regulatory interpretation and unclear laws and enforcement, rising tensions in US–China relations, Chinese tariffs on US goods, difficulty obtaining required licenses, and regulatory compliance risks. See AmCham China and Deloitte, *2019 China Business Climate Survey Report*, https://www2.deloitte.com/content/dam/Deloitte/au/Documents/international-specialist/deloitte-amcham-2019-china-business-climate-survey-report-bilingual-190301.pdf, last accessed on 18 July 2020, p. 9. EU investors in China share similar concerns. The 2019 Business Confidence Survey conducted by the EU Chamber of Commerce in China showed that 53% of respondents reported that doing business in China had become more difficult in 2019 than in the previous year, while

FIEs, investors showed signs of retreat from the Chinese market.[19] Some Asian and European countries voiced concerns over China's allegedly unfair trade and investment policies and practices, and foreign investors have begun to consider moving their production to other growing economies, such as countries in the Association of Southeast Asian Nations, with a cheaper labour force and a fast-growing domestic market for consumption.[20] But most important, it was believed that the US demand for more market access for foreign investment amid the US–China Trade War was the major catalyst for the pre-establishment national treatment commitment in the FIL.[21] The FIL is considered in part an attempt to reconcile and de-escalate with the US and to demonstrate signs of improvement in the domestic investment environment to global investors.

2.1.3 The current legal framework of market access for foreign investment

The pre-establishment national treatment commitment in the FIL mandates the elimination of differentiated market access rules between domestic and foreign investors in principle, but certain legitimate derogations to the commitment are acknowledged, namely the *Negative List for Foreign Investment*, the national security review, the Unreliable Entity List and the Countermeasure List, enumerated as steps 1–4 in Table 2.1. Moreover, pre-establishment

---

48% of respondents reported so in 2018. Specifically, although China's reform and opening-up agenda in the past two years progressed rapidly and saw significant improvement, there was a 'reform deficit' as a result of discontent from European businesses. Some long-lasting problems included insufficient market opening (the still closing of market entry in certain sectors such as legal services, and information and communications technology), regulatory obstacles, forced transfer of technology, restrictive Internet and the cybersecurity laws, the lack of equal treatment and level playing field, dominance of SOEs in critical industries, Made in China 2025 that unfairly favours Chinese companies, and stalled IP rights protection. European Union Chamber of Commerce in China, *Business Confidence Survey 2019*, https://static.europeanchamber.com.cn/upload/documents/documents/Business_Confidence_Survey_2019_updated[663].pdf , last accessed 18 July 2020, pp. 10-47.

19 In 2019, withdrawal of some large foreign companies in China became noticeable. Examples include Samsung, Olympus, Epson, Carrefour, Tesco and Walmart. The reasons behind this withdrawal wave are the rising costs of labour, land, environmental standards and other business factors; the US–China Trade War; foreign manufacturers' strategy to shift production capacity out of China; and foreign investors' sentiment that China makes appealing promises for reform but delivers very few of them in practice. Gong Chen and Zhongxin Yu, 'What Makes China's Latest Wave of Foreign Capital Withdrawal Different? It's Structural', *South China Morning Post*, 29 July 2019, https://www.scmp.com/comment/opinion/article/3020234/what-makes-chinas-latest-wave-foreign-capital-withdrawal-different, last accessed on 18 July 2020.

20 Patrick Heimann and Roger Bischof, 'China's New Foreign Investment Law: An Effort to Reform Chinese Investment Regime in Favour of Foreign Investors', *Diritto Tributario Internazionale e Dell'UE*, December 2020, pp. 785–789, at 786.

21 For a detailed discussion on the impact of the US–China Trade War to China's foreign investment law regime, see the Introduction and Chapter 1.

Table 2.1 The current legal framework of market access for foreign greenfield investment

Step	Measure	Agency	Applicable to	Legal basis
1	Sectoral prohibition and restriction	NDRC and MOFCOM	Foreign investments	Negative List for Foreign Investment Negative List for Foreign Investment in the PFTZs[a]
2	National security review	NDRC and MOFCOM	Foreign investments	Measures for National Security Review of Foreign Investment Trial Measures for National Security Review of Foreign Investment in the PFTZs[b]
3	Unreliable Entity List	MOFCOM	Foreign individuals and entities	Provisions on the Unreliable Entity List
4	Countermeasure List	Relevant department of State Council	Foreign individuals and entities	Anti-Foreign Sanctions Law
5	Sectoral approval and licencing	Depending on the specific sector	All investments	Negative List for Market Access
6	Registration of establishment	Local AMR	All investments	Regulation on the Registration and Administration of Legal Persons
7	Fixed-asset investment approval	NDRC, or State Council, or the local government (depending on the size of investment)	All investments	Measures for the Approval and Recordation of Foreign-Invested Projects Catalogue of Investment Projects Subject to Government Approval

8	Land use rights	Local Land and Resources Department	All investments	Land Administration Law
9	Environmental impact assessment	Local Environmental Protection Departments	All investments	Law on Environmental Impact Assessment
10	Zoning approval	Local Planning Department	All investments	Law on Urban and Rural Planning

Note: For a discussion on the market access for foreign M&A, see Chapter 3.

[a] 自由贸易试验区外商投资准入特别管理措施（负面清单）(2020年版) (Special Administrative Measures for the Market Access of Foreign Investment in the PFTZs – Negative List for Foreign Investment in the PFTZs) (2020 Revision) (Promulgated by NDRC and MOFCOM on 23 June 2020, effective on 23 July 2020).

[b] 自由贸易试验区外商投资国家安全审查试行办法 (Trial Measures for National Security Review of Foreign Investment in the PFTZs) (Promulgated by the General Office of the State Council on 8 April 2015, effective on 8 May 2015).

national treatment in the FIL does not eliminate market access barriers that equally apply to both foreign and domestic investors. Therefore, certain market access procedures adopted prior to the FIL continue to apply, enumerated as steps 5–10 in Table 2.1.

Steps 1 to 4 apply only to foreign investors and their investments. First, in the event that an investment is made within the *Negative List for Foreign Investment*, foreign investors should either be denied market entry (in the prohibited sectors) or comply with the restrictive conditions and relevant approval procedures for market entry (in the restricted sectors).[22] Second, in the event that a foreign investment, including both greenfield and mergers and acquisitions (M&A), is made in the sectors of national defence, important agriculture, important energy and resources, critical equipment manufacturing, critical infrastructure, important transportation, important cultural products and services, important information technology (IT) and Internet products and services, important financial services and critical technology, the foreign investor may be required to file for an *ex ante* national security review.[23] Third, foreign corporations, organizations and individuals that are admitted on China's Unreliable Entity List are prohibited from engaging in trade, investment and mobility of people with China.[24] Fourth, foreign individuals and entities who are included on China's Countermeasure List according to *Anti-Foreign Sanctions Law* are prohibited from entering Chinese territory or any type of business presence in China.[25]

Steps 5 to 10 apply to both foreign and domestic investors. Fifth, if an investment is to be made in special sectors, a foreign investor must obtain additional approval or licences from the industry regulators pursuant to the *Negative List for Market Access*.[26] Sixth, registration of establishment at the local Administration for Market Regulation (AMR) is required according to the *Regulation on the*

---

22 FIL (2019), Art. 28. Negative List for Foreign Investment (2020), Explanations 1 and 3.

23 FIL (2019), Art. 35. 外商投资安全审查办法 (Measures for National Security Review of Foreign Investment) (Promulgated by NDRC and MOFCOM on 19 December 2020, effective on 18 January 2021), Art. 4. For a detailed discussion on the national security review of foreign investment, see Chapter 4.

24 不可靠实体清单规定 (Provisions on the Unreliable Entity List) (Promulgated by MOFCOM on 19 September 2020, effective on promulgation).

25 中华人民共和国反外国制裁法 (Anti-Foreign Sanctions Law) (Promulgated by the Standing Committee of the NPC on 10 June 2021, effective on promulgation).

26 市场准入负面清单 (Negative List for Market Access) (Promulgated by MOFCOM and NDRC on 10 December 2020, effective on promulgation). The Negative List for Market Access is a regime first established in 2016, including a prohibited and a restricted category. Applicable to all market participants, and regardless of their domestic or foreign origin, the Negative List for Market Access is a compilation of *ex ante* review, approval, licencing and qualification requirements in various sectors stipulated in scattered laws and regulations. All market participants are not allowed to enter the prohibited fields and are only allowed for market entry after they gain approval in the restricted fields. The currently effective 2020 version includes five prohibited meta-categories (each includes sub-items) and 118 restricted meta-categories (each includes sub-items).

Registration and Administration of Legal Persons.[27] Seventh, State Council approval, NDRC approval or local government approval is required for all investment in fixed-asset investment projects listed in a Catalogue of the State Council.[28] The Catalogue includes ten areas (each includes sub-items) covering agriculture and water conservancy, energy, transportation, IT industry, raw materials, machinery manufacturing, tobacco, high-tech industry, urban construction and social undertakings.[29] Eighth, proposed investment projects are required for the approval of land-use rights from the local Land and Resources Department.[30] Ninth, an environmental impact assessment from the local Environmental Protection Departments is required,[31] followed by tenth, a zoning approval for the planned location of the investment project by the local Planning Department.[32]

2.1.4 Market access for foreign investment post-FIL: A critical appraisal

The pre-establishment national treatment commitment in the FIL receives antithetical responses. Proponents in support of this legislative transformation, with a 'better late than never' sentiment, opine that China's pre-establishment national treatment with a negative list approach eradicates the case-by-case FDI approval that existed for four decades, therefore representing a revolutionary progress in China's FDI governance, despite the long process. In contrast, opponents in criticism of the new scheme, with a 'too little too late' sentiment, argue that there is little practical benefit left to foreign investors now that China has opened up the most strategic and lucrative sectors which have been reserved from foreign capital in the past few decades. This is because there is simply no market left for new competitors, although any reform towards more market access liberalization is in general welcome and laudable.[33]

---

27 中华人民共和国企业法人登记管理条例 (Regulation on the Registration and Administration of Legal Persons) (2019 Amendment) (Promulgated by the State Council on 3 February 2019, effective on promulgation), Art. 2.

28 外商投资项目核准和备案管理办法 (Measures for the Approval and Recordation of Foreign-Invested Projects) (Promulgated by the NDRC on 27 December 2014, effective on promulgation), Art. 2.

29 政府核准的投资项目目录（2016年本）(Catalogue of Investment Projects Subject to Government Approval) (Promulgated by the State Council on 12 December 2016, effective on promulgation).

30 中华人民共和国土地管理法 (Land Administration Law) (2019 Amendment) (Promulgated by the NPC on 26 August 2019, effective on 1 January 2020), Arts. 52 and 53.

31 中华人民共和国环境影响评价法 (Law on Environmental Impact Assessment) (2018 Amendment) (Promulgated by the NPC on 29 December 2018, effective on promulgation), Art. 16.

32 中华人民共和国城乡规划法 (Law on Urban and Rural Planning) (2019 Amendment) (Promulgated by the NPC on 23 April 2019, effective on promulgation), Art. 38.

33 For example, according to EU investors, the revision of Negative List for Foreign Investment 2019 and Negative List for Market Access 2019 did produce positive results for more market openings in a few sectors such as cosmetics, medical devices and pharmaceuticals,

The rationale behind these two lines of argument comes from two different types of comparison. If a historical perspective is adopted and the present situation is compared with China's FDI regulatory regime prior to the FIL, substantial liberalization has taken place. This is evidenced, *inter alia*, by a relatively dilatory but significant decrease in prohibited and restricted sectors in the *Negative List for Foreign Investment* since 2017, and the abolition of the case-by-case approval for FDI. However, if a horizontal perspective is adopted and China's current market access scheme is compared with that of Western countries where China invests heavily, the lack of reciprocity is still a major concern and China's market access scheme overall may still pose significant obstacles. In particular, three recent legal developments post-FIL may have great potential to impede foreign investors' access to the Chinese market, namely the national security review, the *Negative List for Market Access*, and the defensive laws against foreign restrictive measures and foreign sanctions.

First, China's post-FIL national security review envisaged in the *2020 Measures for National Security Review of Foreign Investment* may raise concerns. The concept of national security is not defined and thus subject to arbitrary interpretation, which raises uncertainty and unpredictability for foreign investors in the market entry phase. Further, the sectors subject to review include ambiguous and far-reaching semantics, and the list of sectors is so broadly stipulated that it could practically encompass all foreign investment to be the subject of review.[34] This can be considered by foreign investors as a serious market access impediment.

Another significant obstacle is a shift from the proliferation of barriers to market entry which apply specifically to foreign investors to a new focus on sectoral market entry requirements for all market participants. A most notable change is that many prohibited and restricted items abrogated from the *Negative List for Foreign Investment* have now found their way into the *Negative List for Market Access*, which is applicable to both foreign and domestic investors. The financial sector is a prominent example. Although banking was already excluded from the *Negative List for Foreign Investment* since 2018, establishing a new bank in China requires, among other approvals, case-by-case approval from the People's Bank of China (PBoC) and CBIRC, pursuant to the *2020 Negative*

---

but 'the opening up of sectors that are already in a late stage of development has left international investors struggling' to compete because 'opening up only after market domination is complete does not represent sustainable, nor meaningful, reform', such as financial services, oil and gas exploration, and shipping. And certain sectors, such as legal services, is not likely to open to foreign investors at all. EU Chamber of Commerce in China, *Business Confidence Survey 2020*, http://www.europeanchamber.com.cn/en/publications-archive/774/European_Business_in_China_Business_Confidence_Survey_2020, last accessed on 25 December 2020, pp. 12–15. US investors share similar concerns, expressing that 'there have been too many unfulfilled promises about market access since the WTO accession', and that 'government commitments or promises have not been implemented recently. They stay at the central level or are ignored in local enforcement or practice'. AmCham China and Deloitte, *supra* note 18, p. 55.

34 For a more detailed discussion on national security review, see Chapter 4.

List for Market Access.[35] Therefore, although the *Negative List for Foreign Investment* has become rather succinct, the *Negative List for Market Access* may become a new frontier for complaints from foreign investors. There is a lingering concern over selective enforcement in practice. As the United States Trade Representative (USTR) 301 Investigation claims, these industry-specific approvals and licencing are time-consuming, involve a great deal of government discretion and manoeuvre, and are applied in selective and non-transparent manners.[36] These sectoral approval processes are accused by the US of enabling Chinese administrative authorities

> to favour domestic competitors over foreign investors ... without leaving a paper trail of discriminatory written regulations ... through the application of vaguely worded or unpublished rules or requirements in ways that discriminate against foreign investors, and through the imposition of deal-specific conditions that go beyond any written legal requirements.[37]

Because the *Negative List for Market Access* is essentially a compilation, not a cut-down of sectoral approval and licencing requirements scattered in existing laws and regulations, there is a concern that foreign investors may be less likely to gain sectoral approval or obtain licencing in practice if competing with domestic applicants.

Since 2020, the promulgation of the four defensive laws against foreign restrictive measures and foreign sanctions may dramatically change the principled liberal narrative of the FIL.[38] In particular, the *Provisions on the Unreliable Entity List* and the *Anti-Foreign Sanctions Law* are relevant to market access for foreign investors. Any foreign individuals, corporations and organizations that are blacklisted on the Unreliable Entity List or the Countermeasure List will be prohibited from conducting any form of business activity in China or with Chinese individuals or entities, which certainly renders making an investment impossible. Although both Lists are not yet published and thus not in use, China's new legal toolbox, if extensively implemented in the future, may cast a shadow on investors' confidence in entering the Chinese market and therefore significantly impact inbound FDI growth in the long term.

---

35 Negative List for Market Access (2020), Restricted Catalogue, Item 59.
36 USTR, *Findings of the Investigation into China's Acts, Policies, and Practices related to Technology Transfer, Intellectual Property, and Innovation under Section 301 of the Trade Act of 1974*, 22 March 2018, pp. 37–38.
37 US Chamber of Commerce, *supra* note 2, pp. 35–36.
38 These four laws are Provisions on the Unreliable Entity List (2020), Export Control Law (2020), Rules on Counteracting Unjustified Extra-Territorial Application of Foreign Legislation and Measures (2021) and Anti-Foreign Sanctions Law (2021). For a discussion on their legislative background, see Introduction. For a detailed discussion on their substance, see Chapter 1, Section 1.1.5. For a discussion on their relevance to national security, see Chapter 4, Section 4.1.

2.2 The negative list approach

2.2.1 The origin of pre-establishment national treatment with a negative list approach

Pre-establishment national treatment in tandem with a negative list approach originated from a well-established standard of protection in international law. As 'the core and the standard repertoire' of bilateral investment treaties (BITs), and first found in the Germany–Pakistan BIT signed in 1959, which is often referred to as the birth of modern BITs, national treatment requires the contracting parties to provide treatment to foreign investors and their investment no less favourable than that accorded to their domestic counterparts.[39] A mapping of international investment agreements (IIAs) conducted by the United Nations Conference on Trade and Development (UNCTAD) demonstrates that out of 2,576 mapped IIAs globally, 2,188 of them incorporated a national treatment provision.[40] The majority of national treatment provisions in IIAs, that is 2,020 out of the 2,188 IIAs with national treatment, applies to post-establishment, and only 168 IIAs contain national treatment applicable at both pre-establishment and post-establishment.[41]

Pre-establishment national treatment with a negative list approach grants national treatment to the admission and establishment of foreign investment in the host state, nevertheless subject to a number of national law reservations, which are usually compiled as a list of annexes to the treaty as non-conforming measures. This is a practice that was originated from, and popularized by, the US treaty-making practice.[42] These listed non-conforming measures are therefore referred to as a 'negative list' in IIAs: only sectors or national regulatory measures that are explicitly listed and backed by national law references are allowed to deviate from the national treatment obligation, and foreign investment in non-listed sectors automatically gains the protection of national treatment at both pre-establishment and post-establishment.[43]

Although China has the world's second-largest IIA regime, national treatment provisions remain a relatively scarce occurrence.[44] A study conducted in

39 Rudolf Dolzer and Christoph Schreuer, *Principles of International Investment Law*, 2nd edn. (Oxford: OUP, 2012), pp. 6, 198.
40 UNCTAD, International Investment Agreements Navigator, Mapping of IIA Content, Standards of Treatment, National Treatment, https://investmentpolicy.unctad.org/international-investment-agreements/iia-mapping, last accessed on 22 December 2020.
41 Ibid.
42 Wolfgang Alschner, 'Americanization of the BIT Universe: The Influence of Friendship, Commerce and Navigation (FCN) Treaties on Modern Investment Treaty Law', *Goettingen Journal of International Law*, Vol. 5 Issue 2 (2013), pp. 455–486, at 470.
43 UNCTAD, *Preserving Flexibility in IIAs: The Use of Reservations* (Geneva: UN Publication, 2006), pp. 17–18.
44 According to UNCTAD, China has concluded 145 BITs and 24 Treaties with Investment Provisions (TIPs), second only to Germany with 155 BITs and 77 TIPs concluded. UNCTAD, Investment Policy Hub, IIA Navigator, Country, https://investmentpolicy.unctad

2012 indicated that out of 130 Chinese investment treaties that were mapped, less than half have a national treatment provision, and all these national treatment provisions only apply post-establishment.[45] In 2013, during the negotiation of a prospective China–US BIT, China for the first time in history made a commitment with the US to negotiate a pre-establishment national treatment clause with a negative list approach.[46] This commitment, however, never materialized because of the fallout of the BIT negotiation. The first Chinese IIA to include a pre-establishment national treatment with a negative list approach is the China–Hong Kong Closer Economic Partnership Arrangement (CEPA) Investment Agreement, concluded in 2017.[47] The Regional Comprehensive Economic Partnership (RCEP), concluded in 2020 by China and 14 other States, is another IIA that incorporates a pre-establishment national treatment provision with a negative list approach.[48] The China–European Union (EU) Comprehensive Agreement on Investment, provisionally concluded in 2020, also adopts pre-establishment national treatment with a negative list approach.[49] It appears that this approach may become a new paradigm for China to adhere to in negotiating future IIAs.

2.2.2 China's negative list approach in domestic law

Although the provision of pre-establishment national treatment with a negative list approach is a relatively new occurrence in Chinese IIAs, the Chinese government appears to be enthusiastic about the negative list approach in national law. Since 2013, multiple negative lists have been adopted and updated at regular intervals (see Table 2.2). A negative list applicable to foreign investors was first adopted in the Shanghai PFTZ in 2013 and has been promoted to the rest of the PFTZs since 2015. The *Negative List for Foreign Investment in the PFTZs*

.org/international-investment-agreements, last accessed on 22 December 2020. For a comprehensive understanding of national treatment in Chinese IIAs, see Norah Gallagher and Wenhua Shan, *Chinese Investment Treaties: Policies and Practice* (Oxford: OUP, 2009), pp. 157–173.

45 Wenhua Shan, Norah Gallagher and Sheng Zhang, 'National Treatment for Foreign Investment in China: A Changing Landscape', *ICSID Review*, Vol. 27 No. 1 (2012), pp. 120–144, at 133.

46 Norah Gallagher, 'China's BIT's and Arbitration Practice: Progress and Problems', in Wenhua Shan and Jinyuan Su (eds.), *China and International Investment Law: Twenty Years of ICSID* Membership (Leiden: Brill, 2014), pp. 180–214, at 186–187.

47 China-Hong Kong CEPA Investment Agreement (Concluded and signed on 28 June 2017), Art. 5. Julien Chaisse and Kehinde Folake Olaoye, 'The Tired Dragon: Casting Doubts on China's Investment Treaty Practice', *Berkeley Business Law Journal*, Vol. 17 Issue 1 (2020), pp. 134–193, at 170.

48 Regional Comprehensive Economic Partnership (Signed on 15 November 2020, not yet effective), Art. 10.3.

49 EU–China Comprehensive Agreement on Investment, agreement in principle announced on 30 December 2020, Section II [Investment Liberalisation], Art. 4.1.

Table 2.2 Negative lists in China

Title	Negative List for Foreign Investment in the PFTZs	Negative List for Foreign Investment	Negative List for Market Access
Applicable to	Foreign investors in the PFTZs	Foreign investors nationwide	All market participants nationwide
Content		Prohibited items and restricted items	
Publishing authorities	Shanghai municipality (2013–2014) The State Council (2015–2017) MOFCOM and NDRC (2018–2020)	MOFCOM and NDRC	
2013	Special Administrative Measures (Negative List) for Foreign Investment in Shanghai Pilot Free Trade Zone	—	—
2014	Special Administrative Measures (Negative List) for Foreign Investment in Shanghai Pilot Free Trade Zone	—	—
2015	Special Administrative Measures (Negative List) for Foreign Investment in the PFTZs	—	—
2016	—	—	Draft Market Access Negative List (Trail in Tianjin, Shanghai, Fujian and Guangdong)
2017	Special Administrative Measures (Negative List) for Foreign Investment in the PFTZs	Catalogue of Industries Guiding Foreign Investment (including a Negative List)	Draft Market Access Negative List extended to another 15 provinces and municipalities

	Special Administrative Measures (Negative List) for Foreign Investment in the PFTZs	Special Administrative Measures (Negative List) for Foreign Investment	Market Access Negative List
2018	Special Administrative Measures (Negative List) for Foreign Investment in the PFTZs	Special Administrative Measures (Negative List) for Foreign Investment	Market Access Negative List
2019	Special Administrative Measures (Negative List) for Foreign Investment in the PFTZs	Special Administrative Measures (Negative List) for Foreign Investment	Market Access Negative List
2020 (**currently effective**)	Special Administrative Measures (Negative List) for Foreign Investment in the PFTZs Special Administrative Measures (Negative List) for Foreign Investment in Hainan Free Trade Port	Special Administrative Measures (Negative List) for Foreign Investment	Market Access Negative List

which is currently in effect was published in June 2020, and is applicable to foreign investors in all PFTZs except for Hainan. Separately, the *Negative List for Foreign Investment in Hainan Free Trade Port* was promulgated by MOFCOM and NDRC in 2020.[50] The *Negative List for Foreign Investment* that applies to foreign investors nationwide was first envisaged as a part of the *2017 Catalogue of Industries Guiding Foreign Investment*, became a standalone regulation in 2018, and was last revised in June 2020. The *Negative List for Market Access* was first adopted probationally in 2016 and last revised in December 2020; it is applicable to all market participants, regardless of their domestic or foreign origin.

2.2.3 The Negative Lists for Foreign Investment 2017–2020

As an experimental measure, the *Negative List for Foreign Investment* was first published in June 2017 as a section of the *Catalogue of Industries for Guiding Foreign Investment*, including 63 prohibited and restricted items. This was a salient reduction considering that the previous 2015 Catalogue included 90 prohibited and restricted items, and 180 prohibited and restricted items in the 2011 Catalogue. The *Negative List for Foreign Investment* is updated annually; the currently effective 2020 version is further reduced to 33 prohibited and restricted items.

The progressive liberalization on market access is not only reflected in the sheer diminishing numbers of prohibited and restricted items in the successive *Negative Lists for Foreign Investment* but also the gradual openness to strategic sectors that were previously reserved for domestic investors and especially for state-owned enterprises (SOEs). Compared with previous references, the most significant liberalization in the *2020 Negative List for Foreign Investment* happened in the financial sectors, where all previous restrictions to foreign investors on securities companies, fund management companies, future companies, life insurance companies and banking institutions (since 2018) were completely removed from the List, thus expanding pre-establishment national treatment to the financial sector. This is also considered a fulfilment of China's promise in the Phase I Trade Deal with the US concluded in January 2020.[51]

However, despite the substantial reduction, the *2020 Negative List for Foreign Investment* has received some lukewarm reactions outside of China. The EU Chamber of Commerce in China commented that the complete opening of China's financial sector realized by the *Negative List for Foreign Investment* in 2020 comes 'too little too late': the idea of competing with Chinese banks, especially state-owned banks, is 'a pipe dream' for European banks, because the

---

50 海南自由贸易港外商投资准入特别管理措施(负面清单)(2020年版) (Special Administrative Measures for Market Access of Foreign Investment – Negative List for Foreign Investment in the Hainan Free Trade Port) (Promulgated by NDRC and MOFCOM on 31 December 2020, effective on 1 February 2021).
51 USTR, 'Economic and Trade Agreement between the Government of the United States of America and the Government of the People's Republic of China' (Phase I Trade Deal), 15 January 2020, Arts. 4.6 and 4.7.

Table 2.3 Negative Lists for Foreign Investment 2017–2020

Version	2017	2018	2019	2020
Number of prohibited items	28	27	23	21
Deleted prohibited items from the previous version	–	Production of weapons and ammunitions	Reconnaissance and exploitation of molybdenum, tin, antimony and fluorite Production of Chinese Xuan paper and Chinese ink stick Development of wild fauna and flora resources originated in China under national protection (The prohibitions on reconnaissance and exploitation of rare earth and radioactive minerals are merged from two items in the 2018 List to one item in the 2019 List.)	The smelting and processing of radioactive minerals, production of nuclear fuel Air traffic control

(*Continued*)

Table 2.3 Continued

Version	2017	2018	2019	2020
Number of restricted items	35	21	17	12
Deleted restricted items from previous version	–	Reconnaissance and exploitation of special and rare coal Reconnaissance and exploitation of graphite Rare earth smelting and separation, tungsten smelting Design, manufacturing and repair of vessels Design, manufacturing and repair of special purpose aircrafts Design, manufacturing and repair of general aircrafts Construction and operation of power grids Purchase and wholesale of rice, wheat and corn Construction and operation of gas stations Construction and operation of main railway networks Railroad passenger transportation companies Banking Land surveying and mapping companies Production of broadcasting television programs and films	Reconnaissance and exploitation of petroleum and gas Shipping agency companies The construction and operation of cinemas Performance agency companies	Water supply and drainage pipelines in cities Securities company Futures company Insurance company (The restrictions on public transportation airlines and general airlines are merged from two items in the 2018 List to one in the 2019 List.)

Sources: 外商投资产业指导目录 2017 (Catalogue of Industries Guiding Foreign Investment 2017) (Promulgated by NDRC and MOFCOM in 28 June 2017, effective on 28 July 2017). 外商投资准入特别管理措施 (负面清单) 2018 (Negative List for Foreign Investment 2018) (Promulgated by NDRC and MOFCOM on 28 June 2018, effective on 28 July 2018). 外商投资准入特别管理措施 (负面清单) 2019 (Negative List for Foreign Investment 2019) (Promulgated by NDRC and MOFCOM on 30 June 2019, effective on 30 July 2019). 外商投资准入特别管理措施 (负面清单) 2020 (Negative List for Foreign Investment 2020) (Promulgated by NDRC and MOFCOM on 23 June 2020, effective on 23 July 2020).

Notes: The difference between these successive negative lists not only concerns the cut-off of prohibited or restricted items but also the revision of some items. Due to the limit of space, revised items are omitted in Table 2.3.

market has been monopolized by China's banking giants of their 'lion's share' for decades and thus few opportunities are left now for European banks to compete for what remains of the market.[52] It is also reported that the vice president of the US–China Business Council described the legislative development as a positive signal in general, but expressed disappointment that the telecom and the entertainment industries, where US firms would have the most competitive advantage, are still restricted or prohibited for foreign investment in China.[53]

2.3 National treatment post-establishment in the FIL

2.3.1 Pledges of equal treatment in law

The FIL and its Implementing Regulation emphasize equal treatment of foreign and domestic investors post-establishment. As a general rule of thumb, investment made outside of the *Negative List for Foreign Investment* shall be governed under the principle of equal treatment.[54]

National preferential policies in support of the development of enterprises shall be equally applied to FIEs.[55] Foreign investors and FIEs are qualified to enjoy state preferential policies in the fields of fiscal and financial policies, taxation and land use.[56] Furthermore, the government is obliged to grant equal treatment to foreign and domestic enterprises in the field of funding, land supply, tax reduction, licencing, standard setting, project application, human resources policies and the application process of these policies.[57] It was alleged that the Chinese central and local governments established 'a large number of programs ... that provide financial support to companies but may exclude FIEs ... in a variety of forms including grants, loans, subsidies, and even the provision of land at lower than market prices', in order to 'carry out goals such as promoting indigenous innovation and fostering domestic champions'.[58] This practice, by favouring domestic companies, has put FIEs in a disadvantageous position. The FIL and its Implementing Regulation aim to put these types of concerns at ease, but its success or failure will ultimately depend on the local governments' adamance to implement the rules effectively.

52 Cissy Zhou, 'China Eases Restrictions on Foreign Investors, But Is It Too Little Too Late?', *South China Morning Post*, 25 June 2020, https://www.scmp.com/economy/china -economy/article/3090620/china-eases-restrictions-foreign-investors-it-too-little-too?utm _campaign=Marketing_Cloud&utm_medium=email&utm_source=USCBC%20News%2 0Overview%206.26.2020&%20utm_content=https%3A%2F%2Fwww.scmp.com%2Fecon-omy%2Fchina-economy%2Farticle%2F3090620%2Fchina-eases-restrictions-foreign-inves-tors-it-too-little-too, last accessed on 30 June 2021.
53 Ibid.
54 FIL (2019), Art. 28.
55 FIL (2019), Art. 9.
56 FIL Implementing Regulation (2019), Art. 12.
57 FIL Implementing Regulation (2019), Art. 6.
58 Covington & Burling LLP, *supra* note 13, pp. 32–33.

Government procurement is another venue for favouritism towards domestic companies over FIEs. Central and local governments were accused of making government procurement a tool 'to support domestic industries or indigenous innovation programs' by prioritizing domestically sourced products and services in major government procurement projects or major government-funded projects.[59] The FIL therefore requires that FIEs and their products and services shall be treated equally in the government procurement process.[60] The purchasers of government procurement shall not apply differential or discriminatory treatment of any kind when selecting between FIEs and domestic suppliers.[61] Again, in order to avoid the trap of mere lip service, effective law enforcement, especially at the local level, is pivotal.

In the past, China prioritized the promotion and adoption of unique Chinese standards which were often at odds with, or different from, pertinent international standards, and foreign businesses had little opportunity to provide input in China's standard setting.[62] It is alleged that the reason behind this practice is that China deliberately fostered a misalignment between Chinese standards and prevailing international standards in order to create market access barriers to FIEs, therefore protecting certain indigenous Chinese companies from foreign competition, for instance, in the automobile and IT sectors.[63] To address this complaint, the FIL makes it clear that FIEs and domestic enterprises shall equally participate in the formulation and modification of national, sectoral, local and communal standards.[64] This means that FIEs are now guaranteed, at least in theory, a fair, open and transparent participation in the development of standards administered at all levels. In addition, compulsory national standards shall be equally applied between FIEs and domestic enterprises.[65] However, the FIL does not mandate equal application in voluntary national standards, local-government-issued standards or market-issued standards.

In industries and sectors where approval and licencing are required, applications from foreign investors shall be evaluated on an equal footing with domestic investors.[66] This pledge is relevant in particular with regard to the *Negative List for Market Access*. An underlying concern is that the chances of gaining sectoral approval for a foreign investor according to the *Negative List for Market Access* are arguably less certain in practice than for a domestic applicant, as the relevant authorities in charge of approval may likely consider the investor's foreign origin as a negating factor and reach a rejective decision, especially in sectors

---

59 Ibid, pp. 34–35.
60 FIL (2019), Art. 16.
61 FIL Implementing Regulation (2019), Art. 15.
62 Ming Du, *The Regulation of Product Standards in World Trade Law* (Oxford: Hart Publishing, 2020).
63 Ibid.
64 FIL (2019), Art. 15; FIL Implementing Regulation (2019), Art. 13.
65 FIL (2019), Art. 15; FIL Implementing Regulation (2019), Art. 14.
66 FIL (2019), Art. 30.

that are considered strategic or sensitive and intrinsically repel foreign ownership or involvement, such as the defence or financial sector. It remains to be seen whether and to what extent this positive but succinct guarantee in the FIL can effectively alleviate such a concern in the sectoral approval and licencing process.

Expropriation against foreign investors and their investment can only take place under certain conditions: there has to be a public interest at stake; under extraordinary circumstances; according to laws and regulations; in a non-discriminatory manner; under due process of law; and compensation should be paid on prompt, fair and reasonable terms and per market value.[67] Foreign investors who are in contention with the expropriatory decisions may resort to administrative review or litigation.[68] The FIL and the Implementing Regulation set the standard for compensation for expropriation to an unprecedented high threshold, which requires compensation to be paid on 'prompt, fair and reasonable terms and per market value'. In contrast, the 1990 EJV Law, which first included a non-expropriation clause in Chinese law, only required the compensation to be 'appropriate', and the *Property Law* promulgated in 2007 simply requires to pay compensation.[69]

Despite the high standards set forth in the expropriation provisions in the FIL, certain issues remain problematic, such as the scope of 'extraordinary circumstances' that justifies an expropriation act, and the ways to determine whether and what public interests are at stake.[70] Because the term 'public interest' in expropriation has never been defined in the *Property Law* or in the Constitution, it has been notoriously implemented in China to legitimize wrongful expropriatory acts, as 'the ambiguity that surrounds this term opens it to abuse by local governments that are intent on encroaching on private interests'.[71] The ambiguity of 'public interest' in expropriation also negatively affects the property ownership of foreign investors. In the pending case of *Hela Schwarz GmbH v. China* lodged in 2017, for instance, the Jinan Municipal Government issued an expropriation decision to confiscate the land use rights and the buildings where the German investor's factory was located as part of an urban redevelopment project.[72] The claimant alleged that the expropriation was illegitimate, relying on, *inter alia*, the argument that the purpose of urban redevelopment is not equal to the public

---

67 FIL (2019), Art. 20. FIL Implementing Regulation (2019), Art. 21.
68 FIL Implementing Regulation (2019), Art. 21.
69 Mo Zhang, 'Change of Regulatory Scheme: China's New Foreign Investment Law and Reshaped Legal Landscape', *UCLA Pacific Basin Law Journal*, Vol. 37 Issue 1 (2020), pp. 179–238, at 213.
70 Ibid.
71 Lei Chen, 'Legal and Institutional Analysis of Land Expropriation in China', in Hualing Fu and John Gillespie (eds.), *Resolving Land Dispute in Asia: Exploring the Limits of Law* (Cambridge: CUP, 2014), pp. 59–85, at 67.
72 *Hela Schwarz GmbH v. China*, ICSID Case No. ARB/17/19, Procedural Order No. 2, 10 August 2018, para. 36.

interest, but rather to the private interest of the developers.[73] This case is a prominent example of how an undefined 'public interest' in expropriation can lead to investment disputes. As a result, an arbitral tribunal may become the ultimate interpreter of the term 'public interest' in Chinese law based on its own discretion in the event that a foreign investor decides to challenge the Chinese government's expropriatory measures in investor–state arbitration. This may lead to uncertainty and inconsistency in determining property ownership in China. The FIL and its Implementing Regulation do not define 'public interest', which seems to become another missed opportunity in the Chinese legal system to shed some light on the margin of public interest in the context of expropriation.

2.3.2 The lack of enforceability in practice

There is a concern over the lack of enforceability of equal treatment and a level playing field between foreign and domestic investors in practice, due to the lack of equal treatment in China even between private and state-owned enterprises. As a manifestation of China's state-led economy, Chinese SOEs undertake the role of the monopolistic operator in certain sectors and in certain geographic areas, giving them exclusive dominance and an unparalleled competitive advantage that are impossible for both domestic private businesses and foreign firms to catch up with.[74] It is therefore particularly difficult to apply equal treatment in practice between Chinese SOEs and other market participants including FIEs and private enterprises.

First, Chinese SOEs, despite continuous reform efforts to reduce their size and total numbers in the economy,[75] have already dominated the most strategic, lucrative and critical sectors for decades, making it difficult for foreign investors to compete. In 2006, the State Council published a list of three industry groups in which different ownership goals are pursued.[76] The first group, strategic and key industries, including defence, power generation and distribution, oil and petrochemicals, telecommunication, coal, civil aviation, shipping, and rail, requires

---

73 *Hela Schwarz GmbH v. China*, ICSID Case No. ARB/17/19, Procedural Order No. 4, 15 May 2019, para. 19.

74 Hongyu Fu and Meng Wan, 'Convergences and Divergences in the China–EU and the China–US BIT Negotiations', in Yuwen Li, Tong Qi and Cheng Bian (eds.), *China, the EU and International Investment Law: Reforming Investor-State Dispute Settlement* (London: Routledge, 2019), pp. 26–39, at 37–38.

75 Ligang Song, 'State-Owned Enterprise Reform in China: Past, Present and Prospects', in Ross Garnaut, Ligang Song and Cai Fang (eds.), *China's 40 Years of Reform and Development* (Canberra: ANU Press, 2018), pp. 345–374.

76 关于推进国有资本调整和国有企业重组的指导意见 (Guiding Opinion on Encouraging Transformation and Restructuring of State-Owned Capital) (Issued by the General Office of the State Council on 12 May 2006, effective on promulgation). The State Council, '国资委：国有经济应保持对七个行业的绝对控制力' (SASAC: State-Owned Economy Shall Maintain Absolute Control in Seven Industries), 18 December 2006, http://www.gov.cn/jrzg/2006-12/18/content_472256.htm, last accessed on 2 July 2020.

'100% state ownership or absolute control (50% or above state ownership)'. The second group, pillar industries, which includes machinery, automobiles, IT, construction, steel, base metals, chemicals, land surveying and research and development, requires 'absolute control or conditionally relative controlling stake (less than 50% state ownership but state maintains the biggest shareholder)'. And even in the third group, the normal industries, which are all industries other than those in the first and second groups, the state must 'maintain necessary influence by controlling stakes in key companies'.[77] The absolute dominance of SOEs in the strategic and key industries and relative dominance in the pillar industries suggest the advancement of SOEs at the expense of private and foreign firms.[78] Taking the banking sector as an example, by the end of 2018, although China was host to 4588 banks nationwide, the sector remained highly monopolized and centralized by the state: China's five largest banks, namely the 'big five',[79] are all state-owned and jointly accounted for 37% of the banking sector's total assets and 38% of the total loan balance in China at that time.[80]

Second, Chinese SOEs have much better access to financing. Chinese SOEs have an inherently advantageous position in securing financing from China's banking system, which in itself is a system dominated by state-owned banks, resulting in the strangling of financing to private businesses. The Chinese banking sector has a preference in financing SOEs over private enterprises. In 2016, 83% of the flow of loans from the entire banking sector was directed to SOEs, 11% was directed to private domestic enterprises and the remaining 6% was loaned to foreign firms.[81] China's banking system is more willing to lend to SOEs compared with private or foreign investors, as SOEs are backed with the government's endorsement and favouritism, have better credit ratings and are less likely to default.[82] This systemic bias in the banking system gives Chinese SOEs the unparallel competitive advantage in sourcing cheap financing, and thus causes the inaccessibility of financing to private and foreign enterprises from Chinese banks.

77 Ibid.
78 For a comprehensive discussion on the advancement of SOEs at the expense of private businesses, see Nicholas R. Lardy, *The State Strikes Back: The End of Economic Reform in China?* (Washington D.C.: PIIE Publication, 2019).
79 Industrial and Commercial Bank of China, Bank of China, China Construction Bank. Agricultural Bank of China, and Bank of Communications.
80 'China Host to 4588 Banks, Big Five State-owned Lenders Account for 37% of Assets', *China Banking News*, 6 August 2019, http://www.chinabankingnews.com/2019/08/06 /china-host-to-4588-banks-big-five-state-owned-lenders-account-for-37-of-assets/#:~:text =As%20of%20the%20end%20of,according%20to%20data%20on%20the, last accessed on 2 July 2020.
81 Nicholas Lardy, 'China's Private Firms Continue to Struggle', *PIIE China Economic Watch*, 4 June 2019, https://www.piie.com/blogs/china-economic-watch/chinas-private-firms -continue-struggle, last accessed on 2 July 2020.
82 Gordon Watts, 'China's Private Sector Turns to IOU Drip Feed', *Asia Times*, 7 August 2019, https://asiatimes.com/2019/08/chinas-private-sector-turns-to-iou-drip-feed/, last accessed on 2 July 2020.

Third, Chinese SOEs allegedly receive massive and off-the-record state sub-sidies or equivalents to subsidies. The issue of Chinese subsidies has irritated China's major trading partners such as the US and the EU for years and is tackled in different ways.[83] The EU is particularly sceptical to state subsidies to sectors in Made in China 2025, especially robotics and new energy vehicles, where central and local governments provide various support to favoured domestic companies, especially SOEs, such as direct funding, loans from state-owned banks on non-commercial terms, or the local governments' pledge to not enforce environment standards to reduce the operating cost of these favoured domestic companies.[84] In June 2020, the European Commission published a White Paper addressing foreign subsidies, noting that companies obtaining subsidies from third-country governments gain undue competitive advantage and unfairly distort the EU inter-nal market when they operate in the EU or seek to enter it, and proposes to estab-lish a centralized EU review system to scrutinize, on a case-by-case basis, takeovers of EU undertakings when the acquirer is facilitated by foreign subsidies.[85] In May 2021, the European Commission adopted a proposal for a regulation on foreign subsidies, which gives the Commission the power to prohibit a takeover of EU companies if the third-country acquirer is subsidized at its home state or the power to exclude the subsidized third-country bidder from public procurement in the EU.[86] This is interpreted as a direct response and a tool to address aggres-sive Chinese investors in the EU, especially those with a background of alleged access to Chinese state subsidies.[87] Subsidies strain the China–US relation more significantly, resulting in multiple proceedings in the World Trade Organization (WTO) dispute settlement.[88] The USTR in 2019 identified that China continues

---

83 Jane Cai, 'Why China's Subsidised State-Owned Enterprises Anger US, Europe and Its Own Private Companies', *South China Morning Post*, 21 February 2019, https://www.scmp.com /news/china/diplomacy/article/2184707/why-chinas-subsidised-state-owned-enterprises -anger-us-europe, last accessed on 2 July 2020.

84 European Union Chamber of Commerce in China, *China Manufacturing 2025: Putting Industrial Policy Ahead of Market Forces* (2017), http://docs.dpaq.de/12007-european _chamber_cm2025-en.pdf, pp. 16–17.

85 European Commission, 'White Paper on Levelling the Playing Field as Regards Foreign Subsidies', 17.6.2020, COM(2020) 253 final, https://ec.europa.eu/competition/interna-tional/overview/foreign_subsidies_white_paper.pdf, last accessed on 2 July 2020.

86 European Commission, Proposal for a Regulation of the European Parliament and of the Council on Foreign Subsidies Distorting the Internal Market, COM(2021) 223 final, 2021/0114 (COD), 5 May 2021.

87 David Meyer, 'As Chinese State-Backed Firms Eye Overseas Acquisitions, Europe Considers New Ways to Block Them', *Fortune*, 17 June 2020, https://fortune.com/2020/06/17/ eu-acquisitions-foreign-subsidies-china/, last accessed on 2 July 2020. Sabine Siebold, 'Eye on China, EU Drafts Rules to Curb State-Backed Foreign Buyers', *Reuters*, 5 May 2021, https://www.reuters.com/world/china/eye-china-eu-drafts-rules-curb-state-backed-for-eign-buyers-2021-05-05/, last accessed on 9 June 2021.

88 The US initiated six cases against China at the WTO dispute settlement regarding prohib-ited subsidies, and prevailed in five cases (and one case still pending), resulting in China's subsequent agreement to eliminate all subsidies at issue. These six cases are DS358 (2007),

to provide substantial and unnotified subsidies to its domestic industries, both state owned and private, with more than 500 subsidy programs, which are in violation of the notification requirement of the WTO Subsidies Agreement and distort the global trade market.[89]

The *de facto* favouritism to SOEs in China is deemed to be a prevalent and systematic practice. A survey conducted by the European Union Chamber of Commerce in China in 2019 concluded that Chinese SOEs 'are everywhere and universally privileged' in China, as more than half of the respondents believed that SOEs have greater access to government contracts, greater ability to influence policy, great access to cheap financing, guaranteed access to licences, guaranteed approval in administrative matters, earlier access to regulatory/administrative information and preferential treatment in public procurement.[90] The reason behind this could be ultimately attributed to China's state-led economy, a result of China's fundamental political system. It appears doubtful that ostensible promises of equal treatment to foreign investors in the FIL would likely solve the perennial ascendency of Chinese SOEs in practice. Rather, it is a problem which can only be resolved by deepened structural reform in the long term.

In addition to favouritism for SOEs, another obstacle to equal treatment in practice is selective law enforcement to the detriment of FIEs. European investors complain that 'regulations are often implemented in an unfair manner' as 'they receive unfavourable treatment compared to domestic firms … by the discretionary enforcement of rules and regulations'.[91] Environmental protection measures, for example, are perceived to have a discrepancy in enforcement that is stricter for FIEs but relatively lenient for Chinese private enterprises and SOEs.[92] Despite the FIL's multiple pledges for equal treatment in law, a long-lasting concern yet to be alleviated is that these promises of equality might be stranded at the central level and be ignored during local enforcement.

2.4 Conclusion

The FIL inaugurates pre- and post-establishment national treatment to foreign investors for the first time in China's legislative history. Pre-establishment national treatment with a *Negative List for Foreign Investment* pertains to the liberalization of market access, whilst post-establishment national treatment is

DS387 (2008), DS419 (2010), DS450 (2012), DS489 (2015) and DS519 (2017). WTO, 'Dispute Settlement, China as Respondent', https://www.wto.org/english/tratop_e/dispu_e/find_dispu_cases_e.htm, last accessed on 2 July 2020.

89 USTR, *2019 Report to Congress on China's WTO Compliance*, March 2020, https://ustr.gov/sites/default/files/2019_Report_on_China%E2%80%99s_WTO_Compliance.pdf, p. 85.

90 European Union Chamber of Commerce in China, *European Business in China Position Paper 2019/2020* (2019), https://static.europeanchamber.com.cn/upload/documents/documents/European_Business_in_China_Position_Paper_2019_2020[756].pdf, p. 12.

91 EU Chamber of Commerce in China, *supra* note 33, p. 16.

92 Ibid, p. 18.

achieved by a plethora of pledges and guarantees for equal treatment between foreign and domestic investors.

At the pre-establishment phase, the FIL has become a watershed in defining a new era of China's foreign investment regulatory regime that grants national treatment between domestic and foreign investors. Major relaxation on market access has been introduced, *inter alia*, the *Negative List for Foreign Investment* to replace the Catalogue, the abolition of the three primary foreign investment laws and the replacement of the case-by-case approval *ex ante* by the information reporting system *ex post*. However, certain limitations could undermine the practical effectiveness of the FIL. The national security review system can be considered by foreign investors as a serious market access impediment for its ambiguous terms and broad scope of application. Multiple review, approval, licencing and qualification processes in the *Negative List for Market Access* are in place, giving rise to concerns over selective and discriminatory implementation during those processes that favour domestic investors but prejudices FIEs, and especially at local levels where local protectionism is rampant. And the promulgation of the defensive laws against foreign restrictive measures and foreign sanctions may cast a shadow on foreign investors' confidence in entering the Chinese market.

At the post-establishment phase, the FIL has made unprecedented promises and guarantees to treat foreign investors as equals to domestic ones in business operations, which is certainly a much-welcomed legislative turnout. However, enforcement of these legal promises and guarantees is not without problems. Because of the decades-long dominance of SOEs, the state as a market player has dominated the traditionally strategic and profitable sectors and has the potential to dominate emerging and promising sectors in the future, making it impossible for FIEs to compete with SOEs or have access to the resources exclusively reserved to SOEs. The success or failure in addressing these problems in the future depends on the progress of a more fundamental and structural economic reform in China and the Chinese government's response to international demands. The real challenge ahead is to ensure that the FIL effectively turns into good governance in enforcement, under the inevitable obstacles of deep-rooted local protectionism and the monopolistic interests of SOEs.

3 Foreign mergers and acquisitions of Chinese enterprises

3.1 The *status quo* of foreign takeovers in China

Mergers and acquisitions (M&A) in China conducted by foreign investors have witnessed a stable increase in recent years, both in terms of the value of transactions and their proportion in total foreign direct investment (FDI) in China. According to the Ministry of Commerce (MOFCOM), foreign M&A transactions in China recorded 17.8 billion United States dollars (USD) in 2018, in drastic contrast to merely 0.3 billion USD in 2004 (see Figure 3.1). Further, foreign M&A activities comprise less than 7% of total inward FDI in China from 2004 to 2014 but soared to 11–16% from 2015 to 2018.[1]

The surge of foreign M&A in China in the last two decades is attributed to several factors. M&A provide a preferred channel for foreign investors who seek to inherit the market access, customer base and production capacity of a domestic Chinese company readily available, thus avoiding the hustle of gradually building up an operation from the ground up via greenfield investment.[2] M&A also allow a foreign acquirer to quickly gain knowledge of local preferences, customs and contacts, and enable the foreign investor to expand its business in the Chinese market more efficiently.[3] China's continuous state-owned enterprise (SOE) reform, *inter alia*, the privatization and restructuring of SOEs, has also increased the opportunity for private investors, including foreign investors, to purchase state-owned assets and shares.[4]

---

1 MOFCOM, *Report on Foreign Investment in China 2019*, http://images.mofcom.gov.cn/wzs/202008/20200819101923422.pdf, p. 62. MOFCOM, *Report on Foreign Investment in China 2018*, http://images.mofcom.gov.cn/wzs/201810/20181009090547996.pdf, p. 101. MOFCOM, *Report on Foreign Investment in China 2017*, http://images.mofcom.gov.cn/wzs/201804/20180416161221341.pdf, p. 101. Statistics from 2004 to 2015 are retrieved from MOFCOM, *Report on Foreign Investment in China 2016*, http://images.mofcom.gov.cn/wzs/201612/20161230131233768.pdf, pp. 7–8. All links are accessed on 16 April 2021.
2 Maarten Roos and Rogier van Bijnen, *Corporate Acquisitions and Mergers in China* (Alphen ann den Rijn: Kluwer Law International, 2020), p. 2.
3 Ibid, p. 3.
4 Ibid, pp. 2–3.

DOI: 10.4324/9781003168805-4

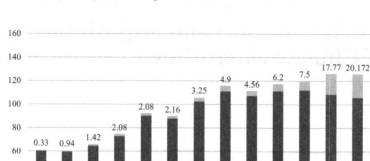

Figure 3.1 Value of greenfield and foreign M&A investment in China 2004–2018
(billion USD) (Source: MOFCOM, *Report on Foreign Investment in China
2019*, http://images.mofcom.gov.cn/wzs/202008/20200819101923422
.pdf, p. 62. MOFCOM, *Report on Foreign Investment in China 2018*,
http://images.mofcom.gov.cn/wzs/201810/20181009090547996.pdf,
p. 101. MOFCOM, *Report on Foreign Investment in China 2017*, http://
images.mofcom.gov.cn/wzs/201804/20180416161221341.pdf, p. 101.
MOFCOM, *Report on Foreign Investment in China 2016*, http://images
.mofcom.gov.cn/wzs/201612/20161230131233768.pdf, pp. 7–8. All
links are accessed on 16 April 2021.)

Notwithstanding the steady increase in value and proportion, foreign M&A
activities in China are still considered less active than in the wider global landscape. According to the United Nations Conference on Trade and Development
(UNCTAD), global cross-border M&A transactions recorded USD 491 billion
in 2019, which accounted for 31.9% of the total value of global FDI inflows
of USD 1,540 billion.[5] By contrast, China, even at its peak of attracting foreign M&A investments in 2016, recorded foreign M&A worth 16% of the total
incoming FDI that year.[6] The relative inactivism of foreign M&A in the context
of the enormous total FDI inflows in China is unlikely to be because of a lack
of enthusiasm from foreign acquirers or a lack of attractiveness of China's ever-
growing market; it is more likely due to China's complicated, multi-level and
restrictive legal environment for cross-border M&A.

5 UNCTAD, *World Investment Report 2020* (Geneva: UN Publication, 2020), p. 16.
6 MOFCOM, *Report on Foreign Investment in China 2017*, http://images.mofcom.gov.cn/
wzs/201804/2018041616122134l.pdf, last accessed on 16 April 2021, p. 101.

The *Foreign Investment Law* (FIL) includes only one provision pertaining to foreign M&A: Art. 2 defines 'foreign investment' to include 'a foreign investor acquiring shares, equities, property rights, or any other similar rights of an enterprise in China', among other types of investment.[7] This means that foreign M&A, greenfield investment and indirect investment are governed under the unified FIL, and should enjoy the same investment liberalization commitments and investors' protection. However, as this chapter demonstrates, the market access regime for foreign M&A is disparate from, and in general more restrictive than, the regime for greenfield investment since the FIL came into force. In addition to laws and regulations specifically governing foreign takeovers of Chinese companies, foreign investors also need to comply with China's takeover legal regime in general that governs all investors at large such as *Company Law*, *Securities Law* and *Measures on Administration of the Takeover of Listed Companies.*[8]

3.2 Foreign takeovers of non-listed companies

3.2.1 *Modalities of foreign takeover of Chinese companies*

In tandem with greenfield investment, foreign investors could enter the Chinese market and establish an initial presence in China through M&A. A merger is a legal combination of two corporate entities which results in the survival of only one entity.[9] China's *Company Law* distinguishes two types of mergers; the first is a merger by absorption, where the acquirer absorbs the target company and the absorbed target is dissolved; and the second is consolidation, where two or more companies combine with each other and cease to exist, resulting in the

---

7 外商投资法 (Foreign Investment Law) (Promulgated by the NPC on 15 March 2019, effective on 1 January 2020). Art. 2 of the FIL defines foreign investment as 'investment activities within China conducted directly or indirectly by foreign natural persons, enterprises, and other organizations alike, including: (1) A foreign investor forms a foreign-invested enterprise within China independently or jointly with other investors; (2) a foreign investor acquires shares, equities, property rights, or other rights alike of an enterprise in China; (3) a foreign investor establishes a new project in China independently or jointly with other investors; and (4) other means according to law'.

8 This chapter will not discuss China's takeover market in general and only focus on the regulatory schemes of foreign takeovers of Chinese private and public companies in specific. For a discussion of China's takeover laws in general, see Chengwei Liu, *Chinese Capital Market Takeover and Restructuring Guide* (Alphen aan den Rijn: Wolters Kluwer, 2011), pp. 7–120. Juan Chen, *Regulating the Takeover of Chinese Listed Companies: Divergence from the West* (Berlin: Springer, 2014). Robin Hui Huang and Juan Chen, 'Takeover Regulation in China: Striking a Balance between Takeover Contestability and Shareholder Protection', in Umakanth Varottil and Wai Yee Wan (eds.), *Comparative Takeover Regulation: Global and Asian Perspectives* (Cambridge: CUP, 2017), pp. 211–240.

9 Cristiana Rizzi, Li Guo and Joseph Christian, *Mergers and Acquisitions and Takeovers in China: A Legal and Cultural Guide to New Forms of Investment* (Alphen aan den Rijn: Wolters Kluwer, 2012), p. 61.

establishment of a new company.[10] An acquisition is defined as the purchase of all or a part of the shares (equity) or assets of the target company by another company as the buyer.[11] The target company may or may not continue to exist after the acquisition, depending on the operational strategy of the acquirer.

According to *Provisions on Mergers and Acquisitions of Domestic Enterprises by Foreign Investors* first promulgated by MOFCOM in 2003 and subsequently revised in 2006 and 2009, alternatively known as Order No. 10, a foreign investor may either conduct an acquisition of shares or an acquisition of assets of a Chinese company.[12] This means that acquisition of shares and acquisition of assets are the only two ways in which foreign M&A are legally permissible in China.[13] In the case of acquisition by shares, the target Chinese company is wholly domestic-owned, and a foreign investor acquires a whole or a part of shares from existing shareholders or subscribes to new shares of the target Chinese company, then converts the target company into a foreign-invested enterprise (FIE).[14] In terms of acquisition by assets, Order No. 10 permits two types: the foreign investor may first establish a new FIE in China, and then purchase assets from a target domestic-owned company through the newly established FIE; alternatively the foreign investor may first purchase the assets of a domestic-owned company, and then establish a new FIE with the assets purchased as registered capital of the new FIE.[15] The former type of acquisition of assets is referred to as asset acquisition after establishment, and the latter as asset acquisition with the establishment.[16]

Because Order No. 10 only permits limited types of foreign M&A transactions, it remains unclear whether foreign investors are allowed to conduct other types of transactions which are not prescribed in the statute. For example, in the case of acquisition by shares, Order No. 10 does not mention indirect acquisition by shares. This would suggest that a foreign investor can only purchase shares of a Chinese domestic company with its offshore financing directly; a foreign investor cannot first establish a new wholly foreign-owned enterprise (WFOE) in China, and then use that WFOE to acquire whole or part of shares of a Chinese company, unless the WFOE is specifically approved by authorities as an investment company. Moreover, in the case of acquisition by assets, Order No. 10 does not specify the legality of the situation where a foreign investor only purchase assets from a Chinese company but does not operate the assets it has acquired.

---

10 公司法 (Company Law) (Promulgated by the NPC on 26 October 2018, effective on promulgation), Art. 172.
11 Cristiana Rizzi, Li Guo and Joseph Christian, *supra* note 9, p. 62.
12 关于外国投资者并购境内企业的规定 (Provisions on Mergers and Acquisitions of Domestic Enterprises by Foreign Investors) (2009 Revision) (Promulgated by MOFCOM on 22 June 2009, effective on promulgation), Art. 2.
13 Cristiana Rizzi, Li Guo and Joseph Christian, *supra* note 9, p. 63.
14 Provisions on Mergers and Acquisitions of Domestic Enterprises by Foreign Investors (2009), Art. 2.
15 Ibid.
16 Maarten Roos and Rogier van Bijnen, *supra* note 2, p. 66.

In recent years China has explored new channels to facilitate foreign M&A activities in private takeovers. Foreign investors can choose to establish a company for the sole purpose of investment in China, which is referred to as a holding company.[17] There are three types of foreign-invested holding companies according to law, namely an investment FIE (外商投资性公司), a foreign-invested start-up investment company (外商投资创业投资企业) and a Qualified Foreign Limited Partner (QFLP) private equity investment fund (境外有限合伙人私募股权投资基金).[18] These three types of foreign-invested holding companies are allowed to conduct equity investment in non-listed Chinese companies. In October 2019, the State Administration of Foreign Exchange (SAFE) issued a Notice, commonly referred to as Order No. 28, which in principle permits all FIEs in China to utilize their own capital in making equity investments in other Chinese companies, under the condition that their equity investment complies with the *Negative List for Foreign Investment* and that the projects to be invested are authentic and legitimate.[19] How Order No. 28 is implemented in practice still remains to be seen.

3.2.2 *Approval procedures for foreign takeovers of domestic companies*

When an acquirer intends to purchase the whole or a part of a non-listed target company, the transaction commences with an inquiry, namely an offer of acquisition, from the buyer to the shareholders of the target company; it is consummated with the successful conclusion of the takeover agreement between the two parties. However, if the acquirer involves a foreign investor, the deal is subject to specific regulatory scrutiny. Table 3.1 provides an inventory of the review and approval procedures a foreign takeover may undergo prior to the conclusion of the deal. A foreign takeover of a non-listed company does not warrant all these procedures, but only the procedures pertinent to the specificity of the deal. Whether a particular review procedure will be triggered or not depends on if the specific conditions are met in the relevant legislation. For instance, an anti-monopoly review will be triggered only when a takeover exceeds the statutory turnover thresholds. It is highly unlikely that a takeover transaction needs to undergo all these approval procedures.

(1) Foreign M&A should first and foremost comply with the *Negative List for Foreign Investment*. The definition of 'foreign investment' in the FIL makes it clear that all forms of foreign M&A in China are subject to the regulation of the FIL. As a result, market access schemes stipulated in the FIL,

---

17 Tarrant Mahony, *Foreign Investment Law in China: Regulation, Practice and Context* (Beijing: Tsinghua University Press, 2015), p. 206.

18 For a detailed discussion of these three types of foreign invested holding companies, see Chapter 1, Section 1.2.2.3.

19 国家外汇管理局关于进一步促进跨境贸易投资便利化的通知 (Notice of the SAFE on Further Facilitating Cross-Border Trade and Investment) (Promulgated by SAFE on 23 October 2019, effective on promulgation), Art. 2.

Table 3.1 Possible approval procedures for foreign takeovers of domestic companies

Measure	Approving agency	Applicable to	Legal basis
Prohibitions and restrictions on certain investment activities	National Development and Reform Commission (NDRC) and MOFCOM	Foreign investments	Negative List for Foreign Investment[a] Negative List for Foreign Investment in the Pilot Free Trade Zones (PFTZs)[b]
National security review	'Working Mechanism' led by NDRC and MOFCOM	Foreign investments that implicate national security	Measures for National Security Review of Foreign Investment[c] Notice of the General Office of State Council on Promulgation of the Trial Measures on National Security Review for Foreign Investment in the Pilot Free Trade Zones[d]
Takeover approval	MOFCOM	Foreign M&A	Provisions on Mergers and Acquisitions of Domestic Enterprises by Foreign Investors (Order No. 10)
Project approval	State Council, or NDRC, or the local government	Investments in fixed asset projects in listed areas	Measures for the Approval and Recordation of Foreign-Invested Projects[e] Notice of the State Council on Issuing the Catalogue of Investment Projects Subject to Government Approval[f]
Sectoral approval and licencing	Dependent on the specific sector	All investments	Negative List for Market Access[g]
State asset transfer approval	Central or local State-owned Assets Supervision and Administration (SASAC); State Council or local government	Transfer of state assets or shares to private investors	Interim Regulation on the Supervision and Administration of State-Owned Assets of Enterprises[h] Law on State-Owned Assets of Enterprises[i] Measures for the Supervision and Administration of State-Owned Shares in Listed Companies[j]

Anti-monopoly review	State Administration for Market Regulation (SAMR)	Takeover in China that might cause monopoly	Anti-Monopoly Law[k]
Registration of enterprise establishment/modification Business licence	SAMR or local AMR	All investments	Regulation on the Administration of the Registration of Enterprise Legal Persons[l]

a 外商投资准入特别管理措施（负面清单）(2020) (Negative List for Foreign Investment) (Promulgated by NDRC and MOFCOM on 23 June 2020, effective on 23 July 2020).

b 自由贸易试验区外商投资准入特别管理措施（负面清单）(2020) (Negative List for Foreign Investment in the Pilot Free Trade Zones) (Promulgated by NDRC and MOFCOM on 23 June 2020, effective on 23 July 2020).

c 外商投资安全审查办法 (Measures for National Security Review of Foreign Investment) (Promulgated by the NDRC and MOFCOM on 19 December 2020, effective on 18 January 2021).

d 国务院办公厅关于印发《自由贸易试验区外商投资国家安全审查试行办法》的通知 (Notice of the General Office of State Council on Promulgation of the Trial Measures on National Security Review for Foreign Investment in the Pilot Free Trade Zones) (Promulgated on 8 April 2015, effective on 8 May 2015).

e 外商投资项目核准和备案管理办法 (Measures for the Approval and Recordation of Foreign-Invested Projects) (Promulgated by the NDRC on 27 December 2014, effective on promulgation).

f 国务院关于发布政府核准的投资项目目录（2016年本）的通知 (Notice of the State Council on Issuing the Catalogue of Investment Projects Subject to Government Approval 2016) (Promulgated by the State Council on 12 December 2016, effective on promulgation).

g 市场准入负面清单 (Negative List for Market Access) (Promulgated by MOFCOM and NDRC on 10 December 2020, effective on promulgation).

h 企业国有资产监督管理暂行条例 (Interim Regulation on the Supervision and Administration of State-Owned Assets of Enterprises) (2019 Revision) (Promulgated by the State Council on 2 March 2019, effective on promulgation).

i 企业国有资产法 (Law on State-Owned Assets of Enterprises) (Promulgated by the NPC on 28 October 2008, effective on 1 May 2009).

j 上市公司国有股权监督管理办法 (Measures for the Supervision and Administration of State-Owned Shares in Listed Companies) (Promulgated by the SASAC, Ministry of Finance, and CSRC on 16 May 2018, effective on 1 July 2018).

k 中华人民共和国反垄断法 (Anti-Monopoly Law of China) (Promulgated by the NPC on 30 August 2007, effective on 1 August 2008).

l 中华人民共和国企业法人登记管理条例 (Regulation on the Administration of the Registration of Enterprise Legal Persons) (2019 Amendment) (Promulgated by the State Council on 3 February 2019, effective on promulgation).

namely pre-establishment national treatment with a negative list approach, apply to foreign M&A as well. Therefore, foreign acquirers are not allowed for takeovers of Chinese companies operating in the prohibited sectors and are subject to a case-by-case approval when acquiring Chinese companies in the restricted sectors, pursuant to the *Negative List for Foreign Investment*.

(2) A foreign acquirer may need approval to proceed with the transaction if it involves national security. A foreign investment, either greenfield or M&A, direct or indirect, that affects or may affect national security is obliged to undergo a national security review prior to the investment being made.[20] A foreign acquirer is subject to notification requirements prior to the closing of the deal if the target Chinese company operates in the defence sector or is located in the vicinity of a military premise, or if the target company operates in any of the listed civil-sensitive sectors and the foreign acquirer seeks control of the target company.[21] Control is ultimately deemed sought after by a judgement that the foreign investor may impose a material influence on significant matters of the target company after the takeover.[22] If a foreign investment, including both greenfield and M&A transactions, takes place in the Pilot Free Trade Zones (PFTZs) and national security may be at stake, a separate set of national security review rules apply.[23]

(3) All foreign takeovers of Chinese domestic companies require a case-by-case approval from MOFCOM. According to Order No. 10, a foreign takeover of the whole or a part of a Chinese company, both non-listed or listed, and by the acquisition of either shares or assets, is subject to *ex ante* approval, regardless of the shareholding ratio in the target, the monetary value of the transaction or the sectors involved.[24] Order No. 10 was promulgated in the context of concerns over the rise of predatory foreign takeovers of Chinese indigenous companies holding time-honoured brands and Chinese national champions, so that the Chinese government could be equipped with a regulatory tool that, on the one hand, selects 'high-quality' takeovers which would bring advanced technology and management skills, and on the other hand wards off undesired M&A transactions that jeopardize China's industrial and economic security.[25] MOFCOM holds a broad scope of discretion

---

20 Measures for National Security Review of Foreign Investment (2020), Art. 2. For a detailed discussion see Chapter 4.
21 Ibid, Art. 4. These ten areas are important agricultural products, important energy and resources, important equipment manufacturing, important infrastructure, important transportation, important cultural products and services, important ICT products and services, important financial services, key technologies, and other important areas.
22 Ibid.
23 Notice of the General Office of State Council on Promulgation of the Trial Measures on National Security Review for Foreign Investment in the Pilot Free Trade Zones (2015).
24 Provisions on Mergers and Acquisitions of Domestic Enterprises by Foreign Investors (2009), Arts. 2 and 6.
25 Hui Huang, 'China's New Regulation on Foreign M&A: Green Light or Red Flag?' *UNSW Law Journal*, Vol. 30 Issue 3 (2007), pp. 804–814, at 810–811.

in this approval process, *inter alia*, the requests to modify the application, documentation and commercial terms of the transaction, whilst the parties of the M&A deal may be under the risk of a prolonged approval process which is ultimately not time-limited.[26]

Following the promulgation of the FIL in 2019, foreign investment, including M&A, enjoys pre-establishment national treatment outside of the *Negative List for Foreign Investment*.[27] This means no more additional approval procedures should be imposed on foreign takeovers compared with domestic takeovers outside of the *Negative List for Foreign Investment*.

(4) The State Council's approval, or National Development and Reform Commission (NDRC) approval, or the local government's approval is required for foreign investment in certain fixed-asset investment projects such as transportation infrastructure, applicable to both greenfield investment and foreign takeovers.[28] The exact scope of investment projects subject to approval is listed separately in the Catalogue of the State Council.[29] The Catalogue includes ten areas (each includes sub-items) covering agriculture and water conservancy, energy, transportation, information technology industry, raw materials, machinery manufacturing, tobacco, high-tech industry, urban construction and social undertakings.[30] For investment in fixed asset projects outside of the Catalogue, a recordation obligation is required.[31] Notably, the Catalogue applies also to domestic investment. Therefore, domestic and foreign investors are essentially subject to an equal level of government scrutiny when conducting fixed asset project investment.

(5) If the target Chinese company operates in specific sectors that require approval or licencing from industry regulators, a foreign acquirer may need to obtain additional sectoral approval or licences according to the *Negative List for Market Access*, which applies to both domestic and foreign investment, including greenfield and M&A.

(6) The transfer of state assets is in principle not limited to private domestic investors but also equally accessible to foreign investors. If an acquirer proposes to purchase state-owned shares or state assets in a target Chinese company, the transaction requires the approval from the central or local State-Owned Assets Supervision and Administration Commission (SASAC), which acts as

---

26 Order No. 10 stipulates that MOFCOM should complete the approval process in 30 days since it has received the full set of documents required from the foreign acquirer. But the preparation of these documents is not time-limited, meaning that the filing of documents can go back and forth between the applicant and MOFCOM until MOFCOM is completely satisfied. Maarten Roos and Rogier van Bijnen, *supra* note 2, p. 57.

27 FIL (2019), Art. 4.

28 Measures for the Approval and Recordation of Foreign-Invested Projects (2014), Art. 2.

29 Ibid, Art. 4.

30 Notice of the State Council on Issuing the Catalogue of Investment Projects Subject to Government Approval (2016).

31 Ibid, Art. 1.

the shareholder or property rights owner.[32] The sale of state assets or equity requires an independent asset appraisal by a qualified institute, the appraisal report should be included as a part of the filings to the SASAC for approval.[33] If the takeover of a state-owned, state-controlled or a state-participated enterprise results in 100% of state shares sold to a private investor, or the change of control of the target Chinese company from the central or local SASAC to a private investor, then the transaction requires approval from the State Council or the corresponding level of local government, in addition to central or local SASAC approval.[34] Publicly listed SOEs and state-owned shares can be traded on the stock market, whereas the transaction is subject to the approval of the SASAC when certain thresholds are met.[35]

(7) A domestic or foreign takeover may require an anti-monopoly review if competition issues are involved. In the event of concentration of business operators, whereby two business entities merge, or one gains control over the other by acquiring shares or assets of the latter, or one gains control of, or may impose material influence over, the other by means such as an agreement, the two business operators are required to seek approval from the State Administration for Market Regulation (SAMR) if the threshold for review is met.[36] In January 2020, a revision draft of the *Anti-Monopoly Law* (AML) was published by SAMR, proposing significant amendments to the current AML effective since 2008.[37] The amendment may bring both benefits and concerns to foreign investors. A new provision is proposed which establishes a 'fair competition review' system that prevents the government, especially

---

32 Interim Regulation on the Supervision and Administration of State-Owned Assets of Enterprises (2019), Art. 23.
33 Law on State-Owned Assets of Enterprises (2008), Arts. 42, 47 and 55.
34 Interim Regulation on the Supervision and Administration of State-Owned Assets of Enterprises (2019), Art. 23.
35 For example, in a listed company with less than one billion shares, the state-owned controlling shareholder needs to seek approval from the SASAC if it plans to transfer 5% or above of the total shares in the listed company in one fiscal year. Measures for the Supervision and Administration of State-Owned Shares in Listed Companies (2018), Art. 12.
36 Anti-Monopoly Law (2007), Arts. 20 and 21. The threshold triggering an anti-monopoly review is that all business entities participating in the concentration in question have a combined global turnover of 10 billion RMB or above in the last fiscal year and at least two among them each has a turnover of 0.4 billion RMB or above within China in the last fiscal year; or that all business entities participating in the concentration in question have a combined turnover of 2 billion RMB or above in the last fiscal year within China and at least two among them each has a turnover of 0.4 billion RMB or above within China in the last fiscal year. If the above threshold is not met, but concrete evidence can prove that a concentration has or may have the effect of eliminating or restricting competition, the SAMR may investigate the transaction. 国务院关于经营者集中申报标准的规定 (Provisions on the Threshold for Declaration of Concentration of Business Operators) (Promulgated by the State Council on 18 September 2018, effective on promulgation).
37 《反垄断法》修订草案 （公开征求意见稿）(Draft Amendment of Anti-Monopoly Law for Public Comments) (Published by SAMR on 2 January 2020).

at the local level, from adopting rules and policies that would exclude and restrict free competition among different market participants.[38] This could be particularly beneficial to foreign investors by alleviating local protectionism and creating a level playing field in competition. At the same time, on the concentration of business operators, newly added provisions propose that, even if the threshold triggering a review is not reached, SAMR may investigate, intervene and prohibit the transaction when it deems that the deal has or may have the effect of eliminating or restricting competition.[39] These provisions appear to add greater regulatory uncertainty to the AML.

(8) Approval is needed from the SAMR for the registration of establishment (设立登记) or registration of modification (变更登记) as a result of a foreign takeover. When a foreign investor acquires all or a part of a wholly domestic-owned company and transforms the target into an FIE, or a foreign investor conducts acquisition by assets which results in the establishment of a new FIE, registration of establishment, approval of the company name, and obtainment of the Business License of Legal Persons at the SAMR or local AMRs authorized by the SAMR is required.[40] When a foreign investor acquires shares owned by others in an existing FIE, the registration of modification (change of shareholding ownership) at the SAMR or the authorized local AMR is required.[41] These registration filing and approval procedures take place on the online Enterprise Registration System.[42]

3.3 Foreign investment in listed companies

A public takeover takes place on the stock market when the target company is a listed company. Foreign investors are subject to approvals and qualifications to gain access to the stock exchange in China, in addition to the approval procedures applicable to a foreign takeover in general, as enumerated in Table 3.1. As a result of rigorous approval and control mechanisms for foreign investors to enter China's stock market, foreign investors hold merely 2.66% of the total shares on China's stock market, according to an Organisation for Economic Co-operation and Development (OECD) survey in 2017.[43] There are four alternatives for a

---

38 Ibid, Art. 9.
39 Ibid, Arts. 24 and 34.
40 Regulation on the Administration of the Registration of Enterprise Legal Persons (2019), Arts. 5, 10 and 16.
41 Ibid, Art. 19.
42 市场监管总局关于贯彻落实《外商投资法》做好外商投资企业登记注册工作的通知 (Notice of the SAMR on Effective Enforcement of the Registration of FIEs for the Implementation of the Foreign Investment Law) (Issued by the SAMR on 28 December 2019, effective on 1 January 2020), Art. 1. The online Enterprise Registration System is accessible at http://wsdj.samr.gov.cn/saicmcdjweb/, last accessed on 3 August 2021.
43 OECD, *OECD Survey of Corporate Governance Frameworks in Asia 2017*, https://www.oecd.org/daf/ca/OECD-Survey-Corporate-Governance-Frameworks-Asia.pdf, last accessed on 3 March 2021, p. 5.

Table 3.2 Qualifications of foreign investors on the Chinese stock market

Alternatives	Qualifications	Approving agency	Applicable to	Legal basis
1	Qualified foreign institutional investor (QFII)	China Securities Regulatory Commission (CSRC)	Foreign investors	Measures for the Administration of Securities and Futures Investment in China by QFIIs and RMB QFIIs[a]
2	Renminbi qualified foreign institutional investor (RMB QFII)	CSRC	Foreign investors	Measures for the Administration of Securities and Futures Investment in China by QFIIs and RMB QFIIs
3	Strategic foreign investor	MOFCOM and CSRC	Foreign investors	Measures for the Administration of Strategic Investment in Listed Companies by Foreign Investors[b]
4	Shanghai–Hong Kong Stock Connect Shenzhen–Hong Kong Stock Connect Shanghai–London Stock Connect	CSRC	Foreign investors	Several Provisions on the Interconnection Mechanism in Mainland China and Hong Kong Stock Markets[c] Provisions on the Interconnection of Depositary Receipts of the Shanghai Stock Exchange and the London Stock Exchange for Trial Implementation[d]

Approval procedures listed in Table 3.1 if applicable

[a] 合格境外机构投资者和人民币合格境外机构投资者境内证券期货投资管理办法 (Measures for the Administration of Securities and Futures Investment in China by QFIIs and RMB QFIIs) (Promulgated by the CSRC, People's Bank of China and State Administration of Foreign Exchange on 25 September 2020, effective on 1 November 2020).
[b] 外国投资者对上市公司战略投资管理办法 (Measures for the Administration of Strategic Investment in Listed Companies by Foreign Investors) (Promulgated by MOFCOM on 28 October 2015, effective on promulgation).
[c] 内地与香港股票市场交易互联互通机制若干规定 (Several Provisions on the Interconnection Mechanism in Mainland China and Hong Kong Stock Markets) (Promulgated by the CSRC on 30 September 2016, effective on promulgation).
[d] 关于上海证券交易所与伦敦证券交易所互联互通存托凭证业务的监管规定（试行）(Provisions on the Interconnection of Depositary Receipts of the Shanghai Stock Exchange and the London Stock Exchange for Trial Implementation) (Promulgated by the CSRC on 12 October 2018, effective on promulgation).

foreign investor to access the Chinese stock market and directly purchase shares of Chinese listed companies.

(1) A foreign investor may obtain *ex ante* approval as a qualified foreign institutional investor (QFII). First launched in 2002, the QFII allows foreign institutional investors, such as fund management organizations, commercial banks, insurance companies, security companies, trust companies, sovereign wealth funds and state pension funds, which have been approved by the China Securities Regulatory Commission (CSRC), to invest in the Chinese stock market with their offshore financing.[44] From 2002 to 2020, 558 foreign financial institutions have been approved as QFIIs in China.[45] Before November 2020, foreign investors as QFIIs were subject to more stringent requirements, namely qualification requirements to the QFII applicants on the minimum period of operation and minimum size of assets under management,[46] limitations on capital entry and exit,[47] limitations on repatriating earnings,[48] shareholding restrictions in a single Chinese listed company,[49] and aggregate investment quota restrictions per QFII upon approval from the SAFE, to the maximum of 5 billion USD per QFII.[50] The purpose behind these control and qualification requirements was to attract those foreign institutional investors that had a sound reputation and experience of good governance, to ensure that they maintained a diversified investment portfolio in China, to prohibit them from building a controlling or influential status in a Chinese listed company, and, most important, to mitigate the risk of capital flight and instability of the Chinese stock market.[51]

Pursuant to the promulgation of *Measures for the Administration of Securities and Futures Investment in China by QFIIs and RMB QFIIs* in 2020, the qualification requirements on asset size and investment quotas of an

---

44 合格境外机构投资者境内证券投资管理暂行办法 (Interim Measures on the Administration of Securities Investment in China by Qualified Foreign Institutional Investors) (Repealed) (Promulgated by the CSRC and PBoC on 5 October 2002, effective on 1 December 2002).

45 CSRC, 合格境外机构投资者名录 (QFII Directory) (until December 2020), http://www .csrc.gov.cn/pub/zjhpublic/G00306205/201511/t20151106_286098.htm, last accessed on 19 February 2021.

46 For instance, for a foreign fund management company as a qualified QFII, its business operation period had to exceed five years and its total assets under management had to exceed 10 billion USD. Interim Measures on the Administration of Securities Investment in China by Qualified Foreign Institutional Investors (2002), Art. 7.

47 Ibid, Arts. 25–28.

48 Ibid, Arts. 29 and 30.

49 Ibid, Art. 20.

50 SAFE, 合格境外机构投资者投资额度审批情况表 (Approved Investment Quota for QFII) (May 2020), http://www.safe.gov.cn/safe/2018/0425/8881.html, last accessed on 19 February 2021.

51 Wenge Wang, 'The Mechanisms of Institutional Activism: Qualified Foreign Institutional Investors in China', *Capital Markets Law Journal*, Vol. 14 Issue 1 (2019), pp. 78–113, at 94, 97.

individual QFII have been repealed, amongst other modifications. Another significant modification of the new rules in 2020 is the expansion of financial products a QFII is allowed to purchase. Instead of stocks, state bonds and corporate bonds that are listed as A-shares in China's stock market, as in the past, the new rules now permit QFIIs to purchase stocks and bonds on the stock market, depositary receipts, bond repos and asset-backed securities traded or transferred on the stock exchanges, stocks listed on the National Equities Exchange and Quotations (NEEQ),[52] the financial products traded on the China Inter-Bank Market, public securities investment funds, private investment funds, financial futures contracts, commodity futures contracts, options, foreign exchange derivatives, and subscriptions to new shares and secondary offering of shares.[53] The shareholding restrictions of QFIIs in a single Chinese listed company remain unaltered: an individual QFII shall hold no more than 10% of the total shares of a listed Chinese company; and the aggregate shareholding percentage of all QFIIs in one Chinese listed company shall not exceed 30% of the total shares of that listed company.[54]

(2) Foreign investors may apply for an Renminbi (RMB) QFII. The program was first introduced in 2011, which allowed the Hong Kong subsidiaries of Chinese fund management and securities companies approved by the CSRC to invest in the Chinese stock market with RMB capital.[55] Since 2013, foreign institutional investors were allowed to trade on the Chinese stock market with their overseas RMB capital, upon the approval of the CSRC for their qualification and the approval of SAFE for investment quota restrictions.[56] In October 2020, there were 259 approved RMB QFIIs in China.[57] The difference between a QFII and an RMB QFII is that the former invests in China's stock market via its offshore foreign currency that subsequently converts to RMB, whereas the latter via its overseas RMB capital directly. Since

---

52 The NEEQ (全国中小企业股份转让系统), also known as 'the New Third board', is an over-the-counter (transactions are done directly between two parties without the supervision of the stock exchange) stock trading market that provides listing for Chinese small and medium enterprises which are not qualified to list on the Main Board in Shanghai and Shenzhen.

53 Measures for the Administration of Securities and Futures Investment in China by QFIIs and RMB QFIIs (2020), Art. 6.

54 Ibid, Art. 7.

55 基金管理公司、证券公司人民币合格境外机构投资者境内证券投资试点办法 (Pilot Measures for Domestic Securities Investment by RMB Qualified Foreign Institutional Investors of Domestic Fund Management Companies and Securities Companies) (Repealed) (Promulgated by CSRC, PBoC, and SAFE on 16 December 2011, effective on promulgation), Art. 2.

56 人民币合格境外机构投资者境内证券投资试点办法 (Measures of the Pilot Program of Securities Investment in China by RMB Qualified Foreign Institutional Investors) (Repealed) (Promulgated by CSRC, People's Bank of China, and SAFE on 1 March 2013, effective on promulgation).

57 CSRC, '人民币合格境外机构投资者名录' (RMB QFII Directories) (October 2020), http://www.csrc.gov.cn/pub/zjhpublic/G00306205/201511/t20151106_286099.htm, last accessed on 22 February 2021.

2020, the qualifications and requirements of QFIIs and RMB QFIIs are unified under the *Measures for the Administration of Securities and Futures Investment in China by QFIIs and RMB QFIIs*, whereby a foreign institutional investor is allowed to submit one application to qualify as both a QFII and an RMB QFII.[58]

(3) A third alternative for a foreign investor to invest in China's securities market is by means of a strategic foreign investor. Since 2005, foreign investors may act as a strategic investor who intends a long-lasting interest and relatively large scale of shareholding in a listed Chinese company.[59] In 2015, the *Measures for the Administration of Foreign Strategic Investors in Listed Companies* was revised, allowing an approved foreign investor to invest A-shares of a listed company. A strategic investor is subject to qualification requirements, *inter alia*, a foreign corporation or a non-legal entity; a total overseas paid-in asset of no less than 100 million USD or a total overseas asset under management of no less than 500 million USD; and sound corporate governance and a good operating record.[60] The qualification of a strategic investor is subject to a case-by-case approval by MOFCOM.[61] A strategic investment should also comply with certain criteria, *inter alia*, the initial purchase of shares of one target listed company shall exceed 10% of the total issued shares of that company and a lock-up period whereby acquired A-shares by the foreign strategic investor shall not be transferred within three years.[62] A strategic investor can purchase A-shares by concluding a shares purchase agreement in a negotiated transfer with the target company or a subscription to new shares in the target listed company's private placement; each transaction requires approval from MOFCOM and CSRC.[63] There are no maximum shareholding limits by which a foreign strategic investor can acquire in the target company, whereas a mandatory tender offer is triggered when an investor acquires more than 30% of shares of a listed company in the stock market.[64] In practice, a foreign strategic investor may combine several

---

58 Measures for the Administration of Securities and Futures Investment in China by QFIIs and RMB QFIIs (2020), Art. 2.
59 外国投资者对上市公司战略投资管理办法 (2005年) (Measures for the Administration of Strategic Investment in Listed Companies by Foreign Investors) (2005 Version) (Promulgated by MOFCOM, CSRC, State Taxation Administration, SAIC, and SAFE on 31 December 2005, effective on 31 January 2006).
60 Measures for the Administration of Strategic Investment in Listed Companies by Foreign Investors (2015), Art. 6.
61 Ibid, Art. 3.
62 Ibid, Art. 5.
63 Ibid, Arts. 7 and 8.
64 The tender offer can be either a general offer to acquire all outstanding shares to all shareholders of the target listed company, or a partial offer to acquire a portion of outstanding shares to all shareholders of the target listed company on a *pro rata* basis. 上市公司收购管理办法 (Measures for the Administration of the Takeover of Listed Companies) (Promulgated by the CSRC on 20 March 2020, effective on promulgation), Arts. 24 and 47.

available methods in order to gain a controlling status in the target company. For instance, in the French SEB–Chinese Supor acquisition completed in 2007, the French acquirer adopted a negotiated transfer, which resulted in the purchase of 11.48% of shares of Supor approved by MOFCOM and CSRC, a subscription of new shares accounting for 18.52% of shares of the target approved by MOFCOM and a partial offer to Supor's shareholders which led to the purchase of 22.74% of shares of Supor approved by CSRC. Altogether SEB acquired 52.74% of shares of Supor and thus became the absolute controlling shareholder of the target.[65]

In June 2020, a consultation draft to further revise the rules on foreign strategic investors was circulated for public comment.[66] The draft proposed significant relaxation of restrictions on strategic foreign investors, including the permission to acquire stakes of A-share companies by tender offer and other methods, the purchase of shares on the NEEQ market, the qualification of foreign natural persons as foreign strategic investors, the reduction of minimum requirements of assets owned or under management by a foreign strategic investor, the reduction of the lock-up period from the current 3 years to 12 months, and the reduction of the proportion of initial shareholding in the target company from a minimum 10% to 5%.[67] It is expected that the proposed revision of the law is to encourage more medium- and long-term foreign investment in the A-share market.[68]

(4) The fourth alternative for foreign investors to access China's stock market and purchase A-shares is through the Stock Connect. The Stock Connect scheme provides a cross-border platform for eligible foreign investors to trade eligible Chinese A-shares at the foreign investors' home exchange and eligible Chinese investors to trade stocks listed overseas through a local Chinese securities exchange. The Shanghai–Hong Kong Stock Connect was first introduced in 2014, which allows eligible Chinese investors to purchase eligible Hong Kong stocks through local Chinese securities companies and foreign investors with an account in Hong Kong Exchange to purchase eligible Chinese stocks through their local Hong Kong brokers. Through the Stock Connect, eligible Chinese A-share stocks are still listed on the Chinese stock market but are accessible and tradable at the Hong Kong Stock Exchange.

---

65 Chengwei Liu, *supra* note 8, pp. 177–180.
66 外国投资者对上市公司战略投资管理办法（修订草案公开征求意见稿）(Measures for the Administration of Strategic Investment in Listed Companies by Foreign Investors – Draft Amendment for Public Opinion) (Published by MOFCOM, CSRC, SASAC, State Taxation Administration, SAMR, and SAFE on 18 June 2020).
67 Ibid.
68 Qing Xie *et al.*, 'Relaxing Requirements on Foreign Strategic Acquisition of Listed Companies – Observations on the Consultation Paper of Strategic Acquisition Measures', *JunHe Legal Updates*, 22 June 2020, http://www.junhe.com/legal-updates/1237, last accessed on 22 February 2021.

In August 2021, 587 A-share stocks listed on the Shanghai Stock Exchange were accessible for foreign investors at the Hong Kong Stock Exchange.[69]

In 2016, the Shenzhen–Hong Kong Stock Connect was initiated following the success of Shanghai–Hong Kong Stock Connect. In August 2021, 847 A-share stocks listed in Shenzhen Stock Exchange were accessible to foreign investors to trade at the Hong Kong Stock Exchange.[70]

The Shanghai–London Stock Connect was launched in 2019, allowing eligible Chinese companies listed on the Shanghai Stock Exchange to issue and trade a global depositary receipt (GDR) on the London Stock Exchange and vice versa. There are so far four Chinese listed companies approved as GDR issuers on the London Stock Exchange and no British companies have yet been successfully approved as GDR issuers on the Shanghai Stock Exchange.[71] The Shanghai–London Stock Connect allegedly encountered significant setbacks and a suspension due to political tension between China and the United Kingdom (UK) during the outbreak of the anti-government movement in Hong Kong.[72] In addition to political risks, the success and vitality of the Shanghai–London Stock Connect are also challenged by the absence of regulatory alignment between China and the UK. Chinese listed companies approved as GDR issuers on the London Stock Exchange need to comply with UK law, and British public companies approved as GDR issuers on the Shanghai Stock Exchange will be governed by Chinese law.[73] Due to the differences between Chinese and British takeover laws, for instance, different defensive tactics available to adopt by the target company against hostile takeovers, investors may be deterred from making a takeover attempt through the Shanghai–London Stock Connect for the lack of a level playing field and significant legal uncertainty.[74]

69 HKEX, 'List of SSE Securities', https://www.hkex.com.hk/-/media/HKEX-Market/Mutual-Market/Stock-Connect/Eligible-Stocks/View-All-Eligible-Securities_xls/SSE_Securities.xls?la=en, last accessed on 11 August 2021.

70 HKEX, 'List of SZSE Securities', https://www.hkex.com.hk/-/media/HKEX-Market/Mutual-Market/Stock-Connect/Eligible-Stocks/View-All-Eligible-Securities_xls/SZSE_Securities.xls?la=en, last accessed on 11 August 2021.

71 London Stock Exchange, 'Shanghai London Stock Connect, Stock Connect Issuers', https://www.londonstockexchange.co m/discover/china/shanghai-london-stock-connec t?lang=en&tab=stock-connect-issuers, last accessed on 14 March 2021.

72 Julie Zhu, Abhinav Ramnarayan and Jonathan Saul, 'China Halts British Stock Link over Political Tensions', *Reuters*, 2 January 2020, https://www.reuters.com/article/us-china-britain-ipos-exclusive-idUSKBN1Z108L, last accessed on 22 February 2021.

73 Joseph Lee and Yonghui Bao, 'The Prospect of Regulatory Alignment for an Interconnected Capital Market between the United Kingdom and China: A Takeover Law Perspective', *The Chinese Journal of Comparative Law*, Vol. 8 No. 2 (2020), pp. 450–484, at 479–480.

74 Ibid.

3.4 Foreign complaints about the Chinese M&A market

3.4.1 A lack of a level playing field

A lack of a level playing field is a complaint about the relatively restrictive Chinese M&A market vis-à-vis the relatively liberal M&A market abroad. As discussed earlier, the Chinese M&A market is heavily regulated for the market entry of foreign investors. The takeover of a non-listed Chinese company may involve multiple approval procedures by different government agencies, and to acquire shares of a listed Chinese company requires additional qualification requirements and approval procedures. These regulatory burdens may contribute to the relatively low proportion of foreign M&A investment to total FDI in China (see Figure 3.1). Compared to the high volume of Chinese outbound M&A investment, inbound M&A demonstrate a significant lag (see Figure 3.2).

The enormous gap between Chinese inbound and outbound M&A investment is perhaps attributed to the lack of a reciprocal regulatory framework over cross-border M&A between China and the Western world. Asymmetrical market access conditions at home and abroad mean that foreign investors face numerous prohibitions and restrictions when acquiring private or public Chinese companies, whilst Chinese investors face far fewer regulatory obstacles when acquiring foreign firms abroad despite the increasing vigilance and control over Chinese takeover attempts in major economies in recent years. For example, the Committee on

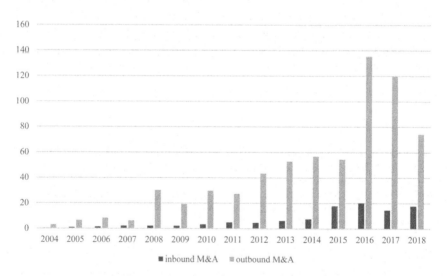

Figure 3.2 Chinese inbound M&A and Chinese outbound M&A 2004–2018 (billion USD) (Sources: Obtained from MOFCOM, *Reports on Foreign Investment in China,* various years (2019–2016); MOFCOM, National Bureau of Statistics, and SAFE, *2019 Statistical Bulletin of China's Outward Foreign Direct Investment* (Beijing: China Commerce and Trade Press, 2020), p. 97.)

Foreign Investment in the United States (CFIUS) is responsible for the national security review of foreign investment, which remains, to date, the only mechanism for foreign acquisitions of US companies.[75] Other developed economies, such as Australia, Canada, and the European Union (EU) and Member States, have adopted similar screening mechanisms on grounds of national security or other public interests, but they are only triggered in exceptional cases when specific thresholds for review are met.[76] However, in the case of China, a national security review is just one of several approval procedures which a foreign investor is required to undergo in order to proceed with the proposed takeover, and failure to gain approval in any of these multiple procedures would result in the abandonment of the whole deal.

The lack of market access symmetry of the takeover market between China and other economies where Chinese buyers tend to invest heavily is perhaps best demonstrated in the China–EU context. Between 2000 and 2017, there were 17 takeovers of European companies successfully conducted by Chinese acquirers, and each of these takeovers had a value of at least 1 billion USD.[77] One study predicted that one-quarter of these deals could not have happened if they had involved a European investor acquiring a Chinese target company in the same sector, as those sectors are legally prohibited or restricted from foreign takeover in China.[78] Furthermore, in half of these Chinese acquisitions of European companies, if the transactions had happened the other way around they would be highly unlikely to be approved by Chinese authorities due to state control and industrial policies, although they would have been legally permissible.[79]

These asymmetrical market access conditions, or a lack of a level playing field, or a lack of reciprocity in the field of M&A have caused significant ramifications to the detriment of China's interest abroad. Chinese acquirers abroad have been recognized, more often than not, as a 'national strategic buyer', whose objective is 'to further the interests of a nation-state in the pursuit of national industrial policy', and to gain control of critical technology and strategic infrastructure abroad, instead of commercial and financial goals.[80] As a result, an increasing number of states have implicitly or explicitly adopted heightened government scrutiny of Chinese takeovers in particular in order to level the playing field.

75 Jeffrey N. Gordon and Curtis J. Milhaupt, 'China as a National Strategic Buyer: Toward a Multilateral Regime for Cross-Border M&A', *Columbia Business Law Review*, No. 1 (2019), pp. 192–251, at 199–200.

76 For a comparative overview of national security review regimes of these jurisdictions, see Carlos Esplugues, *Foreign Investment, Strategic Assets and National Security* (Cambridge: Intersentia, 2018). Cheng Bian, *National Security Review of Foreign Investment: A Comparative Legal Analysis of China, the United States and the European Union* (London: Routledge, 2020).

77 Thilo Hanemann and Mikko Huotari, *EU-China FDI: Working Towards Reciprocity in Investment Relations*, Merics Papers on China No. 3, May 2018, p. 15.

78 Ibid, p. 20.

79 Ibid, p. 20.

80 Jeffrey N. Gordon and Curtis J. Milhaupt, *supra* note 75, at 198.

3.4.2 Targeted law enforcement

Targeted law enforcement is a perennial complaint from foreign investors in China. According to a business confidence survey in 2020 by the EU Chamber of Commerce in China, European companies in China complain that laws and regulations are 'often implemented in a discretionary manner, with 40% reporting enforcement as unfavourable to them', and 27% of respondents regard targeted law enforcement in China as one of the top three challenges in doing business in China.[81] Specifically, discretionary law enforcement manifests as inconsistent interpretation and implementation of the same set of laws among various authorities, across different regions and at different times.[82] Further, the reason why law enforcement is deemed arbitrary and discretionary is that laws and regulations are too ambiguous and unclear, they are either accidentally or intentionally misinterpreted by government officials, and officials cannot adequately enforce laws and regulations due to their limited capacity.[83]

Regarding foreign takeovers in particular, China's anti-monopoly review has become a major area of concern whereby targeted enforcement to the advantage of Chinese SOEs and to the detriment of foreign investors takes place. Art. 7 of AML stipulates that the state protects SOEs in sectors critical to the lifeline of the national economy, national security and statutory state monopolies; this, it is argued, grants special treatment to SOEs over its monopoly 'without objective justification'.[84] The standards of review that determine the approval or rejection of a merger case are criticized for being too vague, *inter alia*, the effect of a proposed takeover on the development of the economy and any other factors the review authority takes into account that affect market competition.[85] These two factors can be interpreted in an excessively expansive way in practice to include non-monopolistic considerations in the assessment of a takeover and to ward off undesired foreign buyers.[86] Art. 55 of the AML stipulates that the law applies to business operators who abuse their intellectual property rights to eliminate or restrict competition, which gives rise to concerns that the Chinese government may cite this broadly worded provision to rattle foreign technology firms in China with a dominant market position.[87]

Those concerns about discriminatory or protectionist enforcement of the AML are evidenced by high-profile foreign merger cases that were argued to lack

---

81 European Union Chamber of Commerce in China, *Business Confidence Survey 2020: Navigating in the Dark*, https://static.europeanchamber.com.cn/upload/documents/documents/BCS_EN2020_final[774].pdf, last accessed on 19 August 2020, pp. 2, 16–17.

82 Ibid.

83 Ibid.

84 Mark Williams, 'Foreign Investment in China: Will the Anti-Monopoly Law Be a Barrier or a Facilitator?' *Texas International Law Journal*, Vol. 45 Issue 1 (2009), pp. 127–156, at 136–137.

85 Anti-Monopoly Law (2007), Art. 27.

86 Mark Williams, *supra* note 84, at 139.

87 Ibid, at 140.

concrete justification. In the merger case of Coca-Cola–Huiyuan Juice Group in 2008, MOFCOM (the statutory anti-monopoly review agency at the time) prohibited the transaction after a six-month-long review procedure and became the first case of rejection since the entry into effect of AML. In its decision, MOFCOM relied on, *inter alia*, the argument that Coca-Cola's dominant position in the carbonated drinks market might extend to juice drinks after the takeover, thus creating a monopoly in the juice drink market.[88] Many have questioned the validity of this argument on the ground that even after the merger, Coca-Cola and Huiyuan would have a combined market share in juice beverages of 28.99%, which was still below the 33.3% threshold by which the AML defines a horizontal dominant market position in Art. 19.[89] Besides the lack of substantial competition concerns, Huiyuan is a private Chinese company in a non-sensitive industry, which makes any concerns about 'national interest', 'public interest' or 'industrial security' appear to be entirely irrelevant to MOFCOM's reason of rejection.[90] It is therefore argued that the prohibition of the deal is really only because of nationalist and protectionist sentiment – the feeling that an iconic domestic brand should not fall into the hands of an American multinational corporation – under the guise of anti-monopoly enforcement.[91] The case was epitomized as an example of 'excessive nationalism and irrational catharsis towards foreign M&As' against 'the tenet of the rule of law'.[92]

Another example in regard to the disadvantageous position of foreign acquirers in M&A transactions involves the sale of state assets. Foreign investors in principle are not excluded from the course of privatization and reconstruction of Chinese SOEs; to the contrary, foreign participation is encouraged in various laws and policies.[93] Laws and regulations governing the transfer of state assets do not distinguish between foreign and domestic buyers, which means that, at

---

88 中华人民共和国商务部公告(2009年)第22号（商务部关于禁止可口可乐公司收购中国汇源公司审查决定的公告）(MOFCOM Notice (2009) No. 22 on the Prohibition of Acquisition of Chinese Huiyuan by Coca-Cola), 18 March 2009, http://fldj.mofcom.gov.cn/aarticle/ztxx/200903/20090306108494.html, last accessed on 24 February 2021.

89 Xinzhu Zhang and Vanessa Yanhua Zhang, 'Chinese Merger Control: Patterns and Implications', *Journal of Competition Law & Economics*, Vol. 6 Issue 2 (2009), pp. 477–496, at 488.

90 Mark Williams, *supra* note 84, at 150.

91 Kevin B. Goldstein, 'Reviewing Cross-Border Mergers and Acquisitions for Competition and National Security: A Comparative Look at How the U.S.A., Europe and China Separate Security Concerns from Competition Concerns in Reviewing Acquisitions by Foreign Entities', *Tsinghua China Law Review*, Vol. 3 Issue 2 (2011), pp. 215–256, at 247–251.

92 Jin Sun, 'The Implementation of China's Anti-Monopoly Law: A Case on Coca-Cola's Abortive Acquisition of Huiyuan Juice', *Frontiers of Law in China*, Vol. 6 Issue 1 (2011), pp. 117–130, at 128.

93 See, for example, 国务院关于积极有效利用外资推动经济高质量发展若干措施的通知 (Notice of the State Council on Certain Measures for Actively and Effectively Utilizing Foreign Investment to Promote Quality Economic Development) (Promulgated by the State Council on 10 June 2018, effective on promulgation), Art. 11 (the state encourages foreign M&A in China … and offers fair and equal opportunities for domestic and foreign investors to participate in the reform of SOEs).

least in theory, they would apply equally to all potentially interested buyers.[94] However, in some cases it has proven difficult for a foreign investor to success-fully acquire a Chinese SOE. In the merger case of Carlyle–Xugong, the US Carlyle group announced in 2005 its bid to buy 85% of the shares of Chinese Xugong Construction Machinery Group, China's largest construction machinery maker and a local SOE owned by the Xuzhou government. The announcement of the deal attracted immediate criticism from the public on the cheap sale of state assets to foreign buyers.[95] The deal was submitted to MOFCOM, SASAC and CSRC for separate approval procedures, but received no response for the next three years.[96] Due to the lack of official approval, the deal was eventually aban-doned in 2008, as the takeover agreements between the two parties expired.[97] It was believed that the Chinese government deliberately stalled the approval process with complete silence until its bureaucracy finally made the foreign buyer withdraw.[98]

As discussed in Sections 3.2 and 3.3, multiple review and approval procedures can take place for foreign takeovers of domestic companies. Some of these pro-cedures, such as anti-monopoly review, sectoral approval and licencing and state asset transfer approval, apply to both domestic and foreign investors equally. This implies that the origin of the acquirer should not play a role in the review and approval procedures. However, targeted law enforcement may complicate the situation in practice.

3.4.3 Ambiguity of the Variable Interest Entity (VIE) structure

The VIE structure was first adopted by Sina, a Chinese Internet company, to solicit offshore investment and complete its initial public offering (IPO) on the New York Stock Exchange (NYSE) in 2000, and is later adopted by other Chinese companies operating in sectors prohibited or restricted from foreign equity ownership and seeking listings abroad.[99] By 2012, almost half of the Chinese

---

94 Maarten Roos and Rogier van Bijnen, *supra* note 2, p. 72.
95 Zhihong Wang, 'Carlyle Abandons Xugong Dream', *China Daily*, 24 July 2008, https://www.chinadaily.com.cn/business/2008-07/24/content_6873004.htm, last accessed on 11 August 2021.
96 Cathleen Hamel Hartge, 'China's National Security Review: Motivations and the Impli-cations for Investors', *Stanford Journal of International Law*, Vol. 49 No. 1 (2013), pp. 239–273, at 246.
97 'China's Xugong Says Carlyle Investment Deal Dead', *Reuters*, 22 July 2008, https://www.reuters.com/article/carlyle-xugong-idUSSHA32313820080722, last accessed on 11 August 2021.
98 Eileen Francis Schneider, 'Be Careful What You Wish For: China's Protectionist Regulations of Foreign Direct Investment Implemented in the Months before Completing WTO Acces-sion', *Brooklyn Journal of Corporate, Financial & Commercial Law*, Vol. 2 No. 1 (2007), pp. 267–288, at 270–271.
99 Thomas Y. Man, 'Policy above Law: VIE and Foreign Investment Regulation in China', *Peking University Transnational Law Review*, Vol. 3 Issue 1 (2015), pp. 215–222, at 217.

companies listed in the US had adopted the VIE structure.[100] By 2019, Chinese companies had raised nearly 1.3 trillion USD of capital in their overseas listings using the VIE structure, most commonly by Internet and e-commerce companies such as Alibaba, Tencent, Baidu and JD.[101]

In a typical VIE structure, three fundamental corporations are at play, namely the Chinese operating company, the offshore listing company and the shell WFOE in China.[102] First, the Chinese operating company, which is owned and controlled by Chinese nationals who are usually the founders and their close associates, conducts substantial business in China.[103] By the Chinese law definition, the Chinese operating company remains a wholly domestic-owned company as its shareholders are Chinese nationals, and thus the company may conduct business that is prohibited or restricted from foreign equity ownership or is in a sector in which it is rather difficult for foreign investors to obtain sectoral licensing, such as telecommunications or e-commerce. Then an offshore listing company is established and controlled through equity ownership by the founders and their close associates of the Chinese operating company, usually at a tax haven such as the Cayman Islands or the Virgin Islands. The offshore listing company will subsequently make its IPO at a major financial hub such as New York or Hong Kong, and act as the vehicle to funnel investment from global investors.[104] Last, the offshore listing company establishes, oftentimes through multi-layered corporate structures, a shell WFOE in China, which does not operate any substantial business. The only purpose of the shell WFOE in China is to serve as a bridge between the Chinese operating company and the offshore listing company.[105] The link between the offshore listing company and the shell WFOE in China is that the offshore listing company owns and controls the shell WFOE in China by conventional shareholding ownership. Meanwhile, the relationship between the shell WFOE in China and the Chinese operating company, which is the core of the whole VIE structure, is that the shell WFOE owns and controls the Chinese

100 Samuel Farrell Ziegler, 'China's Variable Interest Entity Problem: How Americans Have Illegally Invested Billions in China and How to Fix It', *George Washington Law Review*, Vol. 84 Issue 2 (2016), pp. 539–562, at 541.

101 Tim Culpan, 'Wanna Bet $1.3 Trillion on Chinese Regulators?' *Bloomberg*, 22 July 2019, https://www.bloomberg.com/opinion/articles/2019-07-21/variable-interest-entities -are-vulnerable-to-china-s-whims, last accessed on 21 April 2021.

102 Samuel Farrell Ziegler, *supra* note 100, at 547. David Schindelheim, 'Variable Interest Entity Structures in the People's Republic of China: Is Uncertainty for Foreign Investors Part of China's Economic Development Plan?' *Cardozo Journal of International and Comparative Law*, Vol. 21 Issue 1 (2012), pp. 195–234, at 203.

103 Yu-Hsin Lin and Thomas Mehaffy, 'Open Sesame: The Myth of Alibaba's Extreme Corporate Governance and Control', *Brooklyn Journal of Corporate, Financial & Commercial Law*, Vol. 10 Issue 2 (2016), pp. 437–472, at 444–445.

104 Ibid.

105 Samuel Farrell Ziegler, *supra* note 100, at 547.

operating company by a series of contractual agreements, instead of by shareholding ownership.[106]

The particular structure of a VIE serves two main purposes: control by agreement and consolidation of financial statements. First, the VIE structure enables the offshore listing company to 'effectively mimic an ownership relationship' to the Chinese operating company, which is achieved by the setup of control by agreements via the shell WFOE as a bridge.[107] Ultimately, the whole VIE structure is still under the control of the original founders and their close associates of the Chinese operating company, as they are the controlling shareholders in all three corporate vehicles. Second, the control agreements also stipulate a consolidation of financing and accounting among the three corporate vehicles, giving the investors of the offshore listing company access to the profits and liabilities of the Chinese operating company.[108] In turn, the control agreements also give the Chinese operating company access to financing from the offshore listing company.

Take the Alibaba VIE structure, China's biggest e-commerce operator, as an example. Alibaba.com was created in 1999 in China by its founder Jack Ma and 17 of his friends. Alibaba Group Holding Limited (AGH) is established in the Cayman Islands and functions as the offshore listing company, which is controlled by the 'Alibaba Partnership'.[109] The Alibaba Partnership consists of 13 members including Jack Ma and other founding members, all of whom are Chinese nationals. AGH then, through a complex and multi-layered holding structure offshore, established five shell WFOEs in China that do not conduct any substantial business.[110] These five shell WFOEs then control respectively five Chinese operating companies that conduct Alibaba's substantial e-commerce business in China by a series of contractual agreements, including Zhejiang Taobao Network Co., Ltd.; Zhejiang Tmall Network Co., Ltd.; Hangzhou Ali Technology Co., Ltd.; Hangzhou Alibaba Advertising Co., Ltd.; and Alibaba Cloud Computing Ltd.[111] These five Chinese operating companies are controlled by the Alibaba Partnership by majority equity ownership. In September 2014, AGH listed its IPO on the NYSE, the largest IPO at the time in NYSE history.[112] Although AGH is a company registered in the Cayman Islands and listed in the US, it is controlled by the Alibaba Partnership, which collectively only owns a minority stake at AGH. However, investors, such as Yahoo, a US Internet com-

---

106　MacKensie Larson, 'Alibaba's VIE Structure and Erosion of BEPS Goals in China's E-Commerce Industry', *Temple International and Comparative Law Journal*, Vol. 33 Issue 1 (2018), pp. 203–243, at 209–211.

107　Samuel Farrell Ziegler, *supra* note 100, at 547.

108　Ibid, at 548.

109　MacKensie Larson, *supra* note 106, at 231–232.

110　Ibid, at 243.

111　Ibid, at 243.

112　NYSE, 'Alibaba IPO: The Biggest IPO in History', https://www.nyse.com/network/article/Alibaba-Lists-on-the-NYSE, last accessed on 19 July 2021.

pany that at one point owned about 40% of shares of AGH and became the biggest shareholder, as majority shareholders of AGH do not have much of a say in the decision-making of the operation.[113] This is achieved by AGH's preferential stock structure that does not equate shareholding ownership to voting rights and bestows all substantial decision-making power to a handful of shareholders in the Alibaba Partnership.[114]

The existence and proliferation of VIEs can be beneficial to both Chinese companies and foreign investors. For Chinese companies, and especially technology start-ups and Internet companies with few fixed assets, it is difficult to raise sufficient financing from China's state-led banking system, and even more difficult to be listed on China's stock market due to stringent legal requirements.[115] Therefore, in order to seek financing for business, these Chinese companies adopt the VIE structure and raise capital abroad by listing on foreign securities markets. Second, the VIE structure is also welcomed by some foreign investors outside of China, because it gives them the opportunities to invest in promising Chinese companies that are prohibited or restricted from foreign shareholding ownership according to Chinese law.

Because VIE structures have neither been explicitly prohibited nor unequivocally endorsed by the Chinese authorities, they create several compliance and regulatory problems. First, the VIE structure allows tax avoidance and profit shifting from the Chinese operating company to the offshore listing company by the use of tax havens as the base of the offshore listing company.[116] Second, because the VIE is used to circumvent the mandatory prohibitions and restrictions of foreign equity ownership in certain sectors in China, a Chinese court could at one point invalidate the control agreements underlying the VIE structure by invoking Art. 153 of the *Civil Code*, which stipulates that civil activities (including contracts) are null and void if they violate compulsory provisions of laws and administrative regulations.[117] Third, investors in the offshore listing company face high risks, as the Chinese government may deem the whole VIE structure invalid at any point. All of the substantial business conducted and the profits made are under the operating Chinese company, and the offshore listing company only serves the purpose

---

113 Kaitlyn Johnson, 'Variable Interest Entities: Alibaba's Regulatory Work-Around to China's Foreign Investment Restrictions', *Loyola University Chicago International Law Review*, Vol. 12 Issue 2 (2015), pp. 249–266, at 255–256.

114 Ibid.

115 Giulio Santoni, 'Foreign Capital in Chinese Telecommunication Companies: From the Variable Interest Entity Model to the Draft of the New Chinese Foreign Investment Law', *Italian Law Journal*, Vol. 4 Issue 2 (2018), pp. 589–610, at 594–595.

116 MacKensie Larson, *supra* note 106.

117 中华人民共和国民法典 (Civil Code of China) (Promulgated by the NPC on 28 May 2020, effective on 1 January 2021), Art. 153. Before the entry into effect of the Civil Code, Art. 52 of China's Contract Law stipulated that a contract shall be null and void when it purports an illegitimate purpose under the guise of legitimate acts, among other scenarios. One comment noted that this might be particularly the ground for a court to render VIE contracts invalid. David Schindelheim, *supra* note 102, at 218.

of issuing stocks, does not own any substantial business at all and thus has zero profitability. Once the control agreements upholding the conglomerate of the whole VIE structure are deemed illegal and unenforceable by Chinese courts, the offshore listing company's control of the Chinese operating company will be severed, and foreign investors as shareholders of the offshore listing company are eventually left with worthless stock.[118]

Chinese law has developed an approach that appears to be somewhat a tacit consent towards the legality of the VIE structure. First, in 2015, the draft FIL proposed by MOFCOM made an attempt to regulate VIEs by defining 'foreign investment' to include 'control of domestic enterprises or obtaining interests in domestic enterprises through agreements, trust, and so on'.[119] This would suggest that MOFCOM considered legitimizing the VIE structure at the time. Before 2018, only Chinese companies registered in China were allowed to go public on the Chinese stock market. In March 2018, the State Council forwarded a Notice issued by the CSRC, which allows certain eligible red-chip enterprises (红筹企业), namely those companies registered abroad but operating mainly in China using a VIE structure, to make an IPO on the Chinese stock market.[120] The offshore listing company in the VIE may, upon meeting certain requirements and approval from the CSRC, be listed on the Chinese stock market by issuing stocks or depository receipts.[121] And the whole VIE structure at issue may continue to exist. This is considered by some as proof of non-objection of the VIE structure by the Chinese government.[122] However, both the 2019 FIL and the Implementing Regulation remain silent on the concept of control by agreement. This leaves the VIE structure still unregulated and in a legislative grey zone.

In terms of a judicial approach, Chinese courts tend to keep a very prudent position in deciding the validity of VIEs. In 2016, the Supreme People's Court (SPC) gave its appeal ruling in *Changsha Yaxing Properties Development Co.,*

---

118 Kaitlyn Johnson, *supra* note 113, at 253–254, 261.
119 中华人民共和国外国投资法(草案征求意见稿) (Foreign Investment Law Draft for Public Comments) (Published by MOFCOM on 19 January 2015, not adopted), Art. 15(6).
120 国务院办公厅转发证监会关于开展创新企业境内发行股票或存托凭证试点若干意见的通知 (Notice of the General Office of the State Council on Forwarding the Several Opinions of the China Securities Regulatory Commission on Launching the Pilot Program of Innovative Enterprises Domestically Issuing Stocks or Depository Receipts) (Issued by the General Office of the State Council on 22 March 2018, effective on promulgation).
121 Ibid.
122 In October 2020, the Cayman Island based Segway-Ninebot Co., Ltd., became the first red-chip enterprise that was listed on the Chinese stock market. For a detailed discussion, see Kejun Guo *et al.*, '红筹企业境内上市专题系列之一：发行条件、发行股票和CDR的对比、VIE架构相关问题' (Instalment I – IPOs of Red Chip Enterprises in China: Issuing Conditions, Comparison between Stocks and Depository Receipts, and Matters on VIEs), *Zhong Lun Law Firm*, 29 October 2020, http://www.zhonglun.com/Content/2020/10-29/1115385160.html, last accessed on 3 August 2021.

Ltd. v. Beijing Shida Ambow Education and Technology Co., Ltd.[123] The appellee, Beijing Shida Ambow Education and Technology Co., Ltd. (defendant in the first-instance trial), operated in compulsory education in China that is prohibited from the market entry of foreign investment, and adopted a VIE structure using the Ambow Education Holding, Ltd., registered in the Cayman Islands, as the off-shore listing company which was listed on the US stock market.[124] The appellant, Changsha Yaxing Properties Development Co., Ltd. (plaintiff in the first-instance trial), claimed that a cooperation framework agreement signed between the two litigants should be deemed invalid because Beijing Shida Ambow Education and Technology Co., Ltd., was ultimately controlled by Ambow Education Holding, Ltd., which was a Cayman investor, thus in violation of the *Catalogue of Industries Guiding Foreign Investment*. Thus, according to Art. 52 of China's *Contract Law*, the cooperation framework agreement should be invalidated as it violates compulsory provisions of laws and administrative regulations.[125] The SPC, while not directly deliberating on whether a VIE structure itself should be deemed legal, ruled that the cooperation framework agreement is valid, because Beijing Shida Ambow Education and Technology Co., Ltd. was wholly owned by Chinese nationals and thus a domestic company, and Art. 52 of *Contract Law* did not apply in this case because the *Catalogue of Industries Guiding Foreign Investment* acted as departmental rules, not administrative regulations.[126] One comment opines that the SPC deliberately avoided giving its verdict on the valid-ity of VIEs in this case, as it did not yet intend to alter the *status quo* of VIEs, which remains in a regulatory grey area.[127] Also, the SPC's non-objection of VIEs does not necessarily extend to the Internet and telecom sectors where the major-ity of Chinese VIEs operates, as such sectors involve far more national security concerns.[128]

In contrast to the SPC's scrupulous jurisprudence, a local court appears to have taken a more permissible stance on the legality of VIEs. In 2018, in the case of *Yang Lianrong v. Grid (Fujian) Intelligent Technology Co., Ltd.*, the Fuzhou Intermediate People's Court actively confirmed the validity of VIEs.[129]

---

123 长沙亚兴置业发展有限公司与北京师大安博教育科技有限责任公司合作合同纠纷上诉案 (*Changsha Yaxing Properties Development Co., Ltd. v. Beijing Shida Ambow Education and Technology Co., Ltd.*, Appeal on Cooperative Agreement Dispute) (2015) Min Er Zhong Zi No. 117, *ChinaLawInfo*, https://www.pkulaw.com/pfnl/a25051f3312b07f35d085aa4efd 8bab43956e7162ade8418bdfb.html?keyword=%282015%29%E6%B0%91%E4%BA%8C%E7 %BB%88%E5%AD%97%E7%AC%AC117%E5%8F%B7, last accessed on 12 March 2021.

124 Ibid.

125 Ibid.

126 Ibid.

127 '"VIE结构" 第一案: 亚兴公司 vs 安博教育' (First Case of 'VIE Structure': *Yaxing Cor-poration v. Ambow Education*), *Beijing Gangjun Consulting Co., Ltd.*, http://www.gong-sizhuce168.com/lafw/vie/16478.html, last accessed on 2 August 2021.

128 Giulio Santoni, *supra* note 115, at 605.

129 杨连荣诉网格（福建）智能科技有限公司合同纠纷案 (*Yang Lianrong v. Grid (Fujian) Intelligent Technology Co., Ltd.* on Contractual Dispute) (2019) Min 01 Min Zhong No.

The defendant, Grid (Fujian) Intelligent Technology Co., Ltd., established an offshore listing company in Switzerland called VSG AG, which was later listed on the Frankfurt Stock Market.[130] The Court opined that 'at the moment, relevant departments adopt a tacit consent towards the legality of VIEs, and Chinese law does not explicitly prohibit the existence of VIEs', therefore the Court did not support the plaintiff's claim that the plaintiff's investment in the Grid (Fujian) Intelligent Technology Co., Ltd. should be deemed invalid and returned.[131] Court rulings, however, play a rather limited role in dictating the fate of VIEs. Considering the fact that China does not follow precedents as a common law country does and that the invalidation of contracts, i.e., the control agreements that underlie a VIE, requires court litigation on a case-by-case basis, neither consistency nor legal certainty is guaranteed in cases involving the validity of a VIE.

The fate of the VIE structure in the future appears to be precarious both in China and abroad. Some sectoral regulators in China have explicitly forbidden the use of VIEs. For instance, the *Implementing Regulation of the Law on the Promotion of Privately Run Education*, revised in 2021, stipulates that FIEs in China are prohibited from establishing, participating or taking *de facto* control of a privately run school that provides compulsory education.[132] This means that a VIE structure cannot be adopted in compulsory education because the control by agreement between the shell WFOE and the Chinese operating company that is essential to the VIE structure is deemed illegal according to the Implementing Regulation. In July 2021, the US Securities and Exchange Commission decided to suspend all applications of IPOs on the US stock market from Chinese companies using a VIE structure, due to the risks VIEs may pose to US investors and the lack of adequate information disclosure of these VIE structures.[133] It is anticipated that the number of VIEs may witness a dramatic decline in the coming years due to these obstacles in China and abroad.

3.5 Conclusion

The FIL claims to bring a unified governance of greenfield investment, foreign M&A, and indirect investment under the same level of treatment and protection.

948, *ChinaLawInfo*, https://www.pkulaw.com/pfnl/a6bdb3332ec0adc4200b9f22431 72eb9b2e40fdecddfddccbdfb.html?keyword=%E6%9D%A8%E8%BF%9E%E8%8D%A3, last accessed on 2 August 2021.

130 Ibid.

131 Ibid.

132 中华人民共和国民办教育促进法实施条例 (Implementing Regulation of the Law on the Promotion of Privately Run Education) (Promulgated by the State Council on 7 April 2021, effective on 1 September 2021), Art. 5.

133 US Securities and Exchange Commission, 'Statement on Investor Protection Related to Recent Developments in China', 30 July 2021, https://www.sec.gov/news/public -statement/gensler-2021-07-30?utm_medium=email&utm_source=govdeliveryvery, last accessed on 17 August 2021.

This means that foreign M&A are subject to national treatment with a negative list approach at the market entry phase in the same ways greenfield investment would enjoy. However, the question remains as to whether and to what extent pre-establishment national treatment has been realized for foreign M&A in China.

For foreign takeovers of private Chinese companies, significant market entry barriers remain in place. There are eight potential review and approval processes, and three of them apply only to foreign acquirers, namely the *Negative List for Foreign Investment*, national security review and takeover approval by MOFCOM. For the rest of the approval processes, including fixed asset investment project approval, sectoral market access approval, state asset transfer approval, anti-monopoly review and enterprise registration, application does not distinguish between a domestic or a foreign investor. Among these approval procedures, an outstanding issue is the case-by-case approval under Order No. 10, which still remains effective today but is in non-conformity with the pre-establishment national treatment commitment in the FIL. At present, whether the case-by-case approval in Order No. 10 is still applicable in practice is a perplexing question for legislators to answer. Furthermore, for foreign takeovers of public Chinese companies, there appears to be an even more significant discrepancy between foreign and domestic investors in terms of their accessibility to China's securities market. To invest in a listed Chinese company, a foreign investor is required for specific qualifications, namely a QFII, an RMB QFII, a strategic foreign investor or via the Stock Connect. These qualification requirements are in addition to the eight potential review and approval processes if applicable. Compared with the incremental and substantial liberalization of market access for greenfield investment, there is still much to be desired in China's takeover market for foreign investors towards more openness.

Meanwhile, several perennial concerns continue to exist for foreign investors, in particular, a lack of reciprocity on the takeover market in China and abroad, targeted law enforcement that is potentially disadvantageous to foreign buyers, and the ambiguous status of VIEs. It remains to be seen whether and how the FIL and subsequent legislations will eliminate the barriers imposed on foreign takeover transactions and attract more foreign capital into China's takeover market by providing better accessibility.

4 National security review of foreign investment

4.1 The legal framework relating to national security

The concept of national security has become so 'dynamic and continually evolving' that it poses a dichotomy to national and international law attempting to define it: on the one hand, more influence and surveillance of the rule of law are imposed on national security to bring legal predictability and accountability, to confine its scope from being too expansive and ambiguous, and to move away from a matter of purely 'high politics'; on the other hand, although states do have a will to provide a clear definition of national security, they also acknowledge the difficulty of doing so, as national security is a matter of ample discretion and political expediency, is a self-evident concept, and should not be rigidly governed.[1] China's national security legal regime is no exception to this dichotomy between the codification of national security laws and the elusiveness of the very concept.

China's national security conceptualization is comprehensive and inclusive in essence, first coined by President Xi Jinping in 2014 as the 'holistic national security outlook' (总体国家安全观), including (but not limited to) political security, sovereign security, military security, economic security, cultural security, societal security, technological security, information security, ecological security, resource security and nuclear security.[2] At the central level, the Communist Party of China (CPC) established the Central National Security Commission (CNSC) in 2014, chaired by President Xi. The CNSC leads and coordinates a number of pertinent departments such as the Ministry of Public Security, Ministry of State

---

1 Congyan Cai, 'Enforcing a New National Security – China's National Security Law and International Law', *Journal of East Asia and International Law*, Vol. 10 No. 1 (2017), pp. 65–90, at 71–72.
2 '习近平：坚持总体国家安全观，走中国特色国家安全道路' (Xi Jinping: Maintain a Holistic State National Security Outlook, Travel the National Security Road with Chinese Characteristics), *Xinhua Net*, 15 April 2014, http://www.xinhuanet.com//politics/2014-04/15/c_1110253910.htm, last accessed on 12 April 2021.

DOI: 10.4324/9781003168805-5

Security, People's Liberation Army and Ministry of Foreign Affairs, and takes charge of security-related affairs in national defence, public security, diplomacy, intelligence and so on.[3]

In accordance with China's holistic national security outlook, national security legislation has evolved in the past seven years to encompass a broad range of subjects. The overarching law is the *National Security Law*, promulgated in 2015, which codifies the holistic national security outlook and defines national security as 'the status of absence from danger and internal and external threats over state sovereignty, territorial integrity, welfare of the people, sustainable economic and social development, and other material interests of the state'.[4] Art. 59 of the Law further stipulates that China will establish multiple national security review regimes in the area of foreign investment, special products and key technologies, information technology (IT) products and service, construction projects involving national security, and other undertakings of major significance. Art. 59 has been later substantiated by the *Measures for the National Security Review of Foreign Investment* (the 2020 Measures) in the field of foreign investment,[5] *Export Control Law* in the field of special products and key technologies,[6] *Measures for Cybersecurity Review* in the field of IT products and service,[7] and the national security review for construction projects is in principle based on local regulations and administered by local Departments of State Security.[8]

The national security review regime of foreign investment was originally established in 2011 and updated in 2020; it scrutinizes foreign investment in China that poses national security perils. The 2011 system was envisaged in the Notice issued by the State Council and the Provisions adopted by Ministry of Commerce

---

3 For a detailed discussion on the CNSC, see Weixing Hu, 'Xi Jinping's "Big Power Diplomacy" and China's Central National Security Commission (CNSC)', *Journal of Contemporary China*, Vol. 25 No. 98 (2016), pp. 163–177. You Ji, 'China's National Security Commission: Theory, Evolution and Operations', *Journal of Contemporary China*, Vol. 25 No. 98 (2016), pp. 178–196.

4 中华人民共和国国家安全法 (National Security Law of China) (Promulgated by the NPC on 1 July 2015, effective on promulgation), Art. 2.

5 外商投资安全审查办法 (Measures for the National Security Review of Foreign Investment) (Promulgated by the NDRC and MOFCOM on 19 December 2021, effective on 18 January 2021).

6 中华人民共和国出口管制法 (Export Control Law of China) (Promulgated by the NPC on 17 October 2020, effective on 1 December 2020).

7 网络安全审查办法 (Measures for Cybersecurity Review) (Promulgated by Cyberspace Administration of China *et al.* on 13 April 2020, effective on 1 June 2020).

8 For an overview of these local legislations, see 国家安全部建审许可服务网 (Construction Projects Review and Approval Network of the Ministry of State Security), Local Legislations, http://www.jsxk.gov.cn/manage.html, last accessed on 29 July 2021.

(MOFCOM) that implemented the Notice.[9] Almost a decade later, MOFCOM adopted the 2020 Measures that materialize Art. 35 of the *Foreign Investment Law* (FIL), namely the national security review provision. In comparison, the 2020 Measures have significantly expanded the scope of review, *inter alia*, from only reviewing foreign mergers and acquisitions (M&A) to, now, review of all foreign investment, including M&A, greenfield investment and indirect investment. Another significant institutional transformation is the establishment of the Working Mechanism in the 2020 Measures as the review body, which supersedes the *ad hoc* Joint Conference in the 2011 rules. In both the original and current framework, national security in the foreign investment context is not explicitly defined.

The FIL was promulgated in March 2019, and its unprecedented liberalization commitments, such as market access concessions and strong investors' protection, were believed to address concerns of the United States (US) in principle and to mitigate the antagonism of the ongoing US–China Trade War which commenced in early 2018.[10] However, with the global breakout of the Covid-19 pandemic in 2020, US–China bilateral relations have witnessed serious deterioration, leading to a series of restrictive measures and sanctions of the US against Chinese companies and individuals.[11] As countermeasures, China has adopted a series of laws on anti-foreign restrictive measures and anti-foreign sanctions, including the *2020 Provisions on the Unreliable Entity List*,[12] the *2020 Export Control Law*, the *2021 Rules on Counteracting Unjustified Extra-Territorial Application of Foreign Legislation and Measures*,[13] and the *2021 Anti-Foreign Sanctions Law*.[14]

---

9 国务院办公厅关于建立外国投资者并购境内企业安全审查制度的通知 (Notice of the General Office of the State Council on the Establishment of the Security Review System for Mergers and Acquisitions of Domestic Enterprises by Foreign Investors) (Promulgated by the General Office of the State Council on 3 February 2011, effective on promulgation). 商务部实施外国投资者并购境内企业安全审查制度的规定 (Provisions of the Ministry of Commerce on the Implementation of the Security Review System for Mergers and Acquisitions of Domestic Enterprises by Foreign Investors) (Promulgated by the Ministry of Commerce on 25 August 2011, effective on 1 September 2011).

10 For a detailed discussion on the legislative background of the FIL, see Chapter 1, Section 1.1.

11 For a detailed discussion of these US restrictive measures and sanctions against China, see Introduction.

12 不可靠实体清单规定 (Provisions on the Unreliable Entity List) (Promulgated by MOFCOM on 19 September 2020, effective on promulgation).

13 阻断外国法律与措施不当域外适用办法 (The Rules on Counteracting Unjustified Extra-Territorial Application of Foreign Legislation and Measures) (Promulgated by MOFCOM on 9 January 2021, effective on promulgation).

14 中华人民共和国反外国制裁法 (Anti-Foreign Sanctions Law) (Promulgated by the Standing Committee of the NPC on 10 June 2021, effective on promulgation). For a detailed discussion of these four laws on anti-foreign restrictive measures and anti-foreign sanctions, see Chapter 1, Section 1.1.5.

The *Provisions on the Unreliable Entity List* aim at 'protecting national sovereignty, national security, development interest, a fair and liberal international economic order, and legitimate rights of Chinese corporations, organizations and individuals'.[15] The meaning of these terms are not further defined in the law, leaving questions on the scope of their application in practice unanswered. Any foreign corporations, organizations and individuals in China and abroad which are included on the Unreliable Entity List are prohibited from engaging in trade, investment and mobility of people with China, among other ramifications.[16] To date, the Unreliable Entity List has not yet been published. One comment points out that the law could be a double-edged sword: it provides a legal mechanism for China to counter foreign suppression of Chinese entities and individuals, but at the same time, multinational enterprise (MNEs) may fear the uncertainty and ambiguity of the law and be driven away from the Chinese market, which is a result against China's interests.[17]

The *Export Control Law* aims at 'protecting national security and national interests, fulfilling the international obligations of nonproliferation, and strengthening export control'.[18] The jurisdiction of the *Export Control Law* is considered extremely broad and not entirely clear. For example, the law is silent on whether activities of providing controlled items to a foreign individual or entity need to be performed within or outside the territory of China.[19] While it may not be directly relevant to foreign investment, foreign-invested enterprises (FIEs) in China are well advised to adjust their compliance programs in line with the requirements of the law. For instance, FIEs established in China that engage in export activities are also deemed exporters under the governance of the *Export Control Law* if their export businesses involve controlled items and thus may be subject to licensing requirements.

The *Rules on Counteracting Unjustified Extra-Territorial Application of Foreign Legislation and Measures* (Blocking Rules) intend to block the extra-territorial application of foreign laws that prohibit or restrict business between China and a third country when the application of those foreign laws is deemed detrimental to China's 'national sovereignty, national security, development interests, and the legitimate interests of Chinese individuals, corporations and

---

15 Provisions on the Unreliable Entity List (2020), Art. 1.

16 Ibid, Art. 10.

17 Yuanyou Yang, 'China Implements Its Long-Awaited Unreliable Entities List Mechanism', *China Business Review*, 7 October 2020, https://www.chinabusinessreview.com/china-implements-its-long-awaited-unreliable-entities-list-mechanism/, last accessed on 10 August 2021.

18 Export Control Law of China (2020), Art. 1.

19 Lianzhong Pan and Jonathan R. Todd, 'China's New Export Control Law: A Fact Sheet with Practical Applications', *Benesch Friedlander Coplan & Aronoff*, 25 November 2020, https://www.beneschlaw.com/resources/chinas-new-export-control-law-a-fact-sheet-with-practical-applications.html?utm_source=Mondaq&utm_medium=syndication&utm_campaign=LinkedIn-integration, last accessed on 18 March 2021.

organizations'.[20] The law further clarifies that it applies to situations when the extra-territorial application of foreign laws violates 'basic principles of international law and international relations, and normal economic, trade and other related activities'.[21] Many have expressed a concern that China's Blocking Rules may create conflicting compliance obligations for MNEs with business operations both in China and aboard, and a readjustment of their global compliance strategies is well advised.[22]

The objective of the *Anti-Foreign Sanctions Law* is to defend state sovereignty, national security, development interest, and the legitimate rights of Chinese individuals and entities.[23] When foreign states violate the basic principles of international law and international relations, restrict or suppress China according to their national laws, meddle with China's internal affairs, and impose discriminatory restrictive measures against Chinese individuals and entities, the State Council may include individuals and entities who directly or indirectly formulate, determine or implement those discriminatory restrictive measures on China's Countermeasure List.[24] Individuals and entities on the Countermeasure List will be subject to deportation, confiscation of assets, and prohibition to conduct trade and investment transactions or cooperation with Chinese individuals and entities.[25] FIEs in China, their senior executives and actual controlling shareholders, and even their spouses and relatives will be subject to sanctions if they are included on the Countermeasure List.

China's holistic national security outlook has developed into a multi-faceted and multi-institutional framework which has been gradually codified in a series of laws and regulations in addition to the overarching *National Security Law* since 2015. With either direct or indirect relevance to foreign investment, security-related concerns are understood as collective and open-ended terms which not only include traditional national security but also encompass sovereignty, development interests, the legitimate interests of Chinese individuals and entities, the basic principles of international law and international relations, a fair and liberal international economic order, and so on. How these national security-related laws will be implemented in parallel with the FIL that emphasizes investment liberalization and investors' protection is a matter that remains to be observed.

---

20 The Rules on Counteracting Unjustified Extra-Territorial Application of Foreign Legislation and Measures (2021), Art. 1.
21 Ibid, Art. 2.
22 Edward J. Krauland and Bo Yue, 'China's New Blocking Rules May Impact US Sanctions and Export Control Compliance Strategies for Many', *Steptoe*, 10 February 2021, https://www.steptoe.com/en/news-publications/chinas-new-blocking-rules-may-impact-us-sanctions-and-export-control-compliance-strategies-for-many.html, last accessed on 10 August 2021.
23 Anti-Foreign Sanctions Law (2021), Art. 1.
24 Ibid, Arts. 3 and 4.
25 Ibid, Art. 6.

Table 4.1 China's national security-related laws

Area	Law	Time of promulgation	Implementing agency
Holistic national security	National Security Law	1 July 2015	CNSC
Foreign investment	Measures for the National Security Review of Foreign Investment	19 December 2020	National Development and Reform Commission (NDRC) and MOFCOM
Foreign trade and investment	Provisions on the Unreliable Entity List	19 September 2020	'Working Mechanism' led by MOFCOM
Export control of goods and technology	Export Control Law	17 October 2020	State Council, Central Military Commission of the CPC
Block of extra-territorial application of foreign laws	Rules on Counteracting Unjustified Extra-Territorial Application of Foreign Legislation and Measures	9 January 2021	'Working Mechanism' led by MOFCOM
Anti-foreign sanctions	Anti-Foreign Sanctions Law	10 June 2021	State Council

There appears to be a common struggle for foreign companies in China or foreign companies doing business with China to comprehend certain terminologies in China's national security legislation for compliance, for instance, the meaning of national security in general, or some vague terms in specific laws such as 'basic principles of international law and international relations' in the Blocking Rules and the *Anti-Foreign Sanctions Law*. Therefore, it is recommended that these national security-related laws could provide more clarity in their future revisions or be accompanied by more detailed implementing rules.

4.2 The evolutional trajectory of national security review of foreign investment

The menace of foreign investment to national security is not a novel discussion in China. The concept of national security was first raised in 2003 in the *Interim Provisions on Mergers and Acquisitions of Domestic Enterprises by Foreign*

Investors.[26] Art. 19 stipulated that foreign acquirers bore a notification obligation to MOFCOM when a proposed takeover of a Chinese enterprise might seriously impact state economic security, amongst other considerations. In its 2006 revision, alternatively known as Order No. 10, this notification obligation was reiterated.[27] In 2007, China's *Anti-Monopoly Law* called for a national security review in business concentrations involving a foreign investor if national security might be at stake.[28] At this stage, the loosely defined law was merely 'a clarion call for a national security review', which provided little exercisable rules on enforcement.[29]

China's formal national security review for foreign investment was established in 2011, pursuant to the promulgation of *Notice on the Establishment of the Security Review System for Mergers and Acquisitions of Domestic Enterprises by Foreign Investors* and its accompanying *Provisions on the Implementation of the Security Review System for Mergers and Acquisitions of Domestic Enterprises by Foreign Investors.* This formal establishment of China's national security review, notwithstanding some of the ambiguous wording and the ensuing broad discretion of the reviewing authority, was welcomed as a positive development in general because it brought a concrete and workable procedure with greater transparency and predictability.[30]

A separate national security review regime of foreign investment in the Pilot Free Trade Zones (PFTZs) has been established since 2015.[31] The most significant difference between the national security review nationwide and that in the PFTZs is that greenfield investment in the PFTZs is subject to review, whereas in the nationwide scheme it was not. In the same year, the draft FIL published

---

26 外国投资者并购境内企业暂行规定(2003) (Interim Provisions on Mergers and Acquisitions of Domestic Enterprises by Foreign Investors 2003) (Repealed) (Promulgated by the Ministry of Foreign Trade and Economic Cooperation, the State Administration of Taxation, the State Administration for Industry and Commerce, and the State Administration of Foreign Exchange on 2 January 2003, effective on 12 April 2003).

27 关于外国投资者并购境内企业的规定 (2006) (Provisions on Mergers and Acquisitions of Domestic Enterprises by Foreign Investors 2006) (Repealed) (Promulgated by the Ministry of Commerce, State-owned Assets Supervision and Administration Commission of the State Council, China Securities Regulatory Commission, State Administration of Taxation, State Administration for Industry and Commerce, State Administration of Foreign Exchange on 8 August 2006, effective on 8 September 2006).

28 中华人民共和国反垄断法 (Anti-Monopoly Law of China) (Promulgated by the NPC on 30 August 2007, effective on 1 August 2008).

29 Cheng Bian, *National Security Review of Foreign Investment: A Comparative Legal Analysis of China, the United States and the European Union* (London: Routledge, 2020), p. 71.

30 Cathleen Hamel Hartge, 'China's National Security Review: Motivations and the Implications for Investors', *Stanford Journal of International Law*, Vol. 49 Issue 1 (2013), pp. 239–273.

31 国务院办公厅关于印发《自由贸易试验区外商投资国家安全审查试行办法》的通知 (Notice of the General Office of State Council on Promulgation of the Trial Measures on National Security Review for Foreign Investments in Pilot Free Trade Zones) (Promulgated on 8 April 2015, effective on 8 May 2015).

by MOFCOM provided an elaborate chapter on national security review that would have radically overhauled the previous system.[32] One reason for the material modification of the national security review in the draft FIL 2015 was that the system effective since 2011 'suffered several structural defects' which led to its dormancy, as not one single foreign takeover case that warranted a national security review was made public.[33]

The FIL includes one article which reiterates that China establishes a national security review to foreign investment that affects or may affect national security.[34] As the provision in the FIL is not in the least operational, many have anticipated that the Implementing Regulation promulgated six months later would provide some clarification. On the contrary, the Implementing Regulation merely paraphrases the corresponding provision in the FIL, leaving the public with bewilderedness as to its legislative purpose.[35] It is eventually the 2020 Measures that substantiate the national security provision in the FIL. Repealing and replacing the rules promulgated and effective since 2011, the currently effective 2020 Measures are referred to as China's 'National Security Review Version 2.0'.[36] According to an official statement from the NDRC, the 2020 Measures are promulgated to materialize the relevant provision in the FIL, to respond to the ever-changing landscape of foreign direct investment (FDI) screening in other major economies, and to build upon ten years of reviewing practice and experience since the system was first established in 2011,[37] although there was no official announcement of outcomes or cases reviewed in the past decade. In sum, the evolutional trajectory of China's national security review of foreign investment over nearly two decades is a testament to the fact that the regime is not an abrupt legislative turnout, but rather an incremental contemplation over time.

---

32 中华人民共和国外国投资法(草案征求意见稿) (Foreign Investment Law Draft for Public Comments) (Published by MOFCOM on 19 January 2015, not adopted), Arts. 48–74.

33 Xingxing Li, 'National Security Review in Foreign Investments: A Comparative and Critical Assessment on China and U.S. Laws and Practices', *Berkeley Business Law Journal*, Vol. 13 Issue 1 (2016), pp. 255–311, at 266.

34 中华人民共和国外商投资法 (Foreign Investment Law of China) (Promulgated by the NPC on 15 March 2019, effective on 1 January 2020), Art. 35.

35 中华人民共和国外商投资法实施条例 (Implementing Regulation of the Foreign Investment Law of China) (Promulgated by the State Council on 26 December 2019, effective on 1 January 2020), Art. 40.

36 Ping Xu *et al.*, 'China Releases National Security Review Rules Version 2.0', *King and Wood, China Law Insight*, 23 December 2020, https://www.chinalawinsight.com/2020/12/articles/corporate-ma/ma/china-releases-national-security-review-rules-version-2-0/, last accessed on 16 March 2021.

37 NDRC, '健全外商投资安全审查制度 为更高水平对外开放保驾护航——外商投资安全审查工作机制办公室负责人就《外商投资安全审查办法》答记者问' (Strengthen the National Security Review of Foreign Investment, Convoy a Higher Level of Opening-up – Press Conference of the Head of Working Mechanism Office on 'Measures for the National Security Review of Foreign Investment'), 19 December 2020, http://www.gov.cn/zhengce/2020-12/19/content_5571295.htm, last accessed on 8 April 2021.

4.3 The substantive and procedural review regime

4.3.1 Substantive provisions

4.3.1.1 Subject to be protected

National security in the foreign investment context in China has long been criticized of lacking an explicit definition, leading to potentially opaque and arbitrary law enforcement.[38] The 2020 Measures impose an *ex ante* review for the market entry of foreign investment that infringes or may infringe national security.[39] The 2020 Measures provide neither a definition to national security, nor a reference to other laws and regulations to define national security. Presumably, one can make a reference to the *National Security Law* that codifies China's holistic national security outlook which encompasses not only national economic security, but also as many as ten other aspects of security.[40] In this regard, national security concerns could be implicated in a broad range of foreign investment.

4.3.1.2 Transactions subject to review

The 2020 Measures define foreign investment subject to review as direct and indirect investment activities, including (1) establishing new enterprises or investing in new projects in China independently or jointly with other investors; (2) acquiring equity or assets of an enterprise in China by mergers and acquisitions; and (3) any other means of investment.[41] Compared with the 2011 rules, the 2020 Measures considerably expand the scope of transactions subject to review from foreign M&A only to now also greenfield investment and indirect investment. In an indirect transaction, if a foreign investor acquires a foreign company located outside of China and the target foreign company has a Chinese subsidiary located in China, the transaction then constitutes an indirect foreign takeover of a Chinese enterprise and may be subject to review under Chinese law.[42] This

---

38 Mary Ellen Stanley, 'From China with Love: Espionage in the Age of Foreign Investment', *Brooklyn Journal of International Law*, Vol. 40 No. 3 (2015), pp. 1033–1088, at 1070. Kevin B. Goldstein, 'Reviewing Cross-Border Mergers and Acquisitions for Competition and National Security: A Comparative Look at How the United States, Europe, and China Separate Security Concerns from Competition Concerns in Reviewing Acquisitions by Foreign Entities', *Tsinghua China Law Review*, Vol. 3 No. 2 (2011), pp. 215–256, at 227.

39 The Measures (2020), Art. 1.

40 The National Security Law includes political security, sovereign security, military security, economic security, cultural security, societal security, technological security, information security, ecological security, resource security and nuclear security. National Security Law (2015), Arts. 15–34.

41 The Measures (2020), Art. 2.

42 Howard Hao Wu and Tracy Wut, 'China Enacts New Foreign Investment Security Review Measures', *Baker McKenzie Insight*, 4 January 2021, https://www.bakermckenzie.com/en /insight/publications/2021/01/china-enacts-new-foreign-investment-security, last accessed on 11 April 2021.

indicates that the 2020 Measures would have extra-territorial jurisdiction in cases of offshore transactions.

4.3.1.3 Sectors subject to review

Investments in specifically listed sectors require an *ex ante* filing obligation prior to the making of the investment. Investments outside of the listed sectors are not subject to the filing obligation, but are also not deservedly exempted from a potential review, as the review body has the authority to initiate a review *ex officio* over a foreign investment project when deemed necessary.[43] Sectors subject to review fall into two categories. The first comprises military products, national defence and investments to be made in the physical vicinity of military-industrial installations; the second comprises certain sensitive civil sectors where the foreign investor acquires 'actual control' of the target Chinese company.[44] The sensitive civil sectors include 'important agricultural products, important energy and resources, critical equipment manufacturing, important infrastructure, important transportation, important cultural products and services, important IT and Internet products and services, important financial services, key technologies, and other important sectors'.[45]

Compared with those listed in the 2011 rules, the sectors subject to review in the 2020 Measures are significantly more extensive.[46] From the standpoint of Chinese regulators, more inclusiveness of critical sectors subject to review would entail more safeguards to national security. The financial sector, for example, is one that has been incorporated in the 2020 Measures but was absent in the 2011 rules; this absence was once criticized as a dangerous omission considering 'the sector's strategic importance and sensitiveness in Chinese economy'.[47] Whereas from the perspective of foreign investors, sectors subject to review in the 2020 Measures demonstrate considerable ambiguity and thus little operability. In the first category, it remains unknown what the precise radius is for a foreign investment project to be in the 'proximity' of a military premise. In the sensitive civil sectors, the term 'important' is left undefined. It is therefore difficult to determine its semantic reach, namely what investment in a listed sector is deemed

---

43 The Measures (2020), Art. 4.
44 'Actual control' is defined as '(1) the foreign investor holds no less than 50% of shares in the target Chinese company; (2) the foreign investor holds less than 50% of shares in the target Chinese company but its voting rights have a material influence on the resolutions of the board of directors or of the shareholders meeting; and (3) other scenarios whereby the foreign investor is able to impose a material influence on the business decision-making, personnel, finance, technology and so on, of the target Chinese company.' Ibid, Art. 4.
45 Ibid, Art. 4.
46 The 2020 Measures added 'important cultural products and services', 'important IT and Internet products and services', 'important financial services', and 'other important sectors', in comparison to the 2011 rules.
47 Xingxing Li, *supra* note 33, at 286.

'important' and what investment is not.[48] Further, certain sectors that encompass a collective meaning are not explicated, *inter alia*, important infrastructure, or key technologies, leading to concerns over their interpretative uncertainty and unpredictability.[49]

4.3.2 *Procedural provisions*

4.3.2.1 *The review body*

The 2020 Measures establish a 'Working Mechanism' to assume the review process, led by NDRC and MOFCOM and equipped with a permanent office under the NDRC responsible for the daily administration.[50] The Working Mechanism is essentially a continuation of the Joint Conference established in 2011, which was an inter-ministerial and *ad hoc* mechanism led by MOFCOM and NDRC and involved other relevant ministries on a case-by-case basis, and was convened only when specific review cases took place.[51] The new Working Mechanism corrects the interim nature of the obsolete Joint Conference by instituting a permanent office in the NDRC with designated personnel, resources and budget. This amendment provides elevated institutional stability.

However, the Working Mechanism fails to address certain hereditary institutional ambiguities and inefficiencies. As was the case in the Joint Conference, the new Working Mechanism does not clarify the composition of the review body in a specific review case, other than the dual leadership of NDRC and MOFCOM. In contrast, the Committee on Foreign Investment of the United States (CFIUS) consists of 16 statutory head officials of executive departments and offices, which are involved in the review process on a case-by-case basis depending on their diversified expertise.[52] The dual leadership in the Joint Conference is also inherited by the Working Mechanism, which designates NDRC and MOFCOM as two leading agencies, giving rise to 'two parallel decision-makers ... in conflicts', and creating 'unnecessary complications and inefficiency', especially when the two departments hold diverging opinions.[53] It appears that the dual lead agencies set up in the Joint Conference and subsequently in the Working Mechanism is a result of 'political bargaining and compromise' at the State Council in reconciling the competition of regulatory power between NDRC and MOFCOM,[54] not only in national security review but also as a part of a long existing jurisdiction duel

---

48 Howard Hao Wu and Tracy Wut, *supra* note 42.
49 Cheng Bian, *supra* note 29, p. 202.
50 The Measures (2020), Art. 3.
51 Notice of the General Office of the State Council on the Establishment of the Security Review System for Mergers and Acquisitions of Domestic Enterprises by Foreign Investors (2011), Art. 3.
52 Cheng Bian, *supra* note 29, p. 192.
53 Xingxing Li, *supra* note 33, at 301.
54 Ibid, at 301–302.

over foreign investment in China's FDI regulatory regime.[55] Even with the dual leadership setup, the power struggle to become a more potent leader between the two ministries has proven to be inevitable. Since 2011, MOFCOM was the agency responsible for the receipt of investors' applications. MOFCOM's position was superseded by NDRC in 2019 pursuant to a Notice of the NDRC announcing that it will 'take over' MOFCOM's role in national security review,[56] which is further consolidated by the establishment of the Working Mechanism Office within NDRC pursuant to the 2020 Measures. As a result, the prevailing power in China's national security review has been gradually shifted from MOFCOM to NDRC, presumably because of NDRC's stronger bargaining power and lobbying efforts in the State Council.[57]

4.3.2.2 *Initiation of the procedure*

Prior to filing a formal request for review, a foreign investor may consult with the Working Mechanism Office on any relevant matters, for instance, whether its investment falls into the purview of China's national security review.[58] A review can be initiated in two ways. First, a foreign investor may file a voluntary request for review. Upon receiving the full set of requested documents, the Working Mechanism Office shall make a decision on whether a review is necessitated in 15 working days.[59] Second, the Working Mechanism Office may also initiate a review at its own discretion, or make such an initiative based upon the proposition of a third party, such as a governmental agency, an enterprise, a civil entity or the general public.[60]

4.3.2.3 *The two-step review*

The formal review consists of a general review and a special review. A general review should be conducted within 30 working days once the Working Mechanism Office has initiated the review.[61] If it is concluded that national security might be at stake after a general review, the Working Mechanism Office shall conduct a special review to be completed in 60 working days, subject to extension in

---

55 Ibid. Xingxing Li, 'An Economic Analysis of Regulatory Overlap and Regulatory Competition: The Experience of Interagency Regulatory Competition in China's Regulation of Inbound Foreign Investment', *Administrative Law Review*, Vol. 67 No. 4 (2015), pp. 685–750, at 700–708.
56 NDRC, '中华人民共和国国家发展和改革委员会公告 2019 年第4号' (NDRC Announcement No. 4 2019), 30 April 2019, www.ndrc.gov.cn/zcfb/zcfbgg/201904/t20190430 _935337.html, last accessed on 12 April 2021.
57 Ziyu Liu, 'Security Review in the Evolution of Foreign Investment Law with Chinese Characteristics: Part I', *Business Law Review*, Vol. 41 Issue 5 (2020), pp. 172–179, at 178.
58 The Measures (2020), Art. 5.
59 The Measures (2020), Art. 7.
60 The Measures (2020), Art. 15.
61 The Measures (2020), Art. 8.

exceptional circumstances.[62] However, the 2020 Measures do not specify what constitutes 'exceptional circumstances' or the duration allowed for the extension.

The whole review process is also subject to suspension and recount, and therefore is essentially not time limited. During a review, the Working Mechanism Office may request the investor to provide additional materials or make inquiries to the investor, which will temporarily suspend the counting of the statutory time frame of the review.[63] Amid an ongoing review, an investor may be recommended to modify or abandon its investment project; in the former scenario, a new review process will be commenced, and the statutory time frame will be recounted.[64]

4.3.2.4 Review outcomes and legal liabilities

A review can result in three alternatives: approval, approval with conditions and rejection.[65] Investors bear legal ramifications in the event of non-compliance with the law. If a foreign investor fails to file a voluntary request for review and its investment falls within the scope of review, the Working Mechanism Office will mandate the investor to file for review in a given period; failure to do so will result in a mandatory divestment and restoration to the *status quo* if the investment has already been made.[66] When a foreign investor gains approval after a review, but amends its original investment plan afterwards which again involves or may involve national security, the investor is required to re-submit a request for review.[67] If an investor gains approval by fraudulently providing false material or omitting relevant information, the Working Mechanism Office has the authority to revoke the clearing outcome already delivered, and to order a mandatory divestment and restoration to the *status quo* if the investment has been made.[68] As the law does not specify what constitutes 'relevant information' it is possible that an investor may fail to submit certain information in a review, not because of intentional misconduct but because the investor deems such information irrelevant on its own discretion. In such a case of negligence, an investment already reviewed and cleared by the Working Mechanism Office may be subject to a reopening of review, even when the investor has no malicious or fraudulent intention. As was criticized in the 'evergreen provision' of the CFIUS review, the possibility of a completed review procedure being rewound in this way could possibly be a violation of the principle of *res judicata*.[69]

---

62 The Measures (2020), Art. 9.
63 The Measures (2020), Art. 10.
64 The Measures (2020), Art. 11.
65 The Measures (2020), Art. 12.
66 The Measures (2020), Art. 16.
67 The Measures (2020), Art. 14.
68 The Measures (2020), Art. 17.
69 According to the evergreen provision, the CFIUS may reopen a completed review procedure at any time it deems necessary, provided that an investor submitted 'false or misleading material information' or 'omitted material information'. One comment contends that, as

If a foreign investor gains approval with conditions after a review, the Working Mechanism Office, in conjunction with pertinent departments and the local government, is responsible to supervise the implementation of the conditions imposed.[70] Failure to comply with the conditions imposed will result in a mandatory divestment and restoration to the *status quo*.[71]

If a rejection decision is made after a review, the investment plan is then prohibited. If the investment project has already been carried out, the foreign investor is subject to a mandatory divestment and restoration to the *status quo*.[72]

4.4 Potential improvement in the national security review of foreign investment

The newly adopted 2020 Measures aim to commit to further opening-up, to maintain China's continuous endeavour to optimize its business environment and promote foreign investment, and to avoid the trap of protectionism and the generalization of the review mechanism, according to a press release of the NDRC on the promulgation of the Measures.[73] These commendable legislative objectives have been reflected in the 2020 Measures, as Art. 1 provides a guiding principle that the law aims at 'adapting to the need of a new comprehensive opening-up, actively promoting foreign investment, and at the same time preventing and alleviating national security concerns.' Now that the FIL has substantially reduced market access barriers to foreign investors by granting them pre-establishment national treatment, a national security review has become a last line of defence that is necessary to protect China's legitimate security-related interests. The promulgation of the 2020 Measures demonstrates China's willingness and endeavour to formulate a formal legal instrument with regard to national security review. In addition, since 2011 rules came into effect, no official prohibition of foreign investment based on national security grounds has been issued by the Chinese government. This suggests that China's national security review is implemented in the utmost caution and official prohibition will only be adopted in rare and extreme circumstances.

Nonetheless, certain improvements are to be desired. National security review, if implemented in a capricious, arbitrary or unpredictable manner, might deter potential investors, and eventually damage the appeal of a host state to foreign

---

the statute doesn't specify what constitutes 'material information', investors may be subject to recurring reviews even without an intentional breach of the law. This provision would be against the principle of *res judicata*. Jason Cox, 'Regulation of Foreign Direct Investment After the Dubai Ports Controversy: Has the US Government Finally Figured Out How to Balance Foreign Threats to National Security Without Alienating Foreign Companies?' *The Journal of Corporation Law*, Vol. 34 Issue 1 (2008), pp. 293–316, at 313–314.

70 The Measures (2020), Art. 13.
71 The Measure (2020), Art. 18.
72 The Measures (2020), Art. 12.
73 NDRC, *supra* note 37.

investment. It is therefore imperative for host states to bring the impact of the rule of law to their domestic national security review system. International best practices, for example the Organisation for Economic Co-operation and Development (OECD) Guidelines for Recipient Country Investment Policies relating to National Security, call for host states to adhere to a number of principles that are conducive to the rule of law, *inter alia*, predictability, proportionality, procedural fairness and transparency, and accountability.[74] It is well advised that China's national security review may adhere to international best practices such as the OECD Guidelines, as well as draw reference from other jurisdictions such as the US and the European Union (EU), in order to level the playing field for investors. Specifically, the following amendments are recommended.

First, transactions subject to review are advised to be confined to a necessary scope. A most significant change in the 2020 Measures compared with the 2011 rules is the substantial expansion of the purview of China's national security review. While only foreign M&A were subject to review in the 2011 rules, the 2020 Measures now potentially subject all foreign investment to a review, including greenfield investment, M&A, and indirect investment, as long as national security may be at stake. While it is understandable that legislators wish to encompass every type of investment transaction to review in order to safeguard national security in a comprehensive fashion, certain types of thresholds that trigger a review are recommended in order to increase the operability of the system. To make a comparison with the review mechanisms in other jurisdictions, the US only subjects foreign M&A to review,[75] France and Germany require foreign shareholdings in a domestic target company to be above a certain quantitative threshold to trigger a review,[76] and Australia adopts a *de minimis* requirement of the total value of investment in order to trigger a review.[77] China could consider introducing some quantitative thresholds that trigger a review in future revisions of the law, for instance, above a certain total value of investment or above a certain foreign shareholding proportion in a domestic company. This would significantly increase the legal certainty and predictability of the system to both foreign investors and Chinese regulators.

Second, sectors subject to review could benefit from more precision and less ambiguity. The 2020 Measures have prescribed a list of sectors, including the defence sector and ten sensitive civil sectors, that mandates investors to make a voluntary filing pre-market entry. However, as mentioned in some comments

---

74 OECD, 'Guidelines for Recipient Country Investment Policies Relating to National Security', Recommendation Adopted by the OECD Council on 25 May 2009, www.oecd.org/daf/inv/investment-policy/43384486.pdf, last accessed on 9 April 2021.
75 Cheng Bian, *supra* note 29, pp. 113–114.
76 Ibid, pp. 167–168.
77 Vivienne Bath, 'Foreign Investment, the National Interest and National Security – Foreign Direct Investment in Australia and China', *Sydney Law Review*, Vol. 34 No. 1 (2012), pp. 5–34, at 7, 23.

about the 2011 rules,[78] the list in the 2020 Measures also has little operability due to its lack of further definition of terms that are semantically difficult to fathom, for example, the meaning of 'important' or the scope of 'infrastructure'. Further, the sectors subject to review also include a catch-all provision, namely 'other important sectors'; this would mean the sectors subject to review are essentially unlimited. Therefore, it is recommended that subjective terms, such as 'important', in the provisions should either be avoided or accompanied with explanations of their meaning. Certain sectors subject to review appear to suffer from overinclusiveness, for example 'important infrastructure' or 'key technologies'. To avoid the trap of legal vagueness and lack of operability in enforcement, definitions should be prescribed to these terms for all stakeholders to understand the law.

Third, the entire review procedure is advised to be limited to a definite time frame. At first glance, China's national security review procedure appears to be under a definitive time frame. The whole process is *prima facie* bound by a time limitation of up to $(15 + 30 + 60)$ 105 working days, since an investor first files a request for review. However, the process is subject to temporal suspension when the Working Mechanism Office requests additional material submission or makes inquiries, and there is a recount of the time frame when an investor is instructed to modify its investment proposal and submit its filing anew. As there are neither statutory time limits on each suspension nor limits on the frenency of a suspension or a recount of review, the whole process is essentially not time constrained. A definitive time frame is crucial for the national security review to ensure procedural fairness and predictability. Without a clear time constraint in a regulatory procedure, foreign investors may eventually decide to abandon its investment plan amid uncertainty. This was indeed the case in the Carlyle–Xugong deal from 2005 to 2008 which was thwarted by the silent treatment from MOFCOM in its case-by-case takeover approval.[79] Hence, it is advised that the law should also give clear limitations to the usage of suspensions and recounts in addition to the whole 105-working-day time frame.

Fourth, the review system could benefit from more accountability. The accountability of the national security review refers to a situation where the review authorities can be held liable for its actions and decisions. For aggrieved foreign investors, the possibility of judicial recourse in a domestic court of the host state in principle remains the only remedy available for them to hold the review body liable. International best practices such as the OECD Guidelines for Recipient Country Investment Policies relating to National Security recommend the host

---

78 For example, one comment opines that the sectoral scope of the Chinese review is 'much broader than the U.S. model', and 'could cover transactions that have almost no nexus with national security.' Souvik Saha, 'CFIUS Now Made in China: Duelling National Security Review Frameworks as a Countermeasure to Economic Espionage in the Age of Globalization', *Northwestern Journal of International Law & Business*, Vol. 33 Issue 1 (2012), pp. 199–236, at 219–220.

79 For a detailed discussion on the Carlyle–Xugong case, see Chapter 3, Section 3.4.2.

state to adopt internal government oversight, parliamentary oversight, judicial review and periodic regulatory impact assessments to promote accountability.[80] The EU, in its Regulation on FDI screening, mandates Member States to provide 'the possibility to seek recourse against screening decisions of the national authorities'.[81] The US also allows investors to resort to judicial recourse against CFIUS decisions. In the case of *Ralls Corp. v. CFIUS et al.*, the Chinese investor successfully challenged President Obama's Prohibition Order of its investment in wind farms, on the ground that the Presidential Order violated the due process of law by reaching a decision without giving the investor an adequate opportunity to present its explanation.[82] In opposition to prevalent practices in other jurisdictions, China emphasizes in particular the non-litigable nature of national security review, by stipulating in the FIL that decisions made in a national security review are final and not subject to any administrative reconsideration or litigation.[83] Therefore, it is desirable that China's national security review could be subject to some sort of error-correction and supervision mechanisms in the future.

Fifth, the national security review system could avail itself of elevated transparency. Since the formal adoption of China's national security review in 2011, little information has been disclosed to the public about its enforcement. And the system was subject to criticism of a lack of transparency.[84] So far, there is only one known foreign takeover case that has undergone a national security probe. In August 2019, NDRC invited Yonghui Supermarkets, an FIE in China controlled by a Hong Kong-based company operating in the retail industry, to file for a national security review over its proposed acquisition of 40% of shares of Zhongbai Group, another retail company owned by a local State-Owned Assets Supervision and Administration Commission. In December 2019, Yonghui announced its abandonment of the transaction, without disclosing any further information, and the ongoing review came to a halt with no further explanation or decisions given.[85] It remains unknown whether Yonghui's decision to withdraw was a result of the NDRC's intervention or simply a business consideration. This failed Yonghui–Zhongbai deal merely involved two retail companies operating supermarkets, which would appear to be rather extraneous to

---

80 OECD, *supra* note 74.
81 Regulation (EU) 2019/452 of the European Parliament and of the Council of 19 March 2019 Establishing a Framework for the Screening of Foreign Direct Investments into the Union, OJEU, L 79 I, 21.3.2019, Art. 3.5.
82 For a detailed discussion of the case, see Hunter Deeley, 'The Expanding Reach of the Executive in Foreign Direct Investment: How Ralls v. CFIUS Will Alter the FDI Landscape in the United States', *American University Business Law Review*, Vol. 4 Issue 1 (2015), pp. 125–152, at 143.
83 Foreign Investment Law (2019), Art. 35.
84 Xingxing Li, *supra* note 33, at 266.
85 Ding Yi, 'Yonghui Drops Plans to Increase Stake in Chinese Retailer After National Security Probe', *Caixin*, 17 December 2019, https://www.caixinglobal.com/2019-12-17/yonghui -drops-plans-to-increase-stake-in-chinese-retailer-after-national-security-probe-101495178 .html, last accessed on 10 April 2021.

any national security concerns. The case serves to illustrate the fact that China's national security review still leaves some room for improvement when it comes to transparency in enforcement. To that end, more official public disclosure of pertinent information is desirable. In fact, this was proposed in the draft FIL 2015, which called for an annual reporting with regard to national security review. The annual report, if adopted in the future, could provide some essential information to the public, such as the number of cases submitted for review, the number of cases subject to review, the review outcomes and the sectors under scrutiny. This would facilitate a better understanding of the operation of the national security review system, which contributes to public trust and the credibility of the system.

4.5 Conclusion

China's national security review regime is the result of an incremental development of lawmaking since 2003, as opposed to a sudden turn of events or an abrupt spur of the moment following the promulgation of the FIL. Therefore, any allegations suggesting that China's motivation in adopting the 2020 Measures was dishonourable, for instance the claim that China wished to use them as a political and protectionist tool targeting US investment in China in retaliation for the CFIUS censorship against Chinese investment in the US, would be unjustified and untenable. To say the least, China's national security concerns have been addressed in publicly disclosed legal codes and implementing regulations, instead of as an insidious and untraceable *de facto* practice, which is an important manifestation of the rule of law. Be that as it may, a march towards the rule of law calls for deference to certain fundamental principles of law such as proportionality, predictability, procedural fairness, transparency, and accountability in national lawmaking, which is a dynamic and evolving process that takes shape through incremental legal reform. As previously discussed, China's national security review demonstrates some room for improvement, and future legal amendments are recommended for greater adherence to the aforementioned fundamental legal principles contributing to the rule of law. This is to ensure that China's attraction to foreign investment will not be compromised by the national security review system that might not be amply clear yet to foreign investors.

5 Protection of foreign investors' intellectual property

5.1 The legal framework of intellectual property rights

5.1.1 The legal and institutional framework of intellectual property protection

China's intellectual property (IP) law is centred by its *Patent Law*,[1] *Trademark Law*[2] and *Copyright Law*.[3] Each law is accompanied by implementing regulations, administrative regulations, departmental rules, judicial interpretations, and local laws and regulations.[4] For instance, at the central level, the *Patent Law* is accompanied by its *Implementing Regulation*,[5] additional procedural rules on patent litigation,[6] the *Regulation on Patent Agency*,[7] judicial interpretations such as the Supreme People's Court's (SPC) provisions regarding patent

---

1 中华人民共和国专利法 (Patent Law of China) (Promulgated by the NPC on 12 March 1984, 1st revision on 4 September 1992, 2nd revision on 25 August 2000, 3rd revision on 27 December 2008, 4th revision on 17 October 2020, effective on 1 June 2021).
2 中华人民共和国商标法 (Trademark Law of China) (Promulgated by the NPC on 23 August 1982, 1st revision on 22 February 1993, 2nd revision on 27 October 2001, 3rd revision on 30 August 2013, 4th revision on 23 April 2019, effective on 1 November 2019).
3 中华人民共和国著作权法 (Copyright Law of China) (Promulgated by the NPC on 7 September 1990, 1st revision on 27 October 2001, 2nd revision on 26 February 2010, 3rd revision on 11 November 2020, effective on 1 June 2021).
4 For a detailed discussion of these laws and regulations, see Dan Prud'homme and Taolue Zhang, *China's Intellectual Property Regime for Innovation: Risks to Business and National Development* (Cham: Springer, 2019), pp. 22–25. For a comprehensive and historical overview of Chinese IP law, see William P. Alford, *To Steal a Book is an Elegant Offense: Intellectual Property Law in Chinese Civilization* (Stanford: Stanford University Press, 1995). Zhenqing Zhang, *Intellectual Property Rights in China* (Philadelphia: University of Pennsylvania Press, 2019).
5 中华人民共和国专利法实施细则 (Implementing Regulation of the Patent Law) (2010 Revision) (Promulgated by the State Council on 9 January 2010, effective on 1 February 2010).
6 关于专利等知识产权案件诉讼程序若干问题的决定 (Several Issues Concerning Judicial Procedures for Patent and Other Intellectual Property Litigations) (Promulgated by the NPC on 26 October 2018, effective on 1 January 2019).
7 专利代理条例 (Regulation on Patent Agency) (Promulgated by the State Council on 6 November 2018, effective on 1 March 2019).

DOI: 10.4324/9781003168805-6

granting,[8] departmental rules issued by the China National Intellectual Property Administration (CNIPA, successor of State Intellectual Property Office) such as the *Guidelines for Patent Application Examination*,[9] special patents such as the *Regulation on National Defence Patent*,[10] and the sectoral association's regulations such as *Administrative Measures of the All China Patent Attorneys Association on Litigation Agency*.[11] In addition, China has been a party to the World Intellectual Property Organization (WIPO) since 1980, has ratified 15 out of 26 international treaties under WIPO,[12] and is a party to the Agreement on Trade-Related Aspects of Intellectual Property Rights (TRIPS) since 2001. Contrary to popular belief, China performs exceptionally well in its innovation capabilities, as it ranks 14th among 131 economies in the WIPO's Global Innovation Index 2020, which is based on multiple indicators; for instance, China ranks first in the world in terms of the number of inventions granted, the number of utility models granted, the number of industrial designs granted and the number of trademarks registered.[13]

China has built the world's largest IP institution. At the central level, the CNIPA is the national bureau under the governance of the State Administration for Market Regulation (SAMR) that administers patent examination and granting (Patent Office) and trademark registration and administration (Trademark Office) nationwide. At provincial, municipal and district/county levels, local IP offices exist under the auspices of the local AMRs; they are in charge of ceasing IP infringement, seizing infringing goods and imposing penalties to infringers. Copyright is administered by the National Copyright Administration at the central level and Bureaus of Copyright at the local levels. Although the overall institutional capacity and quality of the CNIPA is believed to be improving, some persistent challenges are observed, including long processing time for grants for patents and trademarks due to rising workloads, unsatisfactory quality of patent and trademark examination, concerns over the efficiency and quality of the invalidation process for allegedly infringing patents and trademarks, and insufficient coordination between central and local IP offices.[14]

---

8 最高人民法院关于审理专利授权确权行政案件适用法律若干问题的规定（一）(The Provisions (I) on Several Issues Concerning the Application of Law in the Trial of Administrative Cases Involving the Grant and Confirmation of Patents) (Promulgated by the SPC on 10 September 2020, effective on 12 September 2020).

9 专利审查指南 (Guidelines for Patent Application Examination) (Issued by the CNIPA on 11 December 2020, effective on 15 January 2021).

10 国防专利条例 (Regulation on National Defence Patent) (Promulgated by the State Council and Central Military Commission on 17 September 2004, effective on 1 November 2004).

11 中华全国专利代理师协会诉讼代理管理办法 (Administrative Measures of the All China Patent Attorneys Association (ACPAA) on Litigation Agency) (Promulgated by ACPAA on 24 February 2021, effective on promulgation).

12 WIPO, 'WIPO Administered Treaties, Contracting Parties, China', https://wipolex.wipo.int/en/treaties/ShowResults?country_id=38C, last accessed on 19 January 2021.

13 Soumitra Dutta, Bruno Lanvin and Sacha Wunsch-Vincent (eds.), *Global Innovation Index 2020* (Geneva: WIPO, 2020), p. 239.

14 Dan Prud'homme and Taolue Zhang, *supra* note 4, pp. 120–130.

On paper, China's IP law regime is constantly improving and obliges itself to comply with the international treaties of which China is a party that set IP protection standards, but in practice, the regime has long been stymied by allegations of lax enforcement and rampant IP infringement.[15]

5.1.2　*Foreign complaints about IP law and administrative enforcement*

Foreign companies in China have expressed perennial dissatisfaction and outcry in IP protection and enforcement. In the European Union (EU) Chamber of Commerce Survey in 2020, 36% of EU respondents feared the risks of IP infringement when doing business in China, which deterred them from bringing the latest technology to China, and 35% of respondents reported to have suffered IP infringement in China.[16] According to the German Chamber of Commerce in China, 22% of German investors rated IP rights enforcement as a regulatory business challenge in China in 2020, 'despite undisputed improvements to IP regulations over recent years'.[17] United States (US) investors share very similar concerns. In the 2019 American Chamber of Commerce Survey, 35% of US respondents expressed a lack of sufficient IP protection in China in 2018, 53% of respondents feared that China posed higher IP leakage and data security risks than elsewhere, and 34% of respondents limited their investment in China due to concerns of inadequate IP protection.[18] The most cited IP challenges in China for US investors are insufficient protection of IP rights in laws and regulations, and difficulties prosecuting IP infringements in courts.[19] The Korean government and Korean entertainment conglomerates have continuously demanded stronger copyright protection and enforcement in China over Korean audiovisual works, as pirated Korean television shows, movies and music are rampant in China and unlawfully circulated on the Chinese market, most notoriously on video-sharing websites, causing significant damage to the copyright owners.[20]

15　William Weightman, 'Is the Emperor Still Far Away? Centralization, Professionalization, and Uniformity in China's Intellectual Property Reforms', *UIC Review of Intellectual Property Law*, Vol. 19 Issue 1 (2020), pp. 145–177.

16　EU Chamber of Commerce in China, *Business Confidence Survey 2020*, http://www.europe-anchamber.com.cn/en/publications-archive/774/European_Business_in_China_Business_Confidence_Survey_2020, last accessed on 25 December 2020, pp. 42–43.

17　German Chamber of Commerce in China, *German Business in China Business Confidence Survey 2020/21*, https://china.ahk.de/market-info/economic-data-surveys/business-confidence-survey, last accessed on 17 May 2021, p. 34.

18　AmCham China and Deloitte, *2019 China business Climate Survey Report*, https://www2.deloitte.com/content/dam/Deloitte/au/Documents/international-specialist/deloitte-amcham-2019-china-business-climate-survey-report-bilingual-190301.pdf, last accessed on 18 July 2020, pp. 57, 60 and 62.

19　Ibid, p. 63.

20　Tianxiang He, 'The Big "Ban" Theory and Piracy: Which Way Forward for Effective Transnational Copyright Enforcement in China?' *Journal of the Copyright Society of the U.S.A.*, Vol. 66 (2019), pp. 161–190, at 170–172.

5.1.2.1 High quantity but low quality of patents

The Patent Office of the CNIPA became the world's biggest patent office in terms of the number of applications received since 2011.[21] The drive behind China's explosion of patent applications and its institutional expansion to handle such an explosion is attributed to state financial incentives, and national patenting targets directly related to performance evaluations of the local government, but at the expense of unsatisfied patent quality.[22] The high volume of applications is supported by local government patent subsidy programs to reward granted patents or to subsidize the patent filing and examination fees immediately after a patent filing or examination request; an empirical study indicates that patent subsidies in China increase the number of patent applications by more than 30%, but at the same time generate more requests for low-quality and low-value patent filing.[23] In addition, the pressure-driving mechanism, whereby the central government sets specific numerical targets for annual patent filings nationwide and multiple levels of local governments re-assign, implement, and evaluate the performance of these patent targets, has pressured government officials at all levels to meet the targets in order to secure their future political career.[24]

As a result, despite the enormous quantity of patents applied for and granted, the low quality of patents in China has become a major concern. The surge in utility models and industrial designs, two sub-categories of patents that demand less patentability requirements than invention patents, contributes to the low quality of patents overall in China.[25] China's patent subsidy program has primarily stimulated industrial designs, which in fact deteriorate the overall quality of Chinese patents.[26] One empirical study of 60,000 patent applications worldwide between 2000 and 2010 found that compared with the US, the EU, Japan and Korea, Chinese patents have the longest citation lag, which indicates the lowest overall quality of patents among the rest of the comparators.[27] Another empirical

---

21 WIPO, 'World Intellectual Property Indicators 2012', https://www.wipo.int/edocs/pubdocs/en/intproperty/941/wipo_pub_941_2012.pdf, last accessed on 20 January 2021, p. 47.

22 Dan Prud'homme and Taolue Zhang, *supra* note 4, p. 66.

23 Jianwei Dang and Kazuyuki Motohashi, 'Patent Statistics: A Good Indicator for Innovation in China? Patent Subsidy Program Impacts on Patent Quality', *China Economic Review*, Vol. 35 (2015), pp. 137–155, at 151.

24 Wenting Cheng and Peter Drahos, 'How China Built the World's Biggest Patent Office – The Pressure Driving Mechanism', *International Review of Intellectual Property and Competition Law*, Vol. 49 (2018), pp. 5–40.

25 Dan Prud'homme and Taolue Zhang, *supra* note 4, p. 66.

26 Zhiyuan Chen and Jie Zhang, 'Types of Patents and Driving Forces behind the Patent Growth in China', *Economic Modelling*, Vol. 80 (2019), pp. 294–302, at 301.

27 A citation lag is the time elapsed between the publication of the application of a patent and the first citation it receives. The first citation of a patent is the first time when it has been cited by subsequent patents, indicating that newer patents are built upon the original patent. The longer the citation lag is, the less technological value the patent indicates. Christian Fischa, Philipp Sandnerb and Lukas Regnerc, 'The Value of Chinese Patents: An Empirical Investigation of Citation Lags', *China Economic Review*, Vol. 45 (2017), pp. 22–34.

study found that, while the quantity of Chinese patents surged from 2011 to 2017, the quality declined by measurement of forward citations, especially in information and communication technology (ICT) and semiconductor patents.[28] The dramatically high quantity but low quality of patents incentivized by the 'indigenous innovation' policies and substantial state subsidies don't necessarily result in scientific advancements and innovation capabilities that can generate productivity, leaving China still highly dependent on the importation of foreign goods and technologies in many critical sectors, such as semiconductors, chips, turbofans and commercial aircrafts.[29]

In recent years, several legislative initiatives were adopted to improve patent filing quality. In 2017, the CNIPA promulgated Order No. 75 which curtails, amongst other provisions, 'abnormal patent filing behaviour' such as obviously similar and multiple submissions from the same individual or entity, submissions of obvious plagiarism from previous patents, and submissions based on trial statistics or results that are obviously fabricated.[30] In 2021, the CNIPA issued Notice No. 1 which aims to promote China as an 'innovative superpower', shifting from pursuing mere patent quantity to quality, and stifling irregular patent filing activities that are not intended to protect innovation, among others.[31] Notice No. 1 prohibits setting quantitative patent application goals at local levels as a basis for local government performance evaluation, and as apportion requirements to lower governments and local enterprises in the means of administrative orders. It also modifies China's patent funding policy, which prohibits any forms of funding, rewards or subsidies at all levels of governments at the patent application stage starting June 2021.[32]

5.1.2.2 Trademark squatting

Trademark squatting is a global problem but China is criticized as a place where it is especially rampant. Unlike countries such as the US that follow the 'first to use' rule, China follows the 'first to file' rule for trademark registration. China also doesn't recognize trademarks registered in other jurisdictions and will only grant protection to those who file first in China. Consequently, trademark squatters exploit the differences in trademark laws of different jurisdictions and register

---

28 Renai Jiang, Haoyue Shi and Gary H. Jefferson, 'Measuring China's International Technology Catchup', *Journal of Contemporary China*, Vol. 29 No. 124 (2020), pp. 519–534.

29 Alexander B. Hammer and Shahid Yusuf, 'Is China in a High-Tech, Low-Productivity Trap?' *US International Trade Commission Economic Working Paper Series 2020-07-B*, July 2020, pp. 31–35.

30 关于规范专利申请行为的若干规定 (Several Provisions on Regulating Patent Filing) (Promulgated by the CNIPA on 28 February 2017, effective on 1 April 2017), Art. 3.

31 国家知识产权局关于进一步严格规范专利申请行为的通知 (Notice of the CNIPA on Further Strictly Regulating Patent Application Activities) (Issued on 27 January 2021, effective on promulgation).

32 Ibid, Arts. 4(1) and 4(2).

trademarks that are identical to well-known international brands not yet regis-tered in China. Once the international brand decides to establish its presence in China, the squatters will sell the registered trademark back to the international brand for lucrative profits.[33] Tesla, for example, fell victim to this type of trade-mark squatting in China, among many other aggrieved foreign brands.[34] Other squatters exploit the reputation of an international brand by registering a similar trademark in China, and make huge profits from the original brand's reputa-tion by confusing consumers.[35] In this scenario, the squatter often registers a transliteration in Chinese characters or Chinese Pinyin of the original brand in Roman letters and misleads Chinese consumers to believe that the squatter is sell-ing authentic products from the official foreign brand. The first type of squatter does not intend to use the registered trademark but only to sell it back to the foreign trademark holder, while the second type has an intent to use the regis-tered trademark to conduct theft of the reputation of the original well-known international brands. Both cases are deemed as bad faith trademark registration, causing widespread criticism of China's trademark system.[36]

It is argued that the 2001 Revision of the *Trademark Law* even contributed to bad faith trademark filing practice to a certain extent by allowing a Chinese national who conducts no commercial activity to apply for a trademark, resulting in the proliferation of professional trademark hoarders.[37] The 2019 Amendment of the *Trademark Law* emanates China's efforts to address the outstanding issue of trademark squatting. Art. 4 of the *Trademark Law* first adds bad faith regis-tration with no intent of use as a ground for rejection for registration.[38] It fur-ther stipulates that the Trademark Office, either *ex officio* or upon the request of any third party, may declare a registered trademark invalidated if registered in

---

33 Ming Chen and Xiaohai Liu, 'Bad Faith Filings in the Chinese Trademark Law: Evolution, Status Quo and Improvements', *Queen Mary Journal of Intellectual Property*, Vol. 10 No. 3 (2020), pp. 306–320, at 306.

34 In 2009, a Chinese national named Zhan Baosheng successfully registered Tesla as a trade-mark in China before Tesla Motors, an US electric car manufacturer, entered the Chinese market. Zhan allegedly demanded 32 million USD from Tesla for the company to buy back its own name as a registered trademark in China. The two parties eventually reached an agreement in which Zhan sold its trademark to Tesla at an undisclosed price. 'Tesla Motors Hit with Trademark Obstacle in China', *World Intellectual Property Report*, 15 August 2013, https://www.worldipreview.com/news/tesla-motors-hit-with-trademark-obstacle-in -china, last accessed on 25 May 2021.

35 Ming Chen and Xiaohai Liu, *supra* note 33, at 306.

36 For instance, the USTR accused China of bad faith trademark registration, leading to 'US companies across industry sectors continuing to face Chinese applicants registering their marks and "holding them for ransom" or seeking to establish a business building off of US companies' global reputations'. USTR, *2018 Report to Congress on China's WTO Compli-ance*, February 2019, https://ustr.gov/sites/default/files/2018-USTR-Report-to-Con-gress-on-China%27s-WTO-Compliance.pdf, last accessed on 26 January 2021, p. 38.

37 Ming Chen and Xiaohai Liu, *supra* note 33, at 308.

38 Art. 4.1 of Trademark Law 2019 stipulates: 'A bad faith application for trademark registra-tion for a purpose other than use shall be rejected'.

bad faith without any statutory time limit.[39] However, questions and ambiguities remain. The newly added Art. 4 begs the question of how the intention for use can be proved to be true or otherwise. It opens the possibility that an application for registration of a trademark in bad faith could still potentially be approved as long as an applicant could deceivingly demonstrate an intent of use. Alternatively, a registrant of a trademark in bad faith could potentially defend an invalidation by demonstrating some actual use in business.[40] As a result, this new provision in the *Trademark Law* may not effectively deter trademark squatting behaviour with an intent of use or trademark squatting with some actual use.

Other provisions in the *Trademark Law* stipulate that if one registered trademark is a copy, imitation or translation of another well-known trademark which has not been registered in China and may easily cause confusion, the legitimate holder of the well-known foreign trademark can petition to the Trademark Appeal Board, and subsequently litigate at a Chinese court, for invalidation of the trademark registered in China within five years of the registration.[41] If the existence of a bad faith filing of the Chinese registered trademark can be proved, the five-year statutory limitation doesn't apply.[42] This is regarded as the relative ground on which the foreign legitimate rights holder can rely to oppose trademark squatting in China.[43] However, establishing 'well-known brand' and 'bad faith filing' claims before the Trademark Appeal Board or a Chinese court has proven to be difficult, which compromises the effectiveness in deterring bad faith filings.[44] Trademark squatting behaviour has made brand protection in China difficult for some foreign firms, leading to a significant loss of profits and monetary damages, as well as costs in time and resources in IP legal battles for foreign businesses.

Well-known international brands have fallen victim to trademark squatting in China and have subsequently resorted to legal remedies in Chinese courts. Some foreign sports apparel companies have to constantly combat trademark squatting in China, such as in *Under Armour v. Uncle Martian*, *Michael Jordan v. Qiaodan*, and *Zhou Lelun v. Xin Bai Lun*.[45] The most high-profile IP litigation that came as a success to the foreign IP rights holder is the *Michael Jordan v. Qiaodan* case. The name and image of Michael Jordan, a world-renowned US

---

39 Art. 44 of Trademark Law 2019 stipulates: 'Where a registered trademark violates Art. 4 …, the Trademark Office shall declare invalidation of the registered trademark; any other organization or individual may petition the Trademark Appeal Board to declare invalidation of the registered trademark'.

40 Scott Palmer, 'China's National Legislature Advances Changes to Trademark Law', *Perkins Coie LLP*, 30 April 2019, https://www.perkinscoie.com/en/news-insights/chinas-national-legislature-advances-changes-to-trademark-law.html, last accessed on 26 January 2021.

41 Trademark Law (2019), Arts. 13 and 45.

42 Trademark Law (2019), Art. 45.

43 Ming Chen and Xiaohai Liu, *supra* note 33, at 312–313.

44 Ibid, at 316–317.

45 John Keller Jr., '*Under Armour v. Uncle Martian*: A Case Study in Protecting American Trademarks in China against Homegrown Squatters', *Maryland Journal of International Law*, Vol. 34 (2019), pp. 388–406, at 391.

basketball player, were registered as multiple trademarks by a Chinese company in its Chinese translation (Qiaodan Tiyu), and the Chinese company exploited the reputation of Michael Jordan and sold its products for 20 years in China to confused Chinese consumers. The two parties engaged in a legal battle for eight years. In 2012, Michael Jordan petitioned for an invalidation of the registered trademark 'Qiaodan' and the accompanying image with the Trademark Appeal Board, on the grounds that the disputed trademark violated Art. 31 of the *2001 Trademark Law*, namely trademark registration filing shall not infringe prior rights of others.[46] The Trademark Appeal Board in 2014 rejected Jordan's petition. He then filed an administrative litigation at Beijing First Intermediate People's Court, which ruled in favour of the Trademark Appeal Board.[47] Jordan appealed to the Beijing High People's Court, which sustained the judgement of the court of the first instance.[48] Finally, Jordan in 2018 petitioned for a retrial at the SPC, which ruled in his favour in 2020, repealing all judgements made by lower courts and the decision made by the Trademark Appeal Board.[49] The SPC opined that the Chinese Qiaodan company, fully aware of the long-term and prevalent popularity of Michael Jordan in China, still filed 'Qiaodan', the Chinese Pinyin translation of 'Jordan', for trademark registration, which misled the public to a false perception of the connection between the two and infringed upon the right of the name of Jordan as a prior right.[50] Although this is a victorious landmark case for combating trademark squatting in China, one comment argued that the right of name is a right under Chinese civil law that 'refers exclusively to personality rights, not the economic interests in the name'. However, in this case, it was Michael Jordan's 'control of his name's commercial use on the Chinese market', but not the personality rights of his name such as reputation, that was infringed.[51] Therefore, the SPC's reasoning on the right of name in this case appeared to be problematic.

In the case of *Xin Bai Lun v. New Barlun*, the plaintiff Xin Bai Lun, which is the Chinese subsidiary of the US Sports Apparel Company New Balance, successfully prevailed over the Chinese defendant, New Barlun, for the latter's unfair competition conduct. The Shanghai Pudong People's Court found that the Chinese defendant, New Barlun, used the logo 'N' on its shoes, which was

---

46 迈某乔丹、国家知识产权局商标行政管理(商标) 再审行政判决书, (2018)最高法行再32号 (Administrative Judgement of Retrial of *Michael Jordan v. SIPO* on the Administration of Registered Trademarks) (2018) SPC Xing Zai No. 32, *China Judgements Online*, https:// wenshu.court.gov.cn/website/wenshu/181107ANFZ0BXSK4/index.html?docId=517 5ed72c38840c1bd87ab8a011600ae, last accessed on 9 February 2021.

47 Ibid.

48 Ibid.

49 Ibid.

50 Ibid.

51 Chenguo Zhang, 'The Right of Publicity in Chinese Law? A Comment on the Michael Jeffrey Jordan Case and Comparative Analysis with the US, UK, Germany, and the Asia Pacific', *Queen Mary Journal of Intellectual Property*, Vol. 10 No. 4 (2020), pp. 441–460, at 443, 448.

visually and conceptually similar to the prior original design of the plaintiff, New Balance, and benefited from the similarity and reputation of the US brand New Balance. For that reason, the defendant misled the consumers and distorted the market on purpose, and constituted unfair competition according to *Anti-Unfair Competition Law*. Therefore, the Court in April 2020 ruled in favour of the plaintiff, and damages of 10 million Renminbi (RMB) were to be paid.[52] Prior to this case, the two parties had engaged in legal battles over trademark infringement for more than a decade, but New Balance never succeeded in holding New Barlun liable for trademark squatting or bad faith trademark registration. The case of *New Balance v. New Barlun* demonstrated that foreign investors can not only protect their legitimate IP rights according to IP law but also cite unfair competition claims according to the *Anti-Unfair Competition Law*. The *Trademark Law* does not preclude the application of the *Anti-Unfair Competition Law* in resolving trademark infringement disputes, and the latter provides complementary protection to IP rights when IP laws do not suffice.[53]

But many international brands also encountered significant setbacks in battling trademark squatting in China. For instance, in the case of *Beijing Cottonfield v. Muji*, the Chinese plaintiff, Beijing Cottonfield, obtained '无印良品' as a registered trademark from another Chinese company, Hainan Nanhua, which registered the trademark in 2001, in class 24 (textiles and substitutes for textiles; household linen; curtains of textile or plastic). The defendant, Muji, a Japanese retail company which founded 'Muji' and '無印良品' in 1980, entered the Chinese market in 1999 and registered trademarks on a wide range of goods and services, but not in class 24. When Muji started to sell towels and bed covers in its stores opened in China in 2005 under the trademarks of 'Muji' and '無印良品', the Chinese plaintiff considered it as trademark infringement for two reasons. First, towels belong to class 24 (textiles), on which the rights holder of the trademark '无印良品' is Beijing Cottonfield, not Muji; second, although Muji uses '無印良品' instead of '无印良品' on towels and bed covers, it can be deemed identical from the perspective of an average consumer in China. In 2015, Beijing Cottonfield sued Muji for the defendant's trademark infringement of '无印良品' in class 24.[54] Beijing Intellectual Property Court ruled in favour of the

---

52 新百伦贸易 (中国) 有限公司与纽巴伦 (中国) 有限公司不正当竞争纠纷案一审民事判决书 (2017)沪0115民初1798号 (First Instance Civil Judgement of *Xin Bai Lun (China) v. New Barlun (China)* on Unfair Competition) (2017) Hu 0115 Min Chu No. 1798, https://www.ip-navi.or.kr/board/fileDownload.navi?board_seq=12266&file_server_id=2, last accessed on 23 July 2021.

53 Weijun Zhang and Yuqing Zhuang, '"《商标法》优先适用论" 辨析' (Analysis on the Prioritized Application of Trademark Law), 知识产权 (*Intellectual Property*), No. 6 (2020), pp. 46–59.

54 北京无印良品投资有限公司、北京棉田纺织品有限公司与无印良品（上海）商业有限公司、株式会社良品计画侵害商标权纠纷一审民事判决书 (2015)京知民初字第763号 (Civil Judgement of First Instance *Beijing Wu Yin Liang Pin Co., Ltd. and Beijing Cottonfield Co., Ltd. v. Muji Shanghai Co., Ltd and Ryohin Keikaku Co., Ltd.* on Registered Trademark Infringement) (2015) Jing Zhi Min Chu Zi No. 763. *China Law Info*, https://www

plaintiff in 2016, ordering Muji to stop selling textile products under the trademark '無印良品', and for damages of about 620,000 RMB to be paid to Beijing Cottonfield.[55] This was sustained by Beijing High People's Court in 2019 when Muji appealed.[56] In this case, the 'first to file' rule in the *Trademark Law*, by which Beijing Cottonfield became the legitimate trademark holder of '无印良品' in 2001 in class 24 within China, trumps the 'first to use' principle, whereby the Japanese Muji had established the brand name 'Muji' and '無印良品' as registered trademarks outside of China since 1980. This case demonstrates that foreign brands, if they have not registered their brand names on a comprehensive range of products and services in China, can easily fall victim to trademark squatting in China, and subsequently be entangled in incessant lawsuits with the squatters.

5.1.2.3 Counterfeiting and piracy

Counterfeiting and piracy are the unauthorized copy, imitation and use of other's IP rights, and production, distribution and sale of products that infringe other's IP rights, which include patents, for example, unlicensed pharmaceuticals; trademarks, for example, knock-off consumer products; and copyrights, such as pirated music and movies, and unlicensed computer software.[57] China has a long history and a huge market in counterfeited and pirated goods production and export.[58] Counterfeit goods are even more rampant in China's e-commerce. The most notorious example of a website selling luxury brand counterfeits is Alibaba's online retail platform, Taobao, which sells the products mostly as deceptive counterfeiting goods (the quality of the counterfeit is too good to discern from the original product and the consumer is usually not aware of the fake product).

.pkulaw.com/pfnl/a6bdb3332ec0adc4000a49d9fc81d329d3ac8f38038833a6bdfb.html
?keyword=%E6%97%A0%E5%8D%B0%E8%89%AF%E5%93%81%20%E5%8C%97%E4%BA
%AC%E6%A3%89%E7%94%B0, last accessed on 9 February 2021.

55 Ibid.

56 株式会社良品计画等与北京棉田纺织品有限公司等侵害商标权纠纷上诉案民事判决书 (2018)京民终171号 (Civil Judgement of Appeal *Ryohin Keikaku Co., Ltd. et al. v. Beijing Cottonfield Co., Ltd. et al.* on Registered Trademark Infringement) (2018) Jing Min Zhong No. 171. *China Law Info*, https://www.pkulaw.com/pfnl/a6bdb3332ec0adc43cd1b72 c7daf284777d792f4ff75dc1cbdfb.html?keyword=%E6%97%A0%E5%8D%B0%E8%89%AF %E5%93%81%20%E5%8C%97%E4%BA%AC%E6%A3%89%E7%94%B0, last accessed on 9 February 2021.

57 Daniel C. K. Chow, 'Counterfeiting in the People's Republic of China', *Washington University Law Quarterly*, Vol. 78 Issue 1 (2000), pp. 1–58, at 9–10.

58 According to the 2018 Global Brand Counterfeiting Report, worldwide losses suffered due to counterfeiting equalled to 323 billion USD in 2017, 80% of the world's counterfeit goods come from China, and many counterfeit goods consumers are from the Chinese market as well. Europol estimates that 86% of fakes worldwide originate in China. Europol also estimates the volume of counterfeit goods export at around 12.5% of China's exports and 1.5% of the China's GDP. 'Behind the Counterfeit Product Industry in China', *Daxue Consulting*, 15 June 2020, https://daxueconsulting.com/counterfeit-products-in-china/, last accessed on 9 February 2021.

China's third-largest online platform, Pinduoduo, is notorious for its low-quality counterfeits or copycat products sold at an unreasonably low price, mostly as non-deceptive counterfeiting goods (the consumer is well aware that the product is fake for the low price paid but is intentionally willing to purchase).

The rampancy of counterfeiting in China is attributed to a number of reasons. The first factor is that it is hard to hold counterfeiters accountable for the infringement of trademarks in the first place. Unlike trademark squatters who first seek to legitimize their counterfeiting products by exploiting the legal loopholes and registering trademarks identical or similar to international brands not yet registered in China, counterfeiters simply start to produce unauthorized goods using others' registered trademarks, ignorant of the legal ramifications. If the counterfeited goods are produced under a brand not yet registered in China, the foreign company holding the brand has to register its brand in China first in order to hold the counterfeiters liable, which takes at least one year to process and so would come too late to stop the damages to the brand value and reputation, as well as the financial loss that the counterfeit goods have caused to the foreign company.

Another factor in China's proliferation of counterfeiting and piracy activities is 'a lack of political will' in China to 'engage in an effective crackdown'.[59] Counterfeiting and piracy goods production, consumption and export, even though illegal, result in significant economic benefits to the local economy, create massive job opportunities, create tax revenues to the local government, and provide for the livelihood of workers. Therefore, a high-profile nationwide crackdown would result in the loss of these economic gains and, more important, create disruptive social unrest.[60] A prominent example is Yiwu, a township in Zhejiang Province described as 'the largest and most significant wholesale distribution centre for counterfeit goods' in China.[61] Even if the central government were willing, it is unlikely that local governments would fully enforce the crackdown: local government officials may be directly or indirectly involved, or have an interest in the trade and export of counterfeited and pirated goods.[62]

The third factor is lax IP law enforcement. IP enforcement in China is a dual system that involves administrative enforcement and judicial enforcement. To combat IP infringement, the IP rights holder can either seek administrative remedies at the local AMR against the infringers or file a civil litigation in a court.[63] In the event that the counterfeited goods have infringed a registered trademark in China and the foreign company is able to obtain protection under the *Trademark Law* by securing an administrative decision such as destruction of counterfeit goods or a court judgement against the counterfeit goods producer, it might

---

59 Daniel C. K. Chow, 'Why China Does Not Take Commercial Piracy Seriously', *Ohio Northern University Law Review*, Vol. 32 Issue 2 (2006), pp. 203–226, at 204.
60 Ibid, at 222–223.
61 Daniel C. K. Chow, *supra* note 57, at 19–21.
62 Daniel C. K. Chow, *supra* note 59, at 222.
63 Trademark Law (2019), Art. 60.

be impossible to enforce them because the counterfeiter will simply disappear and relocate. Campaigns are the most common type of IP rights enforcement action in China. They are short periods of time during which several administrative institutions perform a series of quick raids and enforcement actions against infringers.[64] Foreign companies complain about the ineffectiveness of campaigns, because 'shortly after a raid, infringers return to selling counterfeit goods; after numerous raids, counterfeiting operations move on to another town or factory and continue to operate until they are subject to yet another campaign once companies request enforcement measures again'.[65]

The last factor that contributes to piracy in particular relates to China's rigorous censorship in the cultural sectors. Foreign investment is largely prohibited from market entry in the cultural industry. According to the *2020 Negative List for Foreign Investment*, foreign investment is prohibited in Internet services (Internet news and information services, Internet publications, Internet audio and visual services, Internet cultural businesses, Internet information publications); news agencies; publication of books, newspapers and periodicals; electronic publications; distribution and production of audiovisual products; television stations and radio stations; the production, management and import of audiovisual broadcasting programs; production, distribution and importation of films; and cinemas. With regard to foreign trade, foreign cultural goods importation is subject to rigid censorship and licencing on a case-by-case basis. China has *ex ante* and *ex post* censorial mechanisms in publications, broadcasting channels, and online streaming and publishing; import quotas for foreign cultural works such as books and audiovisual products; and top-down enforcement campaigns to eliminate illicit content based on political considerations.[66] China also has a long tradition of abruptly boycotting foreign products, including cultural products such as publications and audiovisual works, due to political incidents with a particular country, a most recent case being the general ban on the import of Korean cultural products due to South Korea's deployment of a US anti-missile defence system named THAAD in 2017.[67] These restrictions 'have limited the ability of Chinese consumers to access the foreign titles they desire', and as a result, Chinese consumers resort to piracy and 'acquire unauthorized copies of foreign titles instead of purchasing legitimate products'.[68]

---

64 Adela Hurtado, 'Protecting the Mickey Mouse Ears: Moving beyond Traditional Campaign-Style Enforcement of Intellectual Property Rights in China', *Fordham Intellectual Property Media & Entertainment Law Journal*, Vol. 28 (2018), pp. 421–475, at 428.

65 Ibid, at 437–438.

66 For a comprehensive discussion on China's censorship in the cultural industry, see Tianxiang He, 'Control or Promote: China's Cultural Censorship System and Its Influence on Copyright Protection', *Queen Mary Journal of Intellectual Property*, Vol. 7 No. 1 (2017), pp. 74–98.

67 For a detailed discussion of the case, see Tianxiang He, *supra* note 20.

68 Tianxiang He, *supra* note 66, at 74–75.

5.1.3 *Foreign complaints in IP litigation*

In general, IP litigation in China is 'more efficient and effective today than in the past'.[69] China is making consistent progress to improve the adjudicative quality in resolving IP disputes. IP disputes can be brought to all levels of courts, depending on the specific type of claims and the monetary amount involved. The foreign identity of a litigant does not affect rules of jurisdiction by court levels. In recent years, China has established designated IP courts to 'centralize authority, create case uniformity, and build professionalism', in an attempt to 'fight local protectionism by taking cases out of local jurisdiction while simultaneously increasing the technical ability and professionalism of judges'.[70] Designated IP courts have jurisdiction over technically complex civil and administrative IP disputes of first instance or appeal, but not exclusive jurisdiction over all IP disputes.[71] In the SPC, an IP Tribunal has been established to adjudicate certain first-instance and certain appeal cases.[72] In addition, three independent IP Courts in Beijing, Shanghai and Guangzhou have been established, equivalent to intermediate people's courts. And 20 IP Tribunals have been established at municipal levels, as an internal tribunal of an intermediate people's court. Specialised IP courts are better positioned to resolve IP disputes because these courts are equipped with technical investigators to facilitate judges, are free from undue interference by the judicial committees that exist in ordinary Chinese courts, can adopt guiding case systems to improve consistency and predictability, generally have faster trial proceedings, and tend to grant increased damages to the infringed litigant.[73]

In addition to specialized IP Courts, since 2017 China has established Internet Courts in Hangzhou, Beijing and Guangzhou, which bring the whole litigation process from case filing to trial and appeal online through the 'e-litigation platform', improving the overall judicial efficiency.[74] Internet Courts are also designed to adjudicate certain IP disputes, for example, copyright disputes on works first published online or copyright infringement on online platforms, amongst other disputes.[75] In April 2019, Beijing Internet Court decided the first case in China

---

69 Dan Prud'homme and Taolue Zhang, *supra* note 4, p. 191.

70 William Weightman, *supra* note 15, at 157–158.

71 最高人民法院关于北京、上海、广州知识产权法院案件管辖的规定 (Provisions of the SPC on the Jurisdiction of the IP Courts in Beijing, Shanghai and Guangzhou) (First issued by the SPC on 31 October 2014, revised on 29 December 2020, effective on 1 January 2021).

72 最高人民法院关于知识产权法庭若干问题的规定 (Provisions of the SPC on Several Issues Concerning the IP Tribunal) (Issued by the SPC on 27 December 2018, effective on 1 January 2019).

73 Jieru Jiang, 'China Specialized IP Courts: Substance or Theater? Part II' *les Nouvelles*, Vol. 54 No. 1 (2019), pp. 19–26, at 25.

74 For a comprehensive discussion on the Internet Court and its innovation, challenges and possible solutions, see Meirong Guo, 'Internet Court's Challenges and Future in China', *Computer Law & Security Review*, Vol. 40 (2021), pp. 1–13.

75 最高人民法院关于互联网法院审理案件若干问题的规定 (Provisions of the SPC on Several Issues Concerning the Trial of Cases by Internet Courts) (Issued by the SPC on 6 September 2018, effective on 7 September 2018), Art. 2.

concerning copyrightability of works generated by artificial intelligence (AI) and ruled that works created solely by AI are not eligible for copyright protection in China because of their lack of a human creation process.[76] Internet Courts are deemed one of the latest endeavours to improve the adjudicative quality in resolving IP-related disputes in China.

Despite these positive developments, two main concerns remain: first, that local Chinese firms allegedly enjoy favouritism in court when litigating against foreign disputants; and second, that low damages are awarded in IP cases due to the fact that Chinese judges prefer to award statutory damages rather than calculating the actual damages according to methods provided by law.[77]

Judicial bias in IP disputes involves a concern that foreign investors as litigants are less likely to win. Foreign investors fear that it might be a futile endeavour to deter IP infringement as a plaintiff in Chinese courts due to a general distrust in China's civil judicial system, as certain perceptions such as 'local protectionism', 'bias', 'corruption', and 'lack of impartiality' permeate the system.[78] Judicial local protectionism, for example, is long argued to be a prevalent practice in China, where a local court is more likely to rule in favour of its local litigant. One empirical study found that in the field of IP, when the dispute is litigated at the court of the plaintiff's domicile, 'the plaintiff's probability of winning the case is significantly higher than in a case when the plaintiff's residence is different from the court's location'.[79] A conventional perception is therefore created that foreign investors as plaintiffs, with a domicile outside of China, find it difficult to prevail against Chinese defendants in Chinese courts to protect their IP rights from infringement. However, other empirical evidence appears to prove otherwise. One empirical study concluded that, although assertions about lax IP enforcement in courts in China are 'strident and commonplace', empirical evidence contradicts these conventional accusations in the case of patent lawsuits.[80] In an investigation of 471 patent lawsuits in China between 2006 and 2011, foreign companies as the patentees and the plaintiffs were found to have won 70% of the cases against Chinese domestic companies as the defendant, as acts of patent infringement were confirmed in these cases by courts; and foreign patentees as plaintiffs were awarded approximately the same amount of

76 北京菲林律师事务所诉百度百家号著作权侵权案一审判决书（2018）京0491民初239号 (First Trial Civil Judgement of *Beijing Feilin Law Firm v. Baidu Inc.* on Copyright Infringement) (2018) Jing 0491 Min Chu No. 239. For a detailed discussion on the case, see Ming Chen, 'Beijing Internet Court Denies Copyright to Works Created Solely by Artificial Intelligence', *Journal of Intellectual Property Law & Practice*, Vol. 14 No. 8 (2019), pp. 593–594.
77 Dan Prud'homme and Taolue Zhang, *supra* note 4, pp. 191–192.
78 Brian J. Love, Christian Helmers and Markus Eberhardt, 'Patent Litigation in China: Protecting Rights or the Local Economy', *Vanderbilt Journal of Entertainment & Technology Law*, Vol. 18 No. 4 (2016), pp. 713–742, at 718.
79 Cheryl Xiaoning Long and Jun Wang, 'Judicial Local Protectionism in China: An Empirical Study of IP Cases', *International Review of Law and Economics*, Vol. 42 (2015), pp. 48–59, at 48.
80 Brian J. Love, Christian Helmers and Markus Eberhardt, *supra* note 78, at 720.

damages as Chinese patentees as plaintiffs.[81] Subsequently, this empirical study concluded that the Chinese patent system appears to 'benefit foreign interests at the expense of domestic ones'.[82] Another empirical investigation based on 318 patent infringement disputes at the Beijing First Intermediate People's Court from 2004 to 2011 found that, in cases where a foreign litigant is present as a plaintiff, the probability of them winning the lawsuit is higher than that in cases where the plaintiff is a Chinese national, suggesting that a foreign patent holder in Chinese courts 'has instead a positive and significant effect on the likelihood of winning the suit'.[83]

China's IP litigation system also receives the constant criticism that foreign litigants' damages are not adequately compensated even when winning the case.[84] Damages awarded to IP rights holders in China are in general low, at approximately 20% of the plaintiff's damages claim, and significantly lower than that in the US, Japan and the EU. One reason is that Chinese judges in more than 90% of the judgements apply statutory damages, which is restricted by an upper limit in the *Patent Law*, instead of calculating the actual suffered damage.[85] Notably, newly introduced punitive damages in IP laws have significantly raised the upper monetary threshold. The *2020 Patent Law* stipulates that damages for patent infringement can be set at a maximum of 5 million RMB at the discretion of a court, compared with that of 1 million RMB in the 2008 Revision.[86] The *2019 Trademark Law* has also set the statutory damage for trademark infringement at a maximum of 5 million RMB, in contrast to 3 million RMB in the 2013 Amendment.[87] In the same vein, the *2020 Copyright Law* raised the maximum statutory damage for copyright infringement at 5 million RMB, as opposed to a mere 500,000 RMB in the 2010 Amendment.[88]

Several recent cases have also demonstrated a trend of certain improvement in judicial quality. In the case of *Lilly Company v. Watson Pharmaceuticals (Changzhou) Co., Ltd.*, the only IP dispute case involving a foreign litigant in the SPC's Guiding Cases, the foreign plaintiff, a British-based pharmaceutical multinational enterprise (MNE), filed to the High People's Court of Jiangsu that Lilly's invention patent, which was a patent method used to produce a drug called Olanzapine, was infringed by Watson Pharmaceuticals (Changzhou) Co., Ltd., because the Chinese defendant used the same method to produce Olanzapine without Lilly's authorization, citing Art. 57 of the *2000 Patent Law*

81 Ibid, at 724, 731–732.
82 Ibid, at 740.
83 Chenguo Zhang and Jin Cao, 'How Fair is Patent Litigation in China? Evidence from the Beijing Courts', *The China Quarterly*, Vol. 241 (2020), pp. 247–261, at 250.
84 Ibid, at 248.
85 Ibid, at 251–252, 254.
86 Patent Law (2020), Art. 71. Patent Law (2008), Art. 65.
87 Trademark Law (2019), Art. 63. Trademark Law (2013), Art. 63.
88 Copyright Law (2020), Art. 54. Copyright Law (2010), Art. 49.

(civil litigation for patent infringement).[89] The High People's Court of Jiangsu ruled in 2014 that Watson's production of Olanzapine violated Lilly's method invention patent, which was overruled and dismissed by the SPC in 2015 in the appeal.[90] The SPC, by investigating complex technical facts using multiple means including consultations with technical investigators, expert auxiliaries, forensic expertise and technology experts in a highly technical patent case, concluded that the two methods of producing Olanzapine were substantially different and did not constitute 'equivalent features', after a comparison between the chemical reaction routes of the two technical solutions that the two companies adopted to make Olanzapine.[91] This case was selected as an SPC guiding case for the court's laudable reference to professional third parties in adjudicating patent disputes with complex technical facts, among other reasons.

In the case of *Lego v. Lepin*, the Shanghai High People's Court in 2020 dismissed the appeal filed by Lepin and sustained the original judgement rendered by Shanghai Third Intermediate People's Court, which sentenced Li, the corporate representative of Lepin, to six years of imprisonment and a fine of RMB 90 million for the crime of copyright infringement (Art. 217 *Criminal Law*).[92] Since 2015, the Chinese Lepin has duplicated without authorization over 40 types of Lego toys, a world-famous Danish toy manufacturer, with a total sales value of more than RMB 300 million.[93] Both the first-instance and the appeal courts found that Lego's toy models were created by Lego independently and originally with unique aesthetics, which undisputedly constitute 'works of fine art' and should enjoy the protection of the *Copyright Law*.[94] As foreign IP rights holders begin to prevail more often in Chinese courts with unprecedented amount of damages awarded and even crimination of the offenders, the case of *Lego v. Lepin* demonstrates the willingness of Chinese courts to render severe punishment to IP infringement, setting a deterrence effect to future offenders.

89 指导案例84号：礼来公司诉常州华生制药有限公司侵害发明专利权纠纷案, (2015)民三终字第1号 (SPC Guiding Case No. 84: *Eli Lilly v. Changzhou Watson Pharmaceuticals Co. Ltd.* on Infringement upon Patent for Invention) (2015) SPC Min San Zhong Zi No. 1, *ChinaLawInfo*, https://www.pkulaw.com/en_case/a25051f3312b07f3fc2c1ff979d7c9c76f1 e9a97dc5609adbdfb.html, last accessed on 9 February 2021.
90 Ibid.
91 Ibid.
92 李海鹏等侵犯著作权案　上海市高级人民法院刑事裁定书 (2020)沪刑终105号 (Criminal Ruling of Shanghai High People's Court: Li Haipeng *et al.* on Infringement of Copyright) (2020) Hu Xing Zhong No. 105, *ChinaLawInfo*, https://www.pkulaw.com/pfnl/c05aeed 05a57db0ae0f5ced4eb88c45e8bdec99178b994aabdfb.html, last accessed on 9 February 2021.
93 Ibid.
94 Ibid.

5.1.4 *IP protection in the Foreign Investment Law (FIL)*

Art. 22 of the FIL stipulates that 'China protects the intellectual property rights of foreign investors and foreign-invested enterprises (FIEs), protects the lawful rights and interests of IP rights holders; and strictly holds IP rights infringement liable according to law'. Art. 23 of the FIL Implementing Regulation reiterates that 'China strengthens the effort to punish IP rights infringement, continuously reinforces IP law enforcement, promotes the establishment of a collaborative IP protection mechanism, establishes a diversified mechanism for IP dispute resolution, and equally protects IP rights between foreign and domestic investors and enterprises'.

The adoption of these provisions, although considered positive progress as China promises to address concerns of foreign investors in IP protection, seems to be 'nothing more than an official declaration that foreign investors' IP will be protected seriously', and might fall victim to 'ceremonial window-dressing' if not rigorously and effectively enforced.[95] That being said, one also has to recognize the limited role that the FIL can play in IP protection. IP rights protection in China and many existing concerns, such as trademark squatting, counterfeiting and piracy, lax administrative IP enforcement, and perceived judicial bias in IP litigation, are best addressed in China's IP lawmaking and enforcement, which are witnessing a continuous melioration. The FIL therefore may not be a primary and substantial source of IP protection for foreign investors in China.

5.2 Forced transfer of technology

5.2.1 *Accusations of forced transfer of technology (FTT) in China*

For years, China has been accused of adopting laws, policies and practices that force foreign companies to transfer their crucial technology to the Chinese government or Chinese firms in order to do business in China. Since 2018, this has become a driving tension in the continuing US–China trade antagonism. FTT policies are defined as government policies that are designed and implemented 'to increase foreign-domestic technology transfer that simultaneously weaken appropriability of foreign innovations'.[96] Appropriability of IP rights refers to the capacity and means a firm 'may use to profit from its inventions or innovations by temporarily enjoying some kind of monopolistic power over the knowledge it creates'.[97] 'Technology' in FTT policies and practices may involve patents

---

95 Jyh-An Lee, 'Shifting IP Battlegrounds in the U.S.-China Trade War', *Columbia Journal of Law & the Arts*, Vol. 43 No. 2 (2020), pp. 147–196, at 169–170.

96 Dan Prud'homme *et al.*, '"Forced Technology Transfer" Policies: Workings in China and Strategic Implications', *Technological Forecasting & Social Change*, Vol. 134 (2018), pp. 150–168, at 150.

97 Andrés López, 'Innovation and Appropriability, Empirical Evidence and Research Agenda', in WIPO, *The Economics of Intellectual Property* (Geneva: WIPO Publication, 2009), pp. 1–40, at 2–3.

(inventions, utility models and industrial designs) where ownership transfer or compulsory licencing may take place, or commercial secrets, know-how and technical information that a foreign investor is forced to disclose to government authorities or to a private domestic party. The term 'forced' implies that 'foreign investors are compelled by repercussions of failing to enter the market or the lack of alternatives to enter the market'.[98]

Although China has adamantly denied, and promised to terminate, the practice of FTT, foreign investors continue to complain about its persistence. The fear of FTT has become one of the most cited obstacles for foreign investors in China to seek new establishment of business or to maintain their business operation, according to surveys conducted by foreign chambers of commerce in China,[99] government reports,[100] the United States Trade Representative (USTR) 301 Investigation,[101] and the World Trade Organization (WTO) dispute settlement proceedings.[102] In principle, three categories of FTT policies and practice are alleged to be rampant in China:

98 Jyh-An Lee, 'Forced Technology Transfer in the Case of China', *Boston University Journal of Science and Technology Law*, Vol. 26 Issue 2 (2020), pp. 324–352, at 348.

99 The US–China Business Council found that 13% of US companies in China as respondents to a survey were asked to transfer technology in 2020. The US–China Business Council, *Member Survey 2020*, https://www.uschina.org/sites/default/files/uscbc_member_survey_2020.pdf, last accessed on 9 February 2021, p. 13. The American Chamber of Commerce in China found in its survey that 13% of US companies as respondents saw technology transfer and IP localization requirements in China as a barrier to their investment in 2018. AmCham China, *2019 China Business Climate Survey Report*, https://www.amchamchina.org/wp-content/uploads/2020/11/BCS2019VF-Feb26-Version-Digital-Print.pdf, last accessed on 9 February 2021, p. 57. The European Chamber of Commerce in China found that 16% of European companies in China as respondents felt compelled to transfer technology to maintain market access in 2020. European Chamber of Commerce in China, *Business Confidence Survey 2020*, http://www.europeanchamber.com.cn/en/publications-archive/774/European_Business_in_China_Business_Confidence_Survey_2020, last accessed on 9 February 2021, p. 43.

100 USTR, *2018 Report to Congress on China's WTO Compliance*, February 2019, https://ustr.gov/sites/default/files/2018-USTR-Report-to-Congress-on-China%27s-WTO-Compliance.pdf, last accessed on 9 February 2021, pp. 132–134.

101 USTR, *Findings of the Investigation into China's Acts, Policies, and Practices Related to Technology Transfer, Intellectual Property, and Innovation Under Section 301 of the Trade Act of 1974*, 22 March 2018.

102 WTO, 'Request for Consultations by the European Union, Revision, China – Certain Measures on the Transfer of Technology', WT/DS549/1/Rev.1, 8 January 2019. WTO, 'Request for Consultations by the United States, China – Certain Measures Concerning the Protection of Intellectual Property Rights', WT/DS542/1/IP/D/38, 26 March 2018.

(1) Market access requirements: Technology transfer requirements as a precondition for market access, such as via performance requirements,[103] government procurement[104] and compulsory joint ventures (JVs).[105]

(2) Discriminatory laws and regulations: Ambiguous laws and regulations that indulge FTT practice, such as technology import/export regulations, compulsory licencing of standard essential patents (SEPs), and the interplay between anti-monopoly law and IP.[106]

(3) Divulgation of commercial secrets: Forced disclosure of sensitive technical information by Chinese administrative agencies in the processes of administrative approval, licencing, anti-monopoly review, national security review and so on.[107]

5.2.1.1 Market access requirements

It is claimed that since 1984 China has implemented a 'trading market for technology' strategy, where FIEs are induced to transfer their technology to China as a pretext for doing business there.[108] The logic behind this policy was to allow China to absorb and catch up with foreign technological advancement, at the expense of exposing infant domestic industries to compete with experienced MNEs. Transfer of technology can be either a natural diffusion process based on market terms and a commercial and voluntary basis or through the practice of FTT. FTT used as market access impediments and preconditions for foreign investment is the most widely condemned practice in China and at the centre of the US–China Trade War.

---

103 A host country's requirement of FTT in exchange for market entry can be deemed one type of performance requirement, which is explicitly forbidden by some IIAs and the WTO Agreement on Trade-Related Investment Measures (TRIMs) to which China is a signatory party. Julia Ya Qin, 'Forced Technology Transfer and the US-China Trade War: Implications for International Economic Law', *Journal of International Economic Law*, Vol. 22 Issue 4 (2019), pp. 743–762, at 752.

104 For instance, US companies claimed that China's policies force them to transfer their technology to China as a precondition to be able to participate in government procurement and sell products to the Chinese government. Daniel C. K. Chow, 'China's Indigenous Innovation Policies and the World Trade Organization', *Northwestern Journal of International Law & Business*, Vol. 34 Issue 1 (2013), pp. 81–124.

105 Dan Prud'homme *et al.*, *supra* note 96, at 157–158. Jyh-An Lee, *supra* note 98, at 331–333. Julia Ya Qin, *supra* note 103, at 746-747. Dan Prud'homme and Max von Zedtwitz, 'Managing "Forced" Technology Transfer in Emerging Markets: The Case of China', *Journal of International Management*, Vol. 25 (2019), pp. 1–14, at 7.

106 Dan Prud'homme *et al.*, *supra* note 96, at 158. Dan Prud'homme and Max von Zedtwitz, *supra* note 105, at 7.

107 Jyh-An Lee, *supra* note 98, at 333–334. Dan Prud'homme and Max von Zedtwitz, *supra* note 105, at 7. Julia Ya Qin, *supra* note 103, at 745–746.

108 Piergiuseppe Pusceddu, 'Hic sunt dracones? Mapping the Legal Framework of China's Innovation Policy: Standardization and IPRs', *International Review of Intellectual Property and Competition Law*, Vol. 51 (2020), pp. 559–593, at 571.

The USTR 301 Investigation conducted in 2018 identified three channels in which FTT takes place in the market entry phase, enumerated as follows.

First, in sectors where either a cooperative or equity joint venture is required according to the *Catalogue of Industries Guiding Foreign Investment* (prior to 2017) or the *Negative List for Foreign Investment* (after 2017), 'as companies negotiate the terms of the joint venture, the foreign side may be asked – or required – to transfer its technology in order to finalize the partnership', which is not explicitly mandated by written laws or regulations but rather as unwritten and oral instructions from the central or local government.[109] A prominent example is China's automobile industry, which requires the mandatory form of a JV in passenger vehicles manufacturing where the share of a Chinese partner must maintain absolute controlling status (no less than 50%) until 2022.[110] In this way, the Chinese partner, usually a state-owned enterprise (SOE) under the ultimate control of the central or local State-Owned Assets Supervision and Administration Commission, would have the leverage to force or pressure the foreign partner to transfer its technology to the JV in order to control 'the JV's core production technology', to develop 'domestic innovation capabilities through control of that core technology', and to gradually upgrade an indigenous brand owned independently by the Chinese partner with the technology obtained from the JV.[111]

Second, even in sectors where a JV is not a mandatory requirement by law, FTT still allegedly takes place as foreign investors may be instructed or pressured to form a JV in order to gain market access approval. Prior to the FIL, China's case-by-case foreign direct investment (FDI) approval by multiple agencies at the central and local levels created the opportunity for the Chinese government to impose technology transfer requirements, not according to traceable provisions in law but to internally circulated customs, as a hidden condition to the approval of market entry.[112] Even after the revocation of the case-by-case FDI approval, China maintains sectoral review, approval, licencing and qualification procedures for market access to all market participants alike in more than 120 fields (each field with multiple sub-categories) pursuant to the *Negative List for Market Access*.[113] By applying these sectoral approval processes, authorities can instruct a foreign investor to enter into partnership with a Chinese private or state-owned enterprise and form a JV, even in sectors where a wholly foreign-owned enterprise is permitted, and require the transfer of core technology to the JV as *quid pro*

---

109 USTR, *supra* note 101, p. 24.
110 外商投资准入特别管理措施（负面清单）(2020) (Negative List for Foreign Investment 2020) (Promulgated by NDRC and MOFCOM on 23 June 2020, effective on 23 July 2020), Item 8.
111 USTR, *supra* note 101, pp. 29–30.
112 Ibid, pp. 38–39.
113 市场准入负面清单2020 (Negative List for Market Access 2020) (Promulgated by MOFCOM and NDRC on 10 December 2020, effective on promulgation).

quo for the foreign investor to gain market access approval.[114] Foreign investors therefore are only given an illusory choice in its corporate form if the technology they possess is sought after, and are subject to a *de facto* JV requirement which may then lead to FTT practice.

A third channel for FTT at the pre-establishment phase is forced disclosure of commercial secrets and sensitive technical information. Because foreign businesses are required to undergo numerous case-by-case FDI approval (prior to 2017) and sectoral approval procedures at different government levels, 'the Chinese government requires the disclosure of unreasonable amounts of sensitive technical information in exchange for necessary administrative approvals'.[115] This sensitive technical information and know-how obtained by the approving authorities is then provided to third parties, including local domestic industries, other government officials, academia or others who hold a competitive interest.[116] Foreign investors are thus faced with a dilemma, forced to choose between, on the one hand, the risk of exposure of their technology, know-how and commercial secrets, and on the other hand, a looming rejection of approval for establishing a business, providing certain services or producing certain products. This practice is alleged to have constantly occurred in sectors such as chemicals, pharmaceuticals, ICT, machinery and finance.[117]

5.2.1.2 *Discriminatory laws and regulations*

The *Regulation on the Administration of Import and Export of Technologies* was heavily accused of imposing restrictions on foreign investors. The 'indemnity terms' mandated the foreign technology transferor to bear all liabilities when a third party's lawful rights were infringed resulting from the domestic transferee's use of the licenced technology.[118] The 'rights in technology improvements terms' mandated the freedom and the ownership of improvements based on the original transferred technology to the domestic transferee, and therefore blocked the foreign transferor from enjoying the benefit of the severable improvement.[119] These two discriminative terms existed from 2001 when the law was first promulgated and until 2019 when the law was revised.

The obsolete JV laws also included unfair conditions on the transfer of technology from a foreign partner to the joint venture. For instance, it was required that the technology transfer agreement between the foreign investor and the JV should not exceed ten years and the JV had the right to continue

---

114 USTR, *supra* note 101, pp. 36–39.
115 Ibid, pp. 41–42.
116 Ibid, p. 42.
117 Jyh-An Lee, *supra* note 98, at 334.
118 中华人民共和国技术进出口管理条例 (Regulation on the Administration of Import and Export of Technologies) (2001 Revision) (Promulgated by the State Council on 10 December 2001, effective on 1 January 2002), Art. 24.
119 Ibid, Arts. 27 and 29(3).

using the transferred technology after the expiration date.[120] US companies complained that this provision only allowed them to control their transferred technology for ten years through the technology transfer agreement, even though some IP rights should be protected far more than ten years; and that the Chinese JV had 'the right to use the US licensor's technology in perpetuity after the technology contract expires, without paying compensation or subject to other terms'.[121]

Another area of law attracting wide criticism is China's compulsory licencing of SEPs. According to the *Interim Administrative Regulation on National Standards Involving Patents*, if a patent is deemed 'essential' and indispensable to the formulation and amendment of a national standard, the patentee is obliged or encouraged to disclose its patent to the Standardization Administration of China, and should opt to licence their patent on 'fair, reasonable, and non-discriminatory (FRAND) terms in order to implement such a national standard'.[122] It is alleged that the ambiguous definition of 'essential' and a rather subjective understanding of the FRAND terms are an intentional legislative outcome, so as to ensure that the Chinese agencies would have room for manoeuvre in practice, and force foreign companies to unreasonably disclose their IP strategies and licence their patents as SEPs.[123]

The prohibition of abuse of IP rights that hinders competition or causes monopoly is another area of policy that raises concerns over potential FTT. According to *Provisions on Prohibiting the Abuse of Intellectual Property Rights to Preclude or Restrict Competition* first promulgated by the State Administration for Industry and Commerce (predecessor of SAMR) in 2015 and revised in 2020, an 'essential facilities doctrine' is introduced.[124] This doctrine, originating from US competition law and adopted in many other jurisdictions including in EU competition law, prescribes that in the event that a business has a dominant market position and that its IP rights constitute a facility essential to other market competitors in the industry, that business is obligated to compulsorily

---

120 中华人民共和国中外合资经营企业法实施条例 (Implementing Regulation for Law on Sino-Foreign Equity Joint Ventures) (2014 Revision) (Promulgated by the State Council on 19 February 2014, effective on 1 March 2014), Art. 43.
121 USTR, *supra* note 101, p. 54.
122 国家标准涉及专利的管理规定（暂行）(Interim Provisions on the Administration of National Standards Involving Patents) (Promulgated by the Standardization Administration of China and the State Intellectual Property Office on 19 December 2013, effective on 1 January 2014), Arts. 4–6, 9.
123 Dan Prud'homme *et al.*, *supra* note 96, at 158. Dan Prud'homme, 'FRAND and Other Requirements in China's Announcement on Releasing (Provisional) Administration Regulations of National Standards Involving Patents', *Journal of Intellectual Property Law & Practice*, Vol. 9 Issue 5 (2014), pp. 346–349.
124 关于禁止滥用知识产权排除、限制竞争行为的规定 (Provisions on Prohibiting the Abuse of Intellectual Property Rights to Preclude or Restrict Competition) (Promulgated by the SAMR on 23 October 2020, effective on promulgation), Art. 7.

licence its IP to others under certain terms.[125] In China, one of the statutory circumstances that triggers the essential facilities doctrine is when the refusal of licencing of such IP rights would lead to 'a negative impact to innovation', 'damage to consumers' interests' or 'damage to public interests'.[126] This broad scope of application of the essential facilities doctrine and its ambiguous terms, for instance, the undefined term 'public interest', are viewed as giving rise to a great potential of limiting the appropriability of foreign investors' IP and forcing technology transfer.[127]

5.2.2 *The paradoxical narrative of FTT in China*

The first paradoxical narrative in the course of China's alleged practice of FTT is that although allegations of FTT practice in China from foreign investors, academics, commerce groups and foreign governments appear to be overwhelmingly convictive,[128] empirical evidence to support the existence of FTT in practice appears to be only circumstantial. Claims that assert to be the victims of FTT are based on the results of anonymous surveys and interviews, without singling out the identity of individual interviewees.[129] This lack of substantial evidence to prove the existence of FTT in China can perhaps be attributed to a number of factors. An often-cited reason is the assumption that FTT in return for market access approval doesn't typically manifest as a direct threat from a Chinese official or a clearly written clause in the JV agreement, but takes place in a murkier manner such as a verbal request behind closed doors from the Chinese government, which makes it difficult to be proved and documented.[130] Another reason might be that foreign companies that have been subject to FTT practice usually prefer to remain anonymous in order to avoid retaliation from the Chinese government so as to continue their business operation in China.

The second paradox pertains to China's response to the allegations of FTT. Since the USTR 301 Investigation, China has responded through official reports,

---

125 Hanna Stakheyeva, 'Intellectual Property and Competition Law: Understanding the Interplay', in Ashish Bharadwaj *et al.* (eds.), *Multi-Dimensional Approaches Towards New Technology* (Singapore: Springer, 2018), pp. 3–19, at 5.

126 Provisions on Prohibiting the Abuse of Intellectual Property Rights to Preclude or Restrict Competition (2020), Art. 7.

127 Dan Prud'homme *et al.*, *supra* note 96, at 158.

128 See *supra* notes 99–102.

129 For example, one comment on China Daily argued for the lack of evidence in the USTR 301 Investigation: 'The US failed to furnish a single real case to prove that the Chinese government had forced or pressured foreign investors to transfer their technologies. And its failure to do so has called into serious question the validity of its claim.' Xiaoming Zhou, 'The Myth of Forced Transfer of Technology', *China Daily*, 3 September 2019, https://www.chinadaily.com.cn/a/201909/03/WS5d6da499a310cf3e355694a7.html, last accessed on 15 January 2021.

130 USTR, *supra* note 101, pp. 19–20.

press conferences and governmental statements at international organizations.[131] China denies the existence of any form of FTT practice, insists that technological cooperation between Chinese and foreign parties only takes place as contractual-based behaviour and strictly on voluntary and commercial terms, and is adamant that all allegations against China lack solid evidentiary support.[132] Meanwhile, China makes high-profile policy and legislative commitments to not conduct FTT against foreign investors, *inter alia*, a dedicated provision in the FIL that prohibits FTT,[133] provisions on the prohibition of FTT and ensuing administrative liabilities in the *Administrative License Law* revised in April 2019,[134] and a dedicated chapter in the US–China Phase I Trade Agreement signed in January 2020 that forbids FTT.[135] The fact that the FIL and *Administrative License Law* incorporate provisions on the prohibition of FTT could indicate that this matter is at least subsistent and imminent enough to be addressed in two national laws.

The third paradox is China's pledge to not pressure or force technology transfer against foreign investors, on the one hand, and a pronounced and consistent national strategy in seeking global technological leadership and dominance by means of attracting and absorbing advanced technology through foreign investment and the localization of innovation, on the other. Since 2006, China has

131 Information Office of the State Council, *The Facts and China's Position on China-US Trade Friction*, September 2018, https://china.usc.edu/sites/default/files/article/attachments /Chinese%20WP%20Sino-Am%20Trade.pdf, last accessed on 2 February 2021, pp. 30–33. MOFCOM, '商务部针对美国《关于301调查的声明》发表声明' (MOFCOM Issues Statement on US Section 301 Investigation), 12 July 2018, http://www.mofcom.gov .cn/article/ae/ai/201807/20180702765543.shtml, last accessed on 14 January 2021. MOFCOM, Permanent Mission of China to the WTO, 'Statement by Ambassador Dr. Zhang Xiangchen at the WTO DSB Meeting', 30 May 2018, http://wto2.mofcom.gov .cn/article/chinaviewpoins/201805/20180502749669.shtml, last accessed on 2 February 2021. Information Office of the State Council, *China's Position on the China-US Economic and Trade Consultations*, June 2019, http://images.mofcom.gov.cn/fj2/201906 /20190606114029957.pdf, last accessed on 2 February 2021.

132 Ibid.

133 FIL (2019), Art. 22.

134 Art. 31 of the Administrative Licensing Law stipulates: 'An administrative agency and its functionaries shall not grant an administrative license on the condition of transfer of technology; nor directly or indirectly require the transfer of technology in the implementation process of an administrative license'. Art. 72 stipulates: 'When an administrative agency or its functionaries conduct any of the following behaviours, its superior administrative agency or the supervisory agency shall order corrective action to be taken; and if the circumstances are serious, administrative penalties shall be imposed on persons held liable ... (6) Granting an administrative license on the condition of transfer of technology, or directly or indirectly requiring transfer of technology in the implementation process of an administrative license'. 行政许可法 (Administrative Licensing Law) (Promulgated by the NPC on 27 August 2003, last revised on 23 April 2019, effective on revision).

135 Economic and Trade Agreement Between the Government of the United States of America and the Government of the People's Republic of China (Phase I Trade Agreement), 15 January 2020, Chapter 2.

issued a series of IP development strategies that pursue 'indigenous innovation'.[136] For instance, the State Council issued the *National Medium- and Long-Term Program for Science and Technology Development (2006–2020)* in 2006, which identified 11 top-priority industries and 8 cutting-edge technologies for development, and set the target for China's reliance on foreign technology to less than 30% by 2020.[137] To achieve that goal, the Program emphasised the cultivation of indigenous IP rights and independence in these industries, and enhancement of the 'digestion, absorbance, and re-invention of imported foreign technology'.[138] In 2010, the State Council issued the *Decision to Accelerate the Development of Strategic Emerging Industries*, which identified seven strategic emerging industries where Chinese firms 'must control key technologies and relevant IP and enhance the independency and capacity of self-development' and should account for 15% of the entire Chinese gross domestic product (GDP) by the end of 2020.[139] One way to achieve this objective is to 'deepen international cooperation in order to expeditiously master key strategic technology', by means of 'guiding foreign investment in China to strategic emerging industries', and 'supporting Chinese enterprises to conduct mergers and acquisitions overseas'.[140] This strategy was reiterated in 2020 and the digital creativity industry has been added as an additional strategic emerging industry.[141] Perhaps the most controversial strategy China has promulgated so far is *Made in China 2025*. It identifies ten significant industries where China must master core technologies by 2020, establish a number of national champions with a strong competitive advantage internationally and significantly increase China's industrial position in the global value chain by 2025, and eventually become a leading global technological superpower by

---

136　Dan Prud'homme and Taolue Zhang, *supra* note 4, pp. 5–6.

137　国家中长期科学和技术发展规划纲要 (2006–2020) (The National Medium- and Long-Term Program for Science and Technology Development 2006–2020) (Promulgated by the State Council on 26 December 2005, effective on promulgation).

138　Ibid.

139　These seven industries included energy conservation and environmental protection, data and ICT, biotechnology, advanced equipment manufacturing, new energy, new materials, and new energy vehicles. 国务院关于加快培育和发展战略性新兴产业的决定 (Decision to Accelerate the Development of Strategic Emerging Industries) (Issued by the State Council on 10 October 2010, effective on promulgation).

140　Ibid.

141　关于扩大战略性新兴产业投资培育壮大新增长点增长极的指导意见 (Guiding Opinions on Expanding Investment in Strategic Emerging Industries and Cultivating and Strengthening New Growth Points and Growth Poles) (Issue by NDRC, Ministry of Science & Technology, Ministry of Industry & Information Technology and Ministry of Finance on 8 September 2020, effective on promulgation).

2049.[142] *Made in China 2025* is challenged for 'using unfair business practices and stealing technology in its efforts to become the world's tech superpower'.[143]

5.2.3 *The potential effectiveness and ineffectiveness of the FIL in curbing FTT*

Art. 22 of the FIL stipulates that

> the state encourages technology cooperation on the basis of volunteerism and business rules. The terms of technology cooperation shall be determined based on the principle of fairness and equal consultation. Administrative agencies and their officials shall not force the transfer of technology against foreign investors by administrative means.

When the FIL was promulgated, Art. 22 was considered to be an overhaul that required further elaboration in order to be implemented. Many have hoped that the later promulgated Implementing Regulation would have served that purpose.[144] Art. 24 of the FIL Implementing Regulation stipulates that

> administrative agencies (including organizations authorized to administer public affairs) and their officials shall not force, or behave to an effect of force, the transfer of technology against foreign investors or FIEs by administrative means such as licensing, inspection, penalty, or compulsion.

The FIL Implementing Regulation seems to be essentially a paraphrase of the equivalent article of the FIL, leaving their effectiveness and enforceability an open question. Reading in context, China's new foreign investment law regime provides both progress and limitations in curbing FTT practice.

In terms of effectiveness, the FIL's liberalized market access regime at large reduces the bargaining chip for China to conduct FTT behaviour. First, with the pre-establishment national treatment with a negative list approach in place, FDI approval, namely the case-by-case approval procedures from the Ministry of

---

142 These ten significant industries are data and ICT, numerical control tools and robotics, aeronautics and aerospace equipment, marine engineering equipment and high-tech ships, rail transit equipment, new energy vehicles, electric power equipment, agricultural machinery, new material, and biotechnology and medical equipment. 国务院关于印发《中国制造2025》的通知 (Made in China 2025) (Issued by the State Council on 8 May 2015, effective on promulgation).

143 Max J. Zenglein and Anna Holzmann, *Evolving Made in China 2025: China's Industrial Policy in the Quest for Global Tech Leadership*, Merics Papers on China, No. 8, July 2019, p. 8.

144 Sofia Baliño, 'How Could China's New Foreign Investment Law Impact Trade Debate?' *IISD*, 30 April 2019, https://www.iisd.org/articles/forced-technology-transfers, last accessed on 18 January 2021.

Commerce (MOFCOM), the National Development and Reform Commission (NDRC) and the State Administration for Industry and Commerce (predecessor of SAMR), or their local counterparts, are abolished for investment outside of the *Negative List for Foreign Investment*.[145] This means that in the majority of cases, the government now has significantly less opportunity to use FDI approval as leverage to force or pressure the transfer of technology against foreign investors.

Second, due to the continuous reduction of the *Negative List for Foreign Investment*, mandatory JV requirements have become scarce. The current *2020 Negative List for Foreign Investment* includes only 12 restricted items where a Chinese partner must be present to form a newly established JV. For investment outside of the list, foreign investors are, at least in theory, unrestricted from choosing a corporate form as long as it is pursuant to the *Company Law* or *Partnership Enterprise Law*, without the imposition of a Chinese local partner. Without a JV structure, the channels to practice FTT are substantially reduced.

Third, discriminatory laws and regulations to the detriment of the appropriability of foreign investors' IP rights have been repealed or revised. These include the revision of the *Regulation on the Administration of Import and Export of Technologies* in 2019 that deletes the indemnity terms and the rights in technology improvements terms, and the abolition of the 'three primary foreign investment laws' and their implementing regulations, which incorporated unfair conditions on the transfer of technology from a foreign partner to the joint venture. Be that as it may, certain laws and regulations currently in effect, such as compulsory licencing of SEPs and the essential facilities doctrine in anti-monopoly measures relating to IP, may still leave room to facilitate FTT in enforcement.

Nonetheless, the FIL also leaves much to be desired to effectively curb FTT practice for a number of reasons. First, sectoral review, licencing, qualification and approval procedures envisaged in the *Negative List for Market Access* which covers more than 120 categories (each category includes numerous sub-items) potentially leave some leverage to the sectoral approvers to conduct FTT. Because the *Negative List for Market Access* is essentially a compilation, not a cut-down or a modification of sectoral market access barriers, the danger of FTT practice still persists. For example, sectoral regulators can still pressure a foreign investor to transfer or licence their patents to a third party, or to disclose unreasonable amounts of technological information during the approval procedure, using their market access approving power as a negotiating leverage.

Second, China's expanded national security review regime may become a new avenue for abuse in facilitating FTT. Now that a national security review may be imposed on 'any foreign investment affecting or may affect national security'[146] across a broad range of sectors with far-reaching implications,[147] there is a

---

145 For a detailed discussion on market access of foreign investment, see Chapter 2.
146 FIL (2019), Art. 35.
147 Sectors subject to review include national defence, important agricultural product, important energy and resources, important equipment manufacturing, important infrastructure,

concern 'that the review mechanism has at least the potential to be (ab)used to "force" technology transfer in the name of national security'.[148] For instance, the NDRC and MOFCOM, China's national security review agencies, may require or imply the transfer of technology from a foreign acquirer to a Chinese target company in exchange for clearance of the national security review in the event of a foreign takeover of a Chinese company. For the aforementioned two reasons, some have speculated the real efficacy of the FTT provision (Art. 22) in the FIL and questioned its lack of a robust enforcement mechanism.[149]

5.3 Protection of commercial secrets

Commercial secrets are trade secrets, know-how, sensitive and confidential technological information, and other commercial business information, 'including a formula, pattern, compilation, program, device, method, technique, or process' that 'confer a competitive advantage and value to its holder by virtue of its secrecy'.[150] Unlike patents, trademarks and copyrights that require governmental imprimatur and also full disclosure to the public in order to obtain legal protection, the core value of commercial secrets is their secrecy.[151] Commercial secrets therefore are either those that are not eligible for protection as a patent, a trademark or copyright, or those that are susceptible to reverse engineering if protected as a registered patent and publicly disclosed, for instance, secret formulae like the formula of Coca-Cola.

The Chinese government has been strongly accused of obtaining foreign investors' commercial secrets and sensitive information, mostly by the US government. According to the USTR 301 Investigation, China allegedly commits theft of sensitive commercial information in two principal ways: forced disclosure of sensitive technical information to Chinese administrative agencies; and

---

important transportation, important cultural product and service, important ICT product and service, important financial service, key technologies, and other important areas. 外商投资安全审查办法 (Measures for the Security Review of Foreign Investment) (Promulgated by NDRC and MOFCOM on 19 December 2020, effective on 18 January 2021). For a detailed discussion of China's national security review, see Chapter 4.

148 Weihuan Zhou, Huiqin Jiang and Qingjiang Kong, 'Technology Transfer under China's Foreign Investment Regime: Does the WTO Provide a Solution?' *Journal of World Trade*, Vol. 54 Issue 3 (2020), pp. 455–480, at 476.

149 For example, Lee opines that the FTT provision in the FIL only pays lip service and is 'ceremonial window-dressing'. Jyh-An Lee, *supra* note 95, at 170. Lee also described it as a declaratory exhibition of China's pronounced position against FTT. Jyh-An Lee, *supra* note 98, at 349. Qin described it as 'a gesture of compromise' to the US–China tension. Julia Ya Qin, *supra* note 103, at 750.

150 Tom C. W. Lin, 'Executive Trade Secrets', *Notre Dame Law Review*, Vol. 87 Issue 3 (2012), pp. 911–972, at 940.

151 Ibid, at 942.

intrusions, cyberattacks and economic espionage into foreign commercial computer networks.[152]

The first allegation is described as a requirement of disclosure of sensitive technical information in great detail and beyond reasonable and necessary amounts, such as formulae, designs, models, databases, source codes, and operation costs and revenues, by the central and local governments, in exchange for administrative approval to enter the Chinese market and also to do business in China post-establishment, including (but not limited to) sectoral market access, construction permits, environmental assessment, licence to sell certain products such as pharmaceuticals, or qualifications to provide certain services such as financial services.[153] The Chinese government and its officials who obtain these commercial secrets and sensitive information then allegedly leak the information to other government bodies, local domestic industries, or Chinese academia, in order to develop similar products or services which eventually benefit the competitive advantage of Chinese companies.[154]

The second allegation concerns acts by, or with support from, the Chinese government, the People's Liberation Army and Chinese SOEs to conduct cyber intrusions such as hacking into foreign networks in an attempt to gain unauthorized access to, and steal, foreign companies' confidential and commercially valuable information.[155] It is alleged that China mobilises 'an army' of computer hackers domestically, spies overseas and insiders in US companies, and poaches US scientists, engineers and corporate executives to conduct theft of US technology and commercial secrets.[156]

The FIL only addresses the first allegation. Art. 23 of FIL stipulates that

> administrative agencies and their officials shall keep the information confidential, regarding commercial secrets of foreign investors and FIEs which they have obtained in performing their duties, and shall neither divulge nor illegally provide others with such information.

In the same vein, Art. 25 of the FIL Implementing Regulation provides that

> where an administrative agency requires a foreign investor or an FIE to provide any materials and information relating to commercial secrets, they shall be limited to the necessary extent for the administrative matter, the personnel of knowledge shall be strictly controlled, and irrelevant personnel shall not gain access to those materials and information.

---

152 USTR, *supra* note 101.
153 Ibid, at 41–43.
154 Ibid, at 41–43.
155 Ibid, at 153–154.
156 Mo Zhang, 'Change of Regulatory Scheme: China's New Foreign Investment Law and Reshaped Legal Landscape', *Pacific Basin Law Journal*, Vol. 37 Issue 1 (2020), pp. 179–238, at 217.

Art. 25 further demands administrative agencies to establish and improve their internal management system and take effective measures to protect foreign investors' commercial secrets from leakage.

Violations of the obligation of confidentiality will result in legal liabilities for government officials, as provided in Art. 39 of the FIL:

> When administrative officials abuse powers, neglect duties, engage misconduct for personal gains or divulge or illegally disclose commercial secret to others, sanctions shall be imposed according to law. They shall also be held criminally liable according to law if applicable.

While recognizing the positive aspect of strengthened liability in legislation, the effectiveness of Art. 39 is brought to question. The exact severity of legal liabilities of administrative officials in violating the duty of confidentiality is not defined by the FIL, leading to a speculation that punishment can be rather lenient such as a mere warning.[157] The FIL only imposes sanctions on government officials, which means the theft of commercial secrets conducted by non-administrative bodies in forms other than administrative approval is not deterred.[158] Further, the FIL may provide the convenience for the Chinese government to argue that acts of theft of commercial secrets has now indeed been prohibited in codified legislature, but it is only to be used as a rebuttal to counter any future allegations on China's theft of commercial secrets.[159]

In addition to the FIL, commercial secrets are protected in China's *Anti-Unfair Competition Law*, which defines, forbids and imposes civil liabilities on acts of infringement of commercial secrets between private individuals and entities.[160] In addition, the *Administrative Licensing Law* prohibits the administrative officials from divulging commercial secrets in the process of administrative licencing, and imposes administrative penalties on government officials who violate the obligation of confidentiality.[161] The *Criminal Code* criminalises severe acts of infringement of commercial secrets conducted by individuals, entities and state functionaries.[162]

---

157 Jyh-An Lee, *supra* note 95, at 169–170. Jyh-An Lee, *supra* note 98, at 351.

158 Mo Zhang, *supra* note 156, at 217–218.

159 Jyh-An Lee, *supra* note 95, at 169–170. Jyh-An Lee, *supra* note 98, at 352.

160 中华人民共和国反不正当竞争法 (Anti-Unfair Competition Law) (Promulgated by the NPC on 2 September 1993, last revised on 23 April 2019, effective on revision), Arts. 9, 17 and 21. For a detailed discussion, see Li Chen and Qianqian Yu, 'The Not-So-Secret Secret to Trade Secret Protection in China', *Journal of Intellectual Property Law & Practice* Vol. 14 No. 6 (2019), pp. 445–453.

161 行政许可法 (Administrative Licensing Law) (Promulgated by the NPC on 27 August 2003, last revised on 23 April 2019, effective on revision), Arts. 5 and 72. For a detailed discussion, see Jyh-An Lee, *supra* note 98, at 337–339.

162 中华人民共和国刑法 (Criminal Code) (Promulgated by the NPC on 6 July 1979, last revised on 26 December 2020, effective on 1 March 2021), Art. 219.

5.4 Conclusion

The FIL allocates three designated provisions to the protection of IP rights of foreign investors and FIEs (Art. 22), prohibition of FTT practice (Art. 22), prohibition on divulgation of commercial secrets (Art. 23), and legal liability for the divulgation of commercial secrets (Art. 39). This can be deemed an attentive and laudable attempt at addressing IP issues in relation to foreign investors, especially considering that the whole FIL only includes 42 articles. However, despite the best legislative intentions, the efficacy of these provisions, as discussed in this chapter, has been treated with scepticism, primarily due to concerns over their potential non-enforcement or insufficient enforcement in practice. In protecting the IP rights of foreign investors, certain foreign complaints, such as trademark squatting, counterfeiting and piracy, lax administrative enforcement, and the gradually improving but still questioned judicial fairness and independence, cannot possibly be addressed by a foreign investment law, but can only be resolved by a continuous effort to reform China's IP law and enforcement at large. For the matter of FTT, the FIL still leaves room for improvement that could better mitigate foreign investors' concerns, especially in the implementation process of the *Negative List for Market Access* and the national security review. For the protection of commercial secrets, the detailed liability of government functionaries in the event of a breach of confidentiality is not provided in the FIL, which may undermine its enforceability and effectiveness. In sum, the FIL is likely to play only a limited role in protecting foreign investors' IP rights.

6 Dispute settlement: Foreign-related arbitration

6.1 The dynamics of law on foreign-related arbitration

Legal grounds for arbitration involving parties with foreign elements are mainly reflected in the *Civil Procedure Law* (CPL), the *Arbitration Law* (AL), the judicial interpretations and opinions of the Supreme People's Court (SPC), and arbitration rules of various arbitration commissions. The special provisions provided in these legal instruments with regard to dispute settlement involving foreign elements result in foreign-related arbitration cases being treated to some extent differently from domestic cases. Generally speaking, more international standards are applied to foreign-related arbitration, though the trend is to integrate the two progressively.

The term 'foreign-related civil cases', which includes foreign-related commercial cases, is used to distinguish them from domestic civil cases. A case is foreign-related when it meets one of the following criteria:[1]

(1) One or two parties are foreigners, stateless persons or foreign legal persons.
(2) The habitual residence of one or two parties is outside of China.
(3) The subject matter of the dispute is located in foreign territories.
(4) The establishment, modification or termination of the legal relationship occurs in foreign territories.
(5) Other conditions that can be recognized as foreign related.

The current effective CPL, modified in 2017, contains a chapter with five articles on foreign-related arbitration. Art. 271 provides that in case of a dispute arising from foreign trade, transportation and maritime activities, where the parties concerned have included an arbitration clause in the contract or have reached a written arbitration agreement subsequently for submitting the dispute to an arbitration institution, the parties concerned shall not file a lawsuit to a court.

---

1 最高人民法院关于适用《中华人民共和国民事诉讼法》的解释 (Interpretation of the SPC on the Application of the Civil Procedure Law of the PRC) (First issued on 30 January 2015, last revised on 29 December 2020, effective on 1 January 2021), Art. 522. It should be noted that cases involving Hong Kong, Macao and Taiwan belong to the foreign-related category.

DOI: 10.4324/9781003168805-7

This Article coincides with Art. II (3) of the Convention on the Recognition and Enforcement of Foreign Arbitral Awards (New York Convention). The CPL also stipulates general provisions concerning application for preservation in the arbitration process (Art. 272), enforcement of arbitral awards (Art. 273), standards for refusal to enforce arbitral awards (Art. 274), and the possibility of starting a new arbitration or bringing a lawsuit to a court if a court has given a decision of non-enforcement of an arbitral award (Art. 275).

The first *Arbitration Law of China* was promulgated in 1994 and became effective in 1995. It was amended twice, in 2009 and 2017; however, only minor changes were made for purposes of referring to the number of articles in the CPL and with regard to the qualifications of an arbitrator. Thus, the current effective AL remains essentially the one promulgated in 1994, which contains a total of 80 articles, of which 9 are 'special provisions for arbitration involving foreign elements'.[2] When the AL was enacted the main purpose was to separate arbitration commissions from the government departments. Prior to the 1994 AL, domestic arbitration was a sort of administrative arbitration managed by relevant governmental departments at the central and local levels in which parties had no choice of a particular arbitration institution or arbitrator, arbitrators were governmental officials, and arbitral awards were not binding.[3] The limited number of foreign-related arbitration cases were solely managed by the China International Economic and Trade Arbitration Commission (CIETAC), which used its own personnel as arbitrators, had presiding arbitrators who often lacked legal expertise and practical experience, did not disclose conflicts of interest, did not apply confidentiality to proceedings, and failed to take measures to prevent arbitrators from *ex parte* contacts.[4]

Against such a background, the 1994 AL can be viewed as a significant step toward modernizing the arbitration system in China. Despite some distinctions

---

2 中华人民共和国仲裁法 (The Arbitration Law) (Promulgated by the Standing Committee of the NPC on 1 September 2017, effective on 1 January 2018), Arts. 65–73. For a comprehensive understanding of the arbitration system in China, see Jingzhou Tao, *Arbitration Law and Practice in China*, 3rd edn. (Alphen aan den Rijn: Kluwer Law International, 2012). Weixia Gu, *Arbitration in China: Regulation of Arbitration Agreements and Practical Issues* (Hong Kong: Sweet & Maxwell, 2012). For foreign-related arbitration in China, see Fan Yang, *Foreign-Related Arbitration in China: Commentary and Cases* (Cambridge: CUP, 2016). Qiao Liu, Wenhua Shan and Ren Xiang (eds.), *China and International Commercial Dispute Resolution* (Leiden: Brill, 2016). For a practical approach on using arbitration and litigation to settle foreign-related disputes in China, see Michael J. Moser (ed.), *Managing Business Disputes in Today's China: Duelling with Dragons* (Alphen aan den Rijn: Kluwer Law International, 2007). Dejun Cheng, Michael J. Moser and Shengchang Wang, *International Arbitration in the People's Republic of China: Commentary, Cases and Materials* (Hong Kong: Butterworths Asia, 2000).

3 Weixia Gu, *supra* note 2, p. 26.

4 Jerome A. Cohen, 'Time to Fix China's Arbitration', *Far Eastern Economic Review* (January 2005), pp. 31–37, at 31. See also Russel Thirgood, 'A Critique of Foreign Arbitration in China', *Journal of International Arbitration*, Vol. 17 Issue 3 (2000), pp. 89–101. Charles Kenworthey Harer, 'Arbitration Fails to Reduce Foreign Investors' Risk in China', *Pacific Rim Law & Policy Journal*, Vol. 8 Issue 2 (1999), pp. 393–422, at 402–420.

such as *ad hoc* arbitration and judicial review, the structure of the AL reflects the United Nations Commission on International Trade Law (UNCITRAL) Model Law on International Commercial Arbitration. Apart from general provisions and supplementary provisions, the AL provides for the rules on the establishment of an arbitration commission and the qualification of arbitrators; the components and validity of an arbitration agreement; arbitration proceedings; and enforcement of arbitral awards. The basic principles of international arbitration are also embedded in the AL, such as the principle of party autonomy (Arts. 4, 6), the principle of conducting arbitration independently (Arts. 8, 14), the principle of fairness and reasonableness (Art. 7), and the principle of finality of arbitral award (Arts. 9, 57, 62). Moreover, the AL contains a specific chapter on foreign-related arbitration. However, since 1994 the rapid development of arbitration practice has rendered the AL outdated and flawed.[5] After years of appealing for substantial amendment of the AL, on 30 July 2021, the Ministry of Justice published the revised AL (draft) for public consultation.[6]

Meanwhile, CIETAC and leading local arbitration commissions (LACs) have taken innovative measures to actively engage in foreign-related arbitration, which have brought striking transformation in the landscape of arbitration in China. This is particularly evidenced in the past decade, resulting from the central government policy to promote the usage of arbitration to settle cross-border commercial disputes as a part of its Belt and Road strategy. In December 2018, the General Office of the State Council issued *Several Opinions on Improving the Arbitration System to Strengthen the Credibility of Arbitration.*[7] The Opinions call for enhanced international competitiveness of the arbitration commissions and to enable those with a sound and strong professional capacity to gradually develop into regional or international arbitration brands with high credibility and competitiveness. Moreover, the Opinions emphasise to strengthen international exchange and cooperation and promote Chinese arbitration commissions to 'go out' and 'invite in' foreign arbitration institutions to arbitrate in China.

---

5 For an updated and critical analysis on the Chinese characteristics of the arbitration system, including the foreign-related arbitration, see Weixia Gu, 'Piercing the Veil of Arbitration Reform in China: Promises, Pitfalls, Patterns, Prognoses, and Prospects', *The American Journal of Comparative Law*, Vol. 65 Issue 4 (2017), pp. 799–840.

6 Ministry of Justice, 'Remarks on the Revised Arbitration Law (Draft)', with explanatory notes and the proposed revisions, http://www.moj.gov.cn/pub/sfbgw/zlk/202107/t20210730 _432965.html, last accessed on 5 August 2021. 中华人民共和国仲裁法 (修订) (征求意见稿) (Arbitration Law Amendment – Draft for Comments) (Published by the Ministry of Justice on 30 July 2021), http://www.moj.gov.cn/pub/sfbgw/zlk/202107/t20210730_432958 .html, last accessed on 15 August 2021. The revised AL (draft) contains 99 articles, compared to 80 articles in the 1994 AL. Foreign-related arbitration is specified in Chapter VII with six articles (88 to 93).

7 关于完善仲裁制度提高仲裁公信力的若干意见 (Several Opinions on Improving the Arbitration System to Strengthen the Credibility of Arbitration) (Issued by the General Office of the State Council and General Office of the CPC Central Committee on 31 December 2018, effective on promulgation).

Another key actor in arbitration is the Chinese courts, which play two important roles. One is issuing orders on interim measures of protection to facilitate arbitration proceedings; the other concerns a judicial review of the validity of arbitration agreements and enforcement of arbitral awards. Within the judicial hierarchy, the SPC's leading position in arbitration reflects its binary roles as rule-maker for arbitration-related judicial practice as well as the final decision-maker in judicial review of arbitral awards. As the rule-maker, the SPC has issued the judicial interpretation of the *Arbitration Law* in 2005, and a series of judicial interpretations and notices to guide local courts in conducting judicial review and to fill in the gaps of the AL. In June 2016, the SPC issued *Opinions on Further Deepening the Reform of the Diversified Dispute Settlement Mechanism* which called for strengthening the connection with arbitration institutions and actively supporting the reform of the arbitration system.[8] Based on the CPL, the AL, and taking into account practical problems which have not been clearly addressed in the laws, the SPC issued four documents concerning arbitration judicial review in 2017 and 2018, which consolidated judicial experiences, set forth standards more in alignment with international norms and practice, aiming to create an arbitration-friendly judicial environment, which is politically called for in the context of the Belt and Road Initiative.

6.2 Internationalization of arbitration institutions

CIETAC is the oldest and biggest arbitration institution to arbitrate foreign-related commercial disputes. Its predecessor was called the Foreign Trade Arbitration Commission, which was established in 1956 by the China Council for the Promotion of International Trade. Originally, CIETAC was the only institution designed to admit foreign-related arbitration cases, and it has set up a number of sub-commissions in Shanghai, Shenzhen, Tianjin, Chongqing, Hangzhou, Wuhan, Fuzhou and Hong Kong. So far, CIETAC has maintained the highest foreign-related arbitration caseload.

CIETAC's exclusive competence to deal with foreign-related arbitration cases was terminated in 1996 when the State Council's Notice provided that local arbitration commissions could also admit foreign-related cases if parties voluntarily select them.[9] Responding to this, since 1998 CIETAC has extended its jurisdic-

---

8 最高人民法院关于适用《中华人民共和国仲裁法》若干问题的解释 (Interpretation on Certain Issues Relating to the Application of the Arbitration Law of the PRC) (Issued by the Judicial Committee of the SPC on 23 August 2006, effective on 8 September 2006). 关于人民法院进一步深化多元化纠纷解决机制改革的意见 (Opinions on Further Deepening the Reform of the Diversified Dispute Settlement Mechanism in the People's Courts) (Issued by the SPC on 28 June 2016, effective on promulgation).

9 国务院办公厅关于贯彻实施《中华人民共和国仲裁法》需要明确的几个问题的通知 (Notice on the Clarification of Several Issues Concerning the Implementation of the Arbitration Law) (Issued by the General Office of the State Council on 8 June 1996, effective on promulgation), Art. 3.

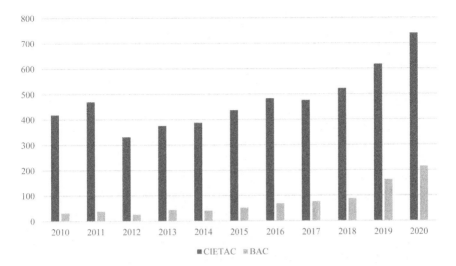

Figure 6.1 Annual foreign-related commercial arbitration cases accepted by CIETAC and BAC (2010–2020) (Figure made by authors. Source: CIETAC, '贸仲委受案总量（涉外、国内）' (CIETAC Caseload, Domestic and Foreign-Related), http://www.cietac.org/index.php?m=Page&a=index &id=24; and BAC, '工作总结2020-2010' (Work Summary 2020-2010), https://www.bjac.org.cn/page/gybh/introduce_report.html, last accessed on 7 June 2021.)

tion to also admit domestic arbitration cases. Consequently, CIETAC and LACs have the same jurisdiction.

At present there are approximately 250 LACs, which are generally named after the administrative area in which they are registered, though their jurisdiction is not confined to their administrative location; instead they can arbitrate domestic and foreign-related cases regardless of the location of the dispute or parties. However, only a few LACs have gained a certain reputation and are used by foreign and domestic companies to settle foreign-related disputes. These include the Beijing Arbitration Commission[10] (BAC is also called the Beijing International Arbitration Center), Shenzhen Court of International Arbitration (SCIA) and Shanghai International Arbitration Center (SHIAC). Over the past two decades, they have gained a substantial reputation as the most progressive LACs in China.

The statistics show a fast-growing number of foreign-related arbitration cases accepted by Chinese arbitration commissions: in 2014 the total number was

10 The BAC has gained growing international recognition even though it was only established in 1995, see Fuyong Chen, 'Striving for Independence, Competence, and Fairness: A Case Study of the Beijing Arbitration Commission', *American Review of International Arbitration*, Vol. 18 No. 3 (2007), pp. 313–352.

1,785, raised to 2,085 in 2015, increased to 3,141 in 2016 and to 3,188 in 2017.[11] These demonstrate the growing popularity of resorting to arbitration to settle foreign-related disputes. In the recent decade, CIETAC and these LACs have accelerated their steps to ascend in worldwide-known arbitration institutions. Their internationalization endeavours can be observed in several ways.

First, they have frequently amended their rules of arbitration by swiftly adopting the most advanced international practices. Taking the BAC as an example, since its first Arbitration Rules were issued in 1995, the Rules have been updated eight times. The newest version was issued in 2019.[12] BAC pioneered the arbitration fee reform in China. In its 2015 Arbitration Rules, it introduced a new arbitration fee system for foreign-related arbitration by separating the fees to the arbitration commission from the fees to the arbitrators. This fundamentally changed the common practice in China that arbitration fees were paid to the arbitration commission, which subsequently decided what portion would be given to the arbitrators. Generally speaking, the fees to the arbitrators are relatively low; this has been criticized as one of the reasons that arbitration services are of relatively low quality as they cannot attract highly qualified professionals to act as arbitrators, or even if they do, these arbitrators will not spend sufficient time and effort when the payment is disproportionate to what they have to do. The BAC's new system enables parties to choose to pay high fees to well-known international arbitrators to arbitrate their cases for the sake of the high quality they pursue. In the BAC's 2019 Arbitration Rules, this system was expanded to cover domestic arbitration as well. Moreover, it introduces hourly fees for arbitrators to be agreed by parties and arbitrators, which is in line with international practice. With respect to the autonomy of parties involved, the fee schedule of the BAC also imposes a cap on an hourly rate of not exceeding 5,000 Renminbi (RMB) in principle.[13] In addition, Chapter VIII of the BAC's 2019 Arbitration Rules stipulates special provisions for international commercial arbitration, which cover interim measures, emergency arbitrators, defence and counterclaims, mediation by the tribunal, and time limits for rendering the award. With regard to the emergency arbitrator procedure, it can be noted that the 1994 AL does not offer such a system. In 2017, the BAC administered the first case in mainland China on interim measures made by the emergency arbitrator, which was successfully enforced in Hong Kong.[14] Art. 63 of the 2019 BAC Arbitration Rules clarifies the emergency arbitrator procedure, and Annex II provides fees

11 The numbers are obtained from CIETAC, 中国国际商事仲裁年度报告 (China International Commercial Arbitration Annual Reports 2014–2017), http://www.cietac.org/index.php?m=Article&a=index&id=251, last accessed on 7 June 2021.
12 For the English version, see BAC, Arbitration Rules (2019), https://www.bjac.org.cn/english/page/data_dl/zcgz_en_2019.pdf, last accessed on 7 July 2021.
13 BAC Arbitration Rules (2019), Annex I, 6(4).
14 Helen Tang and Briana Young, 'First Emergency Arbitration Procedure in China', *Herbert Smith Freehills*, 19 October 2018, https://hsfnotes.com/arbitration/2018/10/19/first-emergency-arbitration-procedure-in-china/, last accessed on 7 July 2021.

involved for the emergency arbitrator. As to the efficiency of the proceedings, Art. 59 of the 2019 BAC Arbitration Rules provides that in the case of an expedited procedure, an arbitral tribunal should render its award within 75 days from the date of its constitution. Under specific circumstances, an extended time limit can be approved by the Secretary-General upon the request of a sole arbitrator. Compared to the 2021 UNCITRAL Expedited Arbitration Rules, the time limit to render an award is set for within six months, and under exceptional circumstances an extension is limited to nine months.[15]

Second, internationalization also reflects on expanding the jurisdiction of arbitration commissions. In 2016, the Shenzhen Court of International Arbitration was the first one to expand its jurisdiction to administer investor–state arbitration in its Arbitration Rules. In managing investor–state arbitration (ISA) cases, the SCIA applies the UNCITRAL Arbitration Rules and the SCIA Guidelines for the Administration of Arbitration under the UNCITRAL Arbitration Rules.[16] An innovative provision in the Guidelines provides, in case parties have not agreed on the place of arbitration, that Hong Kong should be the place, unless otherwise determined by the arbitral tribunal.[17] In 2017, CIETAC issued its International Investment Arbitration Rules (For Trial Implementation),[18] which contain 58 articles and 2 appendixes. This is the first set of specific rules on investor–state arbitration issued by an arbitration commission in China. Following CIETAC, in 2019 the BAC issued its Rules for International Investment Arbitration, which contain 54 articles and 4 appendixes.[19] These investment arbitration rules demonstrate Chinese arbitration institutions' ambitions to ascend in the ISA market. Nevertheless, it should be noted that under the current AL, some fundamental legal obstructions cast doubts on the legal ground of these expanded jurisdictions and their practicability. Art. 2 of the AL set forth the scope of arbitration to settle contractual disputes and other property disputes between 'equal subjects' of citizens, legal persons and other organizations. Art. 65 of the AL defines foreign-related arbitration to settle disputes occurring from economic, trade, transportation and maritime activities involving foreign element. A foreign investor and a state in an ISA case cannot be reasonably deemed as 'equal sub-

---

15 Art. 16 of UNCITRAL Expedited Arbitration Rules, https://uncitral.un.org/sites/uncitral .un.org/files/media-documents/uncitral/en/acn9-1082-e.pdf, last accessed on 21 July 2021.

16 SCIA, Arbitration Rules (2016), http://www.scia.com.cn/index.php/Home/index/rule/ id/798.html, last accessed on 7 July 2021, Arts. 2(2) and 3(5),

17 SCIA, Guidelines for the Administration of Arbitration under the UNCITRAL Arbitration Rules (2019), http://www.scia.com.cn/files/fckFile/file/SCIA%20Guidelines %20for%20the%20Administration%20of%20Arbitration%20under%20the%20UNCITRAL %20Arbitration%20Rules.pdf, last accessed on 7 July 2021, Art. 3.

18 CIETAC, International Investment Arbitration Rules (For Trial Implementation) (2017), http://www.cietac.org/index.php?m=Page&a=index&id=390&l=en, last accessed on 7 July 2021.

19 BAC, Rules for International Investment Arbitration (2019), https://www.bjac.org.cn/ page/data_dl/2019%E6%8A%95%E8%B5%84%E4%BB%B2%E8%A3%81%E8%A7%84%E5 %88%990905%20%E8%8B%B1%E6%96%87.pdf, last accessed on 7 July 2021.

jects' under Art. 2 or Art. 65, which obviously does not imply a state as one party to the dispute. Moreover, when China acceded to the New York Convention in 1987, the Chinese government made an explicit commercial reservation and reciprocity reservation according to Art. 1 of the Convention.[20] In the SPC's *Notice on Implementing the Convention on the Recognition and Enforcement of Foreign Arbitral Awards Acceded to by China*, it also distinctly states that 'the dispute between foreign investor and the host government' is not deemed to be a 'commercial legal relationship'.[21] If an ISA award was rendered by a Chinese arbitration institution, parties may invoke Art. 58 or Art. 70 of the AL to apply for setting aside the award. A straightforward solution is to remove the legislative restriction from the AL. In the revised AL (draft) the words 'equal subjects' were deleted, which is deemed to leave space for investment arbitration and sport arbitration to be handled by arbitration commissions.[22]

Third, a few Chinese arbitration commissions have strengthened their 'going-out' actions to extend international impact. For instance, in 2018 CIETAC opened its North American arbitration centre in Vancouver, Canada and its European arbitration centre in Vienna, Austria.[23] CIETAC's initiative was echoed as a way of learning from international experience in order to advance its own internationalization process, apart from facilitating foreign legal professionals to become familiar with Chinese arbitration practice.[24] In 2018, SCIA and ICSID signed a cooperation agreement which grants the two parties to provide each other with court hearings and supporting facilities. The services of ICSID will be 'landed' in Qianhai.[25] In November 2019, CIETAC, together with eight world-known

20 United Nations, 'Treaty Collection, Convention on the Recognition and Enforcement of Foreign Arbitral Awards, Declarations and Reservations, China', https://treaties.un.org/Pages/ViewDetails.aspx?src=TREATY&mtdsg_no=XXII-1&chapter=22&clang=_en#End-Dec, last accessed on 7 July 2021.

21 最高人民法院关于执行我国加入的《承认及执行外国仲裁裁决公约》的通知 (Notice on Implementing the Convention on the Recognition and Enforcement of Foreign Arbitral Awards in China) (Issued by the SPC on 10 April 1987, effective on promulgation). An English text can be obtained from https://www.newyorkconvention.org/webcore/search?search=china+reservation, last accessed on 7 July 2021.

22 Arbitration Law Amendment – Draft for Comments (2021).

23 Brad Wang and Gloria Ho, 'CIETAC's Fresh Footprint in Norther America: Drawing on Experiences of its Hong Kong Counterpart', *Kluwer Arbitration Blog*, 28 September 2018, http://arbitrationblog.kluwerarbitration.com/2018/09/28/cietacs-fresh-footprint-in-north-america-drawing-on-experiences-of-its-hong-kong-counterpart/, last accessed on 7 July 2021. Adolf Peter, 'The CIETAC European Arbitration Centre – Some Legal Implications of a Vienna-Seated CIETAC Arbitration', *The Singapore Institute of Arbitrators*, https://siarb.org.sg/resources/120-articles/373-the-cietac-european-arbitration-centre-some-legal-implications-of-a-vienna-seated-cietac-arbitration, last accessed on 7 July 2021.

24 Brad Wang and Gloria Ho, *supra* note 23.

25 SCIA, '媒体报道——中国特区国际仲裁的国际影响力进一步提升' (Media Reports – The International Influence of China's Special Economic Zone Has Further Increased), 4 July 2018, http://xn--1nqrdo0mbbz1h9yhp9fsu3a71ojj5bj4w22lsu2a.com/home/index/newsdetail/id/2660.html, last accessed on 20 August 2021.

arbitration institutions, issued the Beijing Joint Declaration, aiming to use inter-national arbitration to serve the Belt and Road Initiative and to build a high-end cooperation platform.[26] In 2019, SCIA and the Hong Kong International Arbitration Centre (HKIAC) signed the Closer Cooperation Agreement aiming to enhance arbitration cooperation between Shenzhen and Hong Kong in the context of 'One Country, Two Systems, Three Jurisdictions', as well as for the Asia-Pacific region.[27] SCIA has also instituted the first 'SCIA Arbitration Hearing Centre' in Los Angeles, the United States.[28] In addition, the Chinese Africa Joint Arbitration Centres have been co-established by the BAC, SCIA and SHIAC with African arbitration institutions in South Africa and Nairobi.[29]

The internationalization efforts of China's arbitration commissions mainly serve two purposes. One is that Chinese arbitration commissions can participate in arbitration abroad when Chinese business is involved. The other is to strive to bring arbitration cases involving Chinese parties to be arbitrated inside of China. To have more cases arbitrated within China, or abroad with the participa-tion of a Chinese arbitration commission, seems equally significant for expand-ing China's impact. Lin Zhiwei, the secretary-general of the BAC, once pointed out that it is their mission to let Chinese arbitration reach out to the world. 'Going out' and 'inviting in' serve the same purpose of allowing more interna-tional arbitration involving Chinese parties to be arbitrated by Chinese arbitra-tion commissions, or at least with their participation, aiming to strengthen the 'home advantage' and to maximally reduce risk.[30] In China, there is a 'three 90%' saying: in China's foreign trade about 90% selected arbitration to settle commercial disputes, 90% of them chose foreign arbitration institutions, and 90% of arbitration cases ended with Chinese parties losing the cases.[31] Chinese arbitration commissions' internationalization endeavours aspire to change such records. According to the 2021 International Arbitration Survey by Queen Mary University of London, Beijing ranks sixth (the same as New York) and Shanghai ranks seventh among the most preferred seats, after London, Singapore, Hong

---

26 '"一带一路"仲裁机构高端圆桌论坛在京成功举行' ('Belt and Road' Arbitration Institutions High-End Roundtable Successfully Held in Beijing), *China-Arbitration*, 11 November 2019, http://www.china-arbitration.com/index/news/detail/id/2123.html, last accessed on 8 July 2021.

27 SCIA, 'SCIA and HKIAC Strengthen Cooperation', 12 July 2019, http://xn--1nq09h1a7994c .com/home/index/newsdetail/id/2779.html, last accessed on 8 July 2021.

28 SCIA, 'About SCIA, Introduction', http://www.scia.com.cn/en/index/aboutdetail/id /15.html, last accessed on 8 July 2021.

29 'Chinese Africa Joint Arbitration Center: A Solution to Trade Disputes between Africa and China', *The Arbitration Brief*, 11 February 2019, https://thearbitrationbrief.com/2019 /02/11/chinese-africa-joint-arbitration-center-a-solution-to-trade-disputes-between-africa -and-china%EF%BB%BF/, last accessed on 8 July 2021.

30 Ruihua Wang, '林志炜：北仲，树立中国仲裁的世界形象' (Lin Zhiwei: BAC, Establishing A Global Image of Chinese Arbitration), *BAC*, 29 July 2014, http://test.bjac.org.cn/news /view.asp?id=2461&title=&cataid=1, last accessed on 8 July 2021.

31 Ibid.

Kong, Paris, and Geneva, and before Stockholm and Dubai. In 2021, CIETAC was also for the first time among the top-five most preferred institutions, after the International Chamber of Commerce (ICC), Singapore International Arbitration Centre (SIAC), HKIAC and London Court of International Arbitration.[32] These figures and developments show that the internationalization of these Chinese arbitration commissions has achieved some initial success and that international recognition and trust of Chinese arbitration institutions are growing.

6.3 Ambiguity and trend on foreign arbitration institutions in China

The 1994 AL does not contain any explicit provision concerning providing arbitration service by foreign arbitration institutions in China. Art. 16 of the AL states that a valid arbitration agreement must meet three components: an expression of intention to apply for arbitration, matters for arbitration and a designated arbitration commission. When the AL was issued in 1994, the meaning of 'a designated arbitration commission' was not deemed to include a foreign arbitration institution. However, in foreign-related contracts a defective arbitration clause can occur, such as applying ICC Arbitration Rules and arbitrating in a city in China. In such case at least three basic questions can be raised: first, whether such arbitration clause is valid; second, whether an arbitral award administered by foreign arbitration institutions can be recognized and enforced in China; and third, whether such an award should be regarded as a foreign arbitral award or foreign-related arbitral award in China, as different laws will apply to their enforcement. Chinese courts have shown an inconsistent stance and delivered contradictory rulings on these issues, especially before and after 2013.[33]

6.3.1 Cases rejecting adjudication by international arbitration institutions in China

Case 1: Zublin (旭普林案)

This case concerns the German company Zublin International GmbH (Zublin)'s application for recognition and enforcement of the arbitral award.[34] In the

---

32 Queen Mary University of London, *2021 International Arbitration Survey: Adapting Arbitration to a Changing World*, http://www.arbitration.qmul.ac.uk/media/arbitration/docs/LON0320037-QMUL-International-Arbitration-Survey-2021_19_WEB.pdf, last accessed on 8 July 2021, pp. 8, 11.

33 For the controversies caused by the 1994 AL concerning the stand of foreign arbitration institutions administrating arbitration seated in China, see Fan Kun, 'Prospects of Foreign Arbitration Institutions Administrating Arbitration in China', *Journal of International Arbitration*, Vol. 28 Issue 4 (2011), pp. 343–353.

34 德国旭普林国际有限责任公司申请承认和执行国外仲裁裁决案　(2004)锡民三仲字第1号 (Application for Recognition and Enforcement of Foreign Arbitral Awards in the Case of

construction contract between Zublin and Wuxi Woke General Engineering Rubber Co., Ltd. in 2000, the arbitration clause states 'ICC Rules, Shanghai shall apply'. The arbitration took place in Shanghai and the ICC International Court of Arbitration issued the arbitral award in 2004, which requested Woke to pay Zublin a considerable amount. Zublin applied to the Wuxi Intermediate People's Court (IPC) to enforce the award and the IPC accepted the case as a matter of recognition and enforcement of a foreign arbitral award. In 2006, the IPC rejected the application for enforcement of the award. The IPC took the view that the central question of the case was to confirm the nationality of the award and the applicable law. Under Chinese CPL, a foreign arbitral award refers to the award rendered by a foreign arbitration institution; the seat of the arbitration institution is used to determine whether an award is domestic or foreign. As the award of the Zublin case was rendered by the ICC Tribunal, it was a 'non-domestic' award under the New York Convention. The IPC refused to recognize and enforce the award because the arbitration clause in the construction contract between the parties had been ruled to be invalid by an earlier decision of a Chinese court on the grounds that the clause did not designate a specific arbitration commission.

Case 2: DMT

This case concerns the plaintiff Cangzhou Donghong Packing Materials Co., Ltd., requesting the invalidity of the arbitral clause in the sales contract it has with the French company DMT Ltd.[35] The arbitration clause in the contract provides that 'the dispute shall be submitted for arbitration. The seat of arbitration shall be in Beijing, China, the arbitration shall be conducted under the relevant ICC rules, and both Chinese and English are working languages'. The plaintiff and the defendant had different views on the meaning of the arbitral clause. The former claims that because the seat of arbitration chosen in the arbitration clause is Beijing, the contract was signed and performed in China, and the place most closely connected to the contract is China, thus Chinese law should apply. The defendant argued that the arbitration rules chosen in the arbitration clause are ICC rules, i.e., the rules of the International Chamber of Commerce in Paris.

Zublin International GmbH v. Wuxi Woke General Engineering Rubber Co., Ltd., (2004) Xi Min San Zhong Zi No. 1), *ChinaLawInfo*, https://www.pkulaw.com/en_case/a25051f 3312b07f3a37ea0a43ed1d2c794f87ed270907b17bdfb.html, last accessed on 8 July 2021.

35 最高人民法院关于仲裁条款效力请示的复函 (2006)民四他字第6号 (Reply of the Supreme People's Court to the Request for Instructions on the Validity of an Arbitration Clause, (2006) Min Si Ta Zi No. 6), *ChinaLawInfo*, https://www.pkulaw.com/en_law/afd4c1a e5ee75be1bdfb.html?keyword=6%20DMT%20case, last accessed on 8 July 2021. This Reply is to the request by the HPC in Hebei concerning the validity of the arbitration clause in the sales contract dispute between Cangzhou Donghong Packing Materials Co., Ltd. and French DMT Ltd.

Based on such an understanding, the DMT filed a request for arbitration with the ICC.

The SPC's opinion is that the arbitration clause in this case is a foreign-related arbitration clause, so the law governing the validity of the arbitration clause should be first determined. According to China's judicial practice and the principles formulated in dealing with foreign-related commercial cases, where the parties have clearly agreed upon the law governing the validity of the arbitration clause in the contract, the law should apply; where the parties fail to agree upon the governing law but agree upon the seat of arbitration, the law of the country where the seat of arbitration is located should apply. In this case, both parties fail to agree upon the law governing the validity of the arbitration clause, thus the law of the seat of arbitration as agreed upon by the parties, i.e., the law of China, should apply to the determination of the validity of the clause. As Art. 18 of the AL clearly provides: 'Where the parties fail to agree or clearly agree upon any arbitration matters or the arbitration commission in the arbitration agreement, they may reach a supplementary agreement; and if no supplementary agreement is reached, the arbitration agreement shall be void'. As both parties in this case failed to agree upon the arbitral institution in the arbitration clause, and could not reach a supplementary agreement subsequently, the arbitration clause was null and void.[36]

The same argument was also used by the SPC in 2011 to reject the validity of the arbitration agreement in the case of Salzgitter Mannesmann International GmbH and Jiangsu Foreign Economic and Trade Corporation;[37] and in the case between Amoi Electronics Co., Ltd. and Belgium Products Co., Ltd. in 2009.[38]

6.3.2 Cases allowing adjudication by international arbitration institutions in China

Case 1: Longlide (龙利得包装印刷案)

Anhui Longlide Packaging and Printing Co., Ltd. (Longlide) and BP Agnati S.R.L. (Agnati) signed a sales contract in 2010, with the following arbitration clause:

---

36 Ibid.
37 最高人民法院关于Salzgitter Mannesmann International GmbH与江苏省对外经贸股份有限公司之间仲裁协议效力的复函 (2011)民四他字第32号 (Reply of the SPC Concerning the Validity of Arbitration Agreement in the Case of *Salzgitter Mannesmann International GmbH v. Jiangsu Foreign Economic and Trade Corporation Co., Ltd.*, (2011) Min Si Ta Zi No. 32), http://www.8law8.com/sfjs/news/sf/arbitration/20110826/1675.html, last accessed on 8 July 2021.
38 最高人民法院关于夏新电子股份有限公司与比利时产品有限公司确认经销协议仲裁条款效力的请示的复函 (2009)民四他字第5号 (Reply of the SPC Concerning the Validity of Arbitration Clause in the Distribution Agreement in the Case of *Amoi Electronics Co., Ltd. v. Belgium Products Co., Ltd.*, (2009) Min Si Ta Zi No. 5), *ChinaLawInfo*, https://www.pkulaw.com/en_law/2338ab2ccb4b0ac8bdfb.html, last accessed on 8 July 2021.

Any dispute arising out of or in connection with this Contract shall be submitted to the ICC International Court of Arbitration for final arbitration in accordance with the Rules of the ICC Court of Arbitration by one or more arbitrators designated in accordance with those rules. The jurisdiction shall be in Shanghai, China, and the arbitration shall be conducted in English.[39]

The key issue of the case concerns the validity of the arbitration agreement. The IPC in Hefei, as the first court to review the case, held that the arbitration agreement in this case does not state the law applicable to the arbitration, however, the agreement provides that the jurisdiction of arbitration is in Shanghai. Thus, based on Art. 16 of the SPC's *Interpretation on Several Issues concerning the Implementation of the Arbitration Law of the People's Republic of China (PRC)*, the Chinese law should be used to decide the validity of the arbitration agreement. The IPC further elaborated that on the question of whether foreign arbitration institutions such as the ICC International Court of Arbitration can engage in arbitration activities in China, China's AL renders no clear answer. However, as parties choose to arbitrate in China, such arbitration in the legal sense should be domestic arbitration. Art. 10 of the AL stipulates that the arbitration commission shall be registered by the judicial administrative department of a provincial-level government. As the Chinese government has not opened the arbitration market to foreign countries, foreign arbitration institutions cannot conduct arbitration in China. Consequently, the IPC took the view that the arbitration clause in this case was invalid.

The IPC's reasoning was not sustained by the SPC. In 2013 the SPC confirmed the validity of the arbitration agreement as a foreign-related arbitration agreement. The legal reasoning was articulated as the following: the parties agreed that the place of jurisdiction shall be Shanghai, which shall be understood to mean that the seat of arbitration is in Shanghai. Based on Art. 16 of the SPC's *Interpretation on Several Issues concerning the Implementation of the Arbitration Law of the PRC*, the law of the place of the arbitration, namely the PRC law, should be applied to confirm the validity of the arbitration agreement. Art. 16 of the AL requires that an arbitration agreement should contain three elements: expression of intention to apply arbitration, matters for arbitration and the designated arbitration committee. The arbitration agreement shall be deemed valid as it meets the intention to resort to arbitration, the matters to arbitration and selection of a specific arbitration commission. This SPC's opinion has a landmark impact, as it declared that a designated arbitration commission, as is required for

---

39 关于申请人安徽省龙利得包装印刷有限公司与被申请人BP Agnati S.R.L.申请确认仲裁协议效力案的复函 (2013)民四他字第13号 (Reply of the SPC to the Application for Confirmation of the Validity of the Arbitration Agreement between the Applicant, Anhui Longlide Packaging and Printing Co., Ltd. and the Respondent, BP Agnati S.R.L., (2013) Min Si Ta Zi No. 13), *ChinaLawInfo*, https://www.pkulaw.com/en_law/bfae3694ffad998cbdfb.html, last accessed on 8 July 2021.

a valid arbitration agreement under Art. 16 of the AL, includes a foreign arbitration institution. Subsequently, this position has been confirmed in other cases.

Case 2: Daesung (大成产业案)

This case concerns a contract dispute between two Korean companies – Daesung Industrial Gases Co., Ltd., and Daesung (Guangzhou) Gases Co., Ltd. – and the Chinese company Praxair (China) Investment Co., Ltd. (普莱克斯公司).[40] The arbitration clause in the contract is that both parties agree that the dispute shall be submitted to the Singapore International Arbitration Centre, following its Arbitration Rules, and to arbitrate in Shanghai. The arbitral award shall be final and binding upon both parties. While the Korean companies submitted the case to SIAC, the subsequently established arbitral tribunal decided it had the jurisdiction. Nevertheless, the Chinese company challenged the tribunal's jurisdiction at the Singapore High Court. This Court supported the decision of the arbitral tribunal, and the Chinese company then appealed to the Singapore Court of Appeal, which overruled the decision of the High Court concerning the seat of arbitration and decided that as Singapore is not the seat of arbitration, the Singapore Court of Appeal will not give any opinion on the dispute. As the parties in this dispute could not agree on the legal effect of the arbitration agreement, the arbitral tribunal had to suspend the arbitration proceedings.

In January 2020, the two Korean companies applied to the No. 1 IPC in Shanghai to recognize the validity of the arbitration agreement. The Shanghai Court first confirmed that the contract in dispute is a foreign-related contract under Art. 1 of the SPC's *Interpretation on Several Issues Concerning Implementation of the Law of the PRC on Choice of Law for Foreign-Related Civil Relations*. Next, it confirmed the foreign-related nature of the arbitration agreement of this case. Then, based on Art. 16 of the AL, the IPC decided that the arbitration agreement is valid, as it meets the criteria of expression of intention to request arbitration, the matters for arbitration were agreed upon and selected a specific arbitration institution, namely SIAC.

In explaining its legal reasoning, the IPC distinctively referred to the SPC's Reply on the Longlide case as in compliance with Art. 16 of the AL. The IPC also pointed out that the respondent's opinion that a foreign arbitration institution shall not administer domestic arbitration is lacking in China's prohibitory legal provisions and is contrary to the trend in the development of international commercial arbitration. The IPC further elaborated that for specific cases, the

---

40 大成产业气体株式会社等与普莱克斯（中国）投资有限公司申请确认仲裁协议效力一案一审民事裁定书 (2020)沪01民特83号 (First-Instance Civil Ruling Concerning the Application of Validity of an Arbitration Agreement in the Case of *Daesung Industrial Gases Co., Ltd., et al. v. Praxair (China) Investment Co., Ltd.*, (2020) Hu 01 Min Te No. 83), *China-LawInfo*, https://www.pkulaw.com/pfnl/a6bdb3332ec0adc403a067c439de9ecfef82d490a79bf8b8bdfb.html?keyword=(2020)%e6%b2%aa01%e6%b0%91%e7%89%b983%e5%8f%b7, last accessed on 8 July 2021.

judiciary cannot refuse to adjudicate on the grounds of unclear legislation. China's AL lacks an international perspective when it was enacted due to its main consideration that was on regulating domestic arbitration, with only a few special provisions on foreign-related arbitration. Obviously, the AL was not comprehensive and lagged behind international commercial arbitration practice. Legislation and adjudication should complement each other. The respondent's understanding of the arbitration commission in the AL is a problem to be solved by the legislator. The shortage of legislation cannot change the effect of the meaning of the SPC judicial interpretation on the issue concerned. The respondent's arguments excessively focused on the inadequacy of the AL, while neglecting the legal effect of relevant judicial interpretations and the progress made by China's judiciary in complying with the trend in the development of international commercial arbitration and making up for the insufficiency of arbitration legislation.

One might notice that such deliberate legal reasonings by the Shanghai IPC illustrate the improvement of judicial quality and confidence in decision-making.

Case 3: *Ningbo Beilun Licheng* (宁波北仑利成案)

This case concerns the validity of an arbitration clause in the sales contract between the Chinese company Ningbo Beilun Licheng Lubricating Oil Co., Ltd., and Formal Venture Corp.[41] In the sales contract the arbitration clause is

> any dispute shall be settled by arbitration in Beijing, and the Rules of Arbitration of the ICC and the award made thereunder shall be binding upon both parties. The arbitration tribunal shall be conducted in accordance with the laws of the PRC and in the Chinese language.

The High People's Court (HPC) in Zhejiang denied the validity of the arbitration clause on the grounds that the parties did not design an arbitration commission as requested in Arts. 16 and 18 of the Chinese AL. However, the SPC recognized the validity of the arbitration clause with the arguments that the parties concerned agreed to apply the ICC Rules of Arbitration to arbitrate, thus the ICC Rules of Arbitration should apply. Art. 6(2) of the ICC Rules of Arbitration (2012) stipulates that: 'By agreeing to arbitration under the Rules, the parties have accepted that the arbitration shall be administered by the Court'. Accordingly, the SPC concludes that the ICC International Court of Arbitration has jurisdiction over a case in which the parties agree to apply the ICC Rules of Arbitration without

---

41 最高人民法院关于宁波市北仑利成润滑油有限公司与法莫万驰公司买卖合同纠纷一案仲裁条款效力问题请示的复函 (2013)民四他字第74号 (Reply of the SPC on the Validity of the Arbitration Clause in the Case of Sales Contract Dispute between Ningbo Beilun Licheng Lubricating Oil Co., Ltd. and Formal Venture Corp., (2013) Min Si Ta Zi No. 74), *ChinaLawInfo*, https://www.pkulaw.com/chl/0f06afca2f3b1aaebdfb.html, last accessed on 8 July 2021.

identifying another arbitration institution. The SPC confirms that where the parties to the case agree to apply the ICC Rules of Arbitration without referring to any arbitration institution, it shall be deemed that 'the arbitration institution can be determined in accordance with the agreed arbitration rules'. Consequently, the SPC pointed out that the opinion of the HPC in Zhejiang is inappropriate. In other words, the SPC recognized the validity of the arbitration clause of this case arbitrated in Beijing, upon the basis of the ICC Rules of Arbitration.[42]

Case 4: Brentwood Industries (布兰特伍德案)

This case concerns the recognition and enforcement of the arbitral award rendered by the ICC International Court of Arbitration, arbitrated in Guangzhou.[43] The American company Brentwood Industries had a sale contract of construction equipment with Guangdong Fa-anlong Mechanical Equipment Manufacture Co., Ltd. (广东阀安龙机械成套设备工程有限公), and Guangzhou Zhengqi Trade Co., Ltd. The latter refused to pay for the equipment they purchased. After failing to persuade the court in China to accept the case, Brentwood Industries brought the dispute to ICC arbitration. The ICC International Court of Arbitration, pursuant to the arbitration agreement in the contract, appointed the single arbitrator, arbitrated in Guangzhou, China, and delivered the award in March 2014. As the Chinese party refused to comply with the award, Brentwood applied to the Guangzhou IPC for recognition and enforcement of the ICC arbitral award in 2015. In August 2020, Guangzhou IPC decided that the arbitral award involved in the case is an arbitral award made in China by a foreign arbitration institution, which can be regarded as a foreign-related arbitral award in China.

This is the first case in which the Chinese court explicitly confirmed that the arbitral award rendered in China by a foreign arbitration institution is a foreign-related arbitral award in China. The Court also confirmed that the legal basis of enforcing the award is China's CPL, not the New York Convention. This illustrates a new trend that China is accepting foreign arbitration institutions to arbitrate in China.[44] One eminent judge at the SPC expounded that arbitration under the management of a foreign arbitration institution in China will not

42 Qingming Li, '境外仲裁机构在中国内地仲裁的法律问题' (Legal Issues Concerning Arbitration in Mainland China Administered by Foreign Arbitration Institutions), 《环球法律评论》 (*Global Law Review*), No. 3 (2016), pp. 181–192.

43 布兰特伍德工业有限公司、广东阀安龙机械成套设备工程有限公司申请承认与执行法院判决、仲裁裁决案件一审民事裁定书 (2015)穗中法民四初字第62号 (First-Trial Civil Ruling on the Application of Enforcement of a Court Judgement and Arbitration Award Concerning the Case of *Brentwood Industries Inc. v. Guangdong Fa-anlong Mechanical Equipment Manufacture Co., Ltd.*, (2015) Sui Zhong Fa Min Si Chu Zi No. 62). For information of the case in English, see Chinese Justice Observer, https://www.chinajusticeobserver.com /law/x/2015-sui-zhong-fa-min-si-chu-zi-no-62-20200806, last accessed on 9 July 2021.

44 Xiaoli Gao, '中国法院承认和执行外国仲裁裁决的积极实践' (Active Practice on Recognition and Enforcement of Foreign Arbitral Awards by Chinese Courts), 《法律适用》 (*Application of Law*), No. 5 (2018), pp. 2–8.

harm China's interests; instead it is conducive to vigorous competition that could stimulate Chinese arbitration commissions and arbitrators to raise their professional quality. If Chinese courts refuse to recognize and enforce arbitral awards rendered by such tribunals on the grounds that there is no legal basis, this will result in the absence of a legal remedy to recognize and enforce such arbitral awards, which indirectly leads to foreign arbitration institutions avoiding administering arbitration in China. Such a consequence is contradictory to both the current trend of international commercial arbitration and China's strategic goal of forging a Belt and Road international dispute settlement centre.[45] The revised AL (draft) explicitly provides that a foreign arbitration institution intending to establish a business operation in China to conduct arbitration involving foreign elements should register with the judicial administration bureau of the province, autonomous region or municipality directly under the central government, and report to the Ministry of Justice for the record.[46] The new AL can be expected to allow foreign arbitration institutions to set up their offices in China to arbitrate foreign-related commercial disputes.

6.4 Changing policies on foreign arbitration institutions

Since 2015, the government policy of 'inviting in' of foreign arbitration institutions to set up business inside China has gradually emerged, reflecting the government's positive attitude towards opening up the arbitration market. In the *Notice on Advancing the Reform and Opening Up in China (Shanghai) Pilot Free Trade Zone* approved by the State Council, it specifically points out to support 'internationally renowned commercial dispute settlement institutions' entry into Shanghai Pilot Free Trade Zone (PFTZ).[47] After this Notice, in November 2015 HKIAC established its representative office in Shanghai PFTZ. This was followed by the ICC International Court of Arbitration and Singapore International Arbitration Center in February and March 2016, respectively.

In August 2019, the State Council's *Notice of Issuing the General Plan for the LinGang New Area in China (Shanghai) Pilot Free Trade Zone*[48] further indicated that foreign arbitral institutions may be permitted to set up business organizations in Shanghai's extended free trade zone to arbitrate commercial disputes

---

45 Xiaoli Gao, '司法应依仲裁地而非仲裁机构所在地确定仲裁裁决籍属' (Nationality of Arbitral Awards Should be Determined by the Seat of Arbitration Instead of the Location of Arbitration Institutions in Judiciary), 《人民司法》 (*People's Judiciary*), No. 20 (2017), pp. 68–74.
46 Arbitration Law Amendment – Draft for Comments (2021), Art. 12.
47 国务院关于印发进一步深化中国(上海)自由贸易试验区改革开放方案的通知 (Notice on Advancing the Reform and Opening Up in China (Shanghai) Pilot Free Trade Zone) (Issued by the State Council on 8 April 2015, effective on promulgation).
48 国务院关于印发中国(上海)自由贸易试验区临港新片区总体方案的通知 (Notice on Issuing the General Plan for the LinGang New Area in China (Shanghai) Pilot Free Trade Zone) (Issued by the State Council on 27 July 2019, effective on promulgation).

resulting from international trade and investment, and such arbitration can be conducted in English.

Subsequently, in October 2019, Shanghai's Municipal Bureau of Justice issued the *Administrative Measures for Business Offices Established by Overseas Arbitration Institutions in LinGang New Area of China (Shanghai) Pilot Free Trade Zone.*[49] The Measures provide general rules for the establishment and operation of a business office by an 'overseas arbitration institution' in the LinGang New Area. The 'overseas arbitration institution' is clarified as 'any non-profit arbitration institution' legally established in foreign countries, or in the Hong Kong Special Administrative Region (SAR), Macao SAR and Taiwan; or established by international organizations of which China is a member. Such an institution should meet three conditions: (1) it has been legally established and duly existing for more than five years; (2) it has administered substantial arbitration activities overseas and enjoys high international reputation; and (3) the principal of the business office has not been subjected to any criminal penalty for any wilful offence.

With regard to the scope of business, Art. 14 of the Administrative Measures provides that a business office may conduct foreign-related arbitration services concerning civil and commercial disputes by (1) acceptance, trial, hearing and awarding of cases; (2) case management and services; and (3) consultancy, guidance, training and seminars.

The World Intellectual Property Organization (WIPO) Arbitration and Mediation Shanghai Service (世界知识产权组织仲裁和调解上海中心), in October 2019, became the first business office of foreign arbitration institution registered in Shanghai, and it started to manage cases in 2020.[50]

Similar to Shanghai, the State Council has also issued policy papers to support the opening-up of the arbitration market in Beijing. The 2017 Reply of the State Council on deepening reform and further opening-up of services sectors in Beijing, allows foreign arbitration institutions to establish representative offices in Beijing.[51] As a step further, in August 2020, the State Council approved the Beijing government's Plan,[52] which allows foreign arbitration institutions to set

49 境外仲裁机构在中国(上海)自由贸易试验区临港新片区设立业务机构管理办法 (Administrative Measures for Business Offices Established by Foreign Arbitration Institutions in LinGang New Area in China (Shanghai) Pilot Free Trade Zone) (Issued by Shanghai Municipal Bureau of Justice on 21 October 2019, effective on 1 January 2020).

50 Wenting Zhou, 'WIPO Arbitration and Mediation Center in Shanghai Established', *China Daily*, 23 October 2020, https://www.chinadaily.com.cn/a/202010/23/WS5f926ab8a31024ad0ba80904.html, last accessed on 9 July 2021.

51 国务院关于深化改革推进北京市服务业扩大开放综合试点工作方案的批复 (Reply of the State Council to Beijing Municipality on Deepened Reform and Promotion for a Comprehensive Pilot Program of Expanding Opening-up in the Service Industry) (Issued by the State Council on 25 June 2017, effective on promulgation).

52 深化北京市新一轮服务业扩大开放综合试点建设国家服务业扩大开放综合示范区工作方案 (Reply of the State Council to Beijing Municipality on a Comprehensive Pilot Plan of a New Round of Opening-up in the Service Sector and Building a National Comprehensive

up business organizations in designated area(s) in Beijing, and to conduct arbitration in settling international commercial and investment disputes. It specifies that a foreign arbitral institution is one that is established outside mainland China, including in Hong Kong, Macao or Taiwan.

The recent government policy papers definitely show a gradual opening-up of the commercial arbitration market in Shanghai and Beijing, and the liberalized opinions of the SPC point in the same direction. It is correct to observe that: 'In Chinese policy formation, a "vision" often precedes implementation or a pilot program. Sometimes, both can even take place before regulations are implemented'.[53] However, before the AL is revised to provide overt legal certainty on the status and nature on arbitral awards rendered by foreign arbitral tribunals in China, foreign parties will prefer to select an arbitration place outside of China. The ambiguity of law will also instigate foreign lawyers to 'continue to recommend against providing for arbitration of foreign-related disputes seated in Mainland China administered by a foreign arbitral institution'.[54]

6.5 Experimentation on interim measures by courts

The CPL covers property preservation, evidence preservation, and conduct preservation. An application for an interim measure is submitted by an arbitration commission to the IPC where the respondent has residence or the respondent's property is located, and the decision to impose the interim measure is made by the court. An applicant must provide security, otherwise the court will not rule on preservation.[55] Under the 1994 AL, neither an arbitration commission nor an arbitral tribunal is competent to grant enforceable interim measures. A criticism of this exclusive competence of courts is that it is time-consuming and procedurally redundant as an 'arbitral tribunal is sufficiently competent to render the decision'.[56]

In recent years, practice has developed beyond the legal restrictions. A new development is that in 2018 two China International Commercial Courts (CICCs) were established in Shenzhen and Xi'an. The SPC has announced that in arbitration cases administered by the CIETAC, SHIAC, SCIA, BAC, and

---

Demonstrative Area for Opening-up in the Service Sector) (Issued by the State Council on 28 August 2020, effective on promulgation).

53 Matthew S. Erie, 'The New Legal Hubs: The Emergent Landscape of International Commercial Dispute Resolution', *Virginia Journal of International Law*, Vol. 60 Issue 2 (2020), pp. 225–298, at 243.

54 Helen Tang, Weina Ye and Briana Young, 'Beijing to Open to Foreign Arbitral Institutions', *Herbert Smith Freehills LLP*, 14 September 2020, https://www.lexology.com/library/detail .aspx?g=f053f6e4-78e4-44c9-bff0-21d6727dce5a, last accessed on 9 July 2021.

55 民事诉讼法 (Civil Procedure Law) (Promulgated by the Standing Committee of the NPC on 27 June 2017, effective on 1 July 2017), Arts. 81, 100, 101 and 272.

56 Jingzhou Tao, 'Salient Issues in Arbitration in China', *American University International Law Review*, Vol. 27 No. 4 (2012), pp. 807–830, at 820.

China Maritime Arbitration Commission, the parties may, either before the commencement of arbitration or during the arbitral proceedings, apply to the CICC for preservation of evidence and assets.[57] This is the so-called 'one-stop' service, in which the CICC is the court to make the first and the final ruling, and there is no need to go through the IPCs as the CPL provides.

Neither the CPL nor the AL contain any clear provision with regard to the application for interim measures by foreign arbitration institutions. An exception is that the SPC and the Government of the Hong Kong SAR issued the specific Arrangement in 2019, allowing parties of Hong Kong-seated arbitrations administered by an eligible arbitration institution in Hong Kong to have the right to apply for interim measures to mainland Chinese courts.[58] Hong Kong is the only jurisdiction outside mainland China that enjoys such privileges. Within one year of the Arrangement becoming effective, mainland courts have granted 32 applications for interim measures, among which were 29 cases on asset preservation, 2 cases on evidence preservation and 1 case on conduct preservation.[59]

In addition, the SPC's judicial interpretation articulates that, for foreign-related maritime disputes arbitrated by foreign arbitration institutions, if the property concerned is in the territory of China, the maritime court where the property is located should accept the case if the parties concerned apply maritime claim preservation.[60] There are a number of cases in which Chinese maritime courts have supported application for maritime claims preservation.[61] Whether this special provision on maritime cases arbitrated by foreign arbitration institutions can be

---

57 最高人民法院办公厅关于确定首批纳入"一站式"国际商事纠纷多元化解决机制的国际商事仲裁及调解机构的通知 (Notice of the General Office of the SPC on the Inclusion of the First Group of Arbitration and Mediation Institutions in the 'One-Stop' Diversified International Commercial Dispute Resolution Mechanism) (Issued by the SPC on 13 November 2018, effective on 5 December 2018).

58 关于内地与香港特别行政区法院就仲裁程序相互协助保全的安排 (Arrangement Concerning Mutual Legal Assistance in Court-Ordered Interim Measures in Aid of Arbitral Proceedings by the Courts of Mainland and Hong Kong Special Administrative Region) (Signed on 2 April 2019, effective on 1 October 2019), Art. 3. The English text is available at https://www.doj.gov.hk/en/community_engagement/press/pdf/arbitration_interim_e.pdf, last accessed on 9 July 2021.

59 SPC, '最高法、司法部相关负责人就《最高人民法院商事仲裁司法审查年度报告（2019年）》答记者问' (Press Conference on the SPC 'Annual Report on Judicial Review of Commercial Arbitration Cases 2019' by Heads of SPC and Ministry of Justice), 24 December 2020, http://www.court.gov.cn/zixun-xiangqing-281201.html, last accessed on 29 July 2021. Despite the announcement, the full text of this Annual Report was not made public at the time of writing this book.

60 最高人民法院关于适用《中华人民共和国海事诉讼特别程序法》若干问题的解释 (Interpretation of the SPC on the Implementation of the Special Maritime Procedure Law of the PRC) (Issued by the SPC on 6 January 2003, effective on 1 February 2003), Art. 21(2).

61 For example, 厦门西凌海运有限公司与非洲海上承运人有限公司海事请求保全申请案 (2005)沪海法商保字第35号 (Application for Preservation of Maritime Claims in the Case of *Xiamen Xiling Maritime Co., Ltd. v. African Maritime Carriers Co., Ltd.*, (2005) Hu Hai Fa Shang Bao Zi No. 35), *ChinaLawInfo,* https://www.pkulaw.com/pfnl/a25051f3312b07f3f08d4376526c32bba68926c19f47fe8ebdfb.html, last accessed on 9 July 2021.

extended to other cases is a matter to be addressed in the future revision of the CPL and the AL.

The revised AL (draft) contains a groundbreaking change by empowering arbitral tribunals to grant interim measures and other short-term measures deemed necessary by the arbitral tribunal.[62]

6.6 New developments on judicial review

The most important function of courts in this field consists of judicial review of arbitration agreements and arbitral awards. With regard to the validity of arbitration agreements, the prevalent international practice follows the 'competence to competence' principle, which entails that an arbitral tribunal has the power to decide the validity of an arbitration agreement and consequently its jurisdiction.[63] Unlike this international practice, the 1994 AL does not empower an arbitral tribunal with such competence, though this can be changed in the revised AL.[64] Art. 20 of 1994 AL provides that if parties disagree on the validity of arbitration agreement, they may apply to an arbitration institution to make a decision or apply to a court for a ruling. If one party applies to an arbitration institution and the other party applies to a court, the court shall give the ruling. Empowering arbitration institutions with the competence is criticised as being incompatible with the function of such institution, which is to manage cases rather than to determine the jurisdiction of an arbitral tribunal. This role of courts in the Chinese context also raises concerns, as Chinese courts 'have the tendency to enlarge its jurisdiction by implementing strictly the Arbitration Law'.[65] Accordingly, it is expounded that: 'The frequent use of judicial review in arbitration procedures could not make the arbitration more "legal," but rather it adversely affected the development of arbitration as a dispute resolution mechanism by parties' free choice'.[66]

Nevertheless, the SPC has strived to formulate coherent rules in guiding Chinese courts in dealing with arbitration-related judicial review. Based on judicial practice and the need to effectively conduct judicial review and to create an arbitration-friendly judiciary, the SPC issued four important judicial documents in 2017 and 2018 concerning arbitration judicial review. They are

---

62 Arbitration Law Amendment – Draft for Comments (2021), Art. 43.
63 Art. 16(1) of UNCITRAL Model Law on International Commercial Arbitration (2006) states: 'The arbitral tribunal may rule on its own jurisdiction, including any objections with respect to the existence or validity of the arbitration agreement'.
64 Arbitration Law Amendment – Draft for Comments (2021), Art. 28. It provides that an arbitral tribunal shall make a decision if parties to a case have objection to the validity of the arbitration agreement or to the jurisdiction of the arbitration case.
65 Jingzhou Tao, *supra* note 56, at 814.
66 Ibid, at 818. For academic analysis and case study on the validity of international commercial arbitration agreement in China, see Jin Qiu and Xu Shi-Jie, '中国国际商事仲裁协议效力认定问题研究' (Study on the Validation of China's International Commercial Arbitration Agreement), 《仲裁研究》 (*Arbitration Research*), Vol. 28 Issue 4 (2018), pp. 193–208.

1. *Provisions of the SPC on Several Issues Concerning Conduct of Arbitration Judicial Review* (Judicial Review Provisions)[67]
2. *Provisions of the SPC on Issues of Reporting and Verification of Arbitral Judicial Review* (Reporting Provisions)[68]
3. *Notice of the SPC on Some Issues Concerning Centralised Administration of Judicial Review of Arbitration Cases* (Centralised Notice)[69]
4. *Provisions of the SPC on Several Issues Concerning People's Courts' Handling of Enforcement Cases of Arbitral Awards* (Enforcement Provisions)[70]

The new developments of key issues reflected in these judicial documents are briefly analysed next.

6.6.1 Scope of judicial review

The power of arbitration judicial review is provided in both the CPL and the AL. The SPC's Judicial Review Provisions enumerate details in performing this power. Art. 1 provides an exhaustive list of six types of cases to be reviewed:

(1) Application for confirmation of the validity of arbitration agreement.
(2) Application for recognition and enforcement of arbitral awards by arbitration institutions in China.
(3) Application for setting aside of arbitral award of arbitration institutions in China.
(4) Application for recognition and enforcement of arbitral awards of arbitral award from Hong Kong, Macao and Taiwan.
(5) Application for recognition and enforcement of foreign arbitral awards.
(6) Other arbitration-related judicial review cases.

While the first five types of cases are clear, the last one – 'other cases' – leaves a space for including any potentially new type of case. For instance, on 30 December 2016 the SPC issued the *Opinions on Providing Judicial Guarantee for the*

---

67 最高人民法院关于审理仲裁司法审查案件若干问题的规定 (Provisions of the SPC on Several Issues Concerning the Trial of Arbitration Judicial Review) (Issued by the SPC on 26 December 2017, effective on 1 January 2018).
68 最高人民法院关于仲裁司法审查案件报核问题的有关规定 (Provisions of the SPC on Issues of Reporting and Verification of Arbitration Judicial Review) (Issued by the SPC on 26 December 2017, effective on 1 January 2018).
69 最高人民法院关于仲裁司法审查案件归口办理有关问题的通知 (Notice of the SPC on Some Issues Concerning Centralized Administration of Arbitration Judicial Review) (Issued by the SPC on 22 May 2017, effective on promulgation).
70 最高人民法院关于人民法院办理仲裁裁决执行案件若干问题的规定 (Provisions of the SPC on Several Issues Concerning People's Courts' Handling of Enforcement Cases of Arbitral Awards) (Issued by the SPC on 22 February 2018, effective on 1 March 2018).

Construction of Pilot Free Trade Zones,[71] which provide that if 'enterprises registered in the pilot free trade zone agree to arbitrate their dispute in a *specific* place in mainland China, in accordance with *specific* arbitration rules, by *specific* personnel, the arbitration agreement may be deemed to be valid'. The 'three specifics' of arbitration cases here actually refer to *ad hoc* arbitration in mainland China. While *ad hoc* arbitration is a prevalent international practice, it is not recognized in China's AL. The cover clause in Art. 1 of the Judicial Review Provisions provides a bellwether for such cases.[72] The arbitration circle in China has long recommended incorporating *ad hoc* arbitration in the AL. This has resulted in a partial attainment, as the revised AL (draft) provides *ad hoc* arbitration can only be used to settle 'foreign-related commercial disputes'.[73]

6.6.2 Jurisdiction and governing law

To start with, IPC is the first level of court for arbitration judicial review cases. A distinction can be made between recognition and enforcement of arbitral awards delivered by either Chinese or foreign arbitration institutions. For foreign-related arbitral awards rendered by Chinese arbitration institutions in China, Art. 273 of the CPL provides generally that if an arbitration award is rendered, the parties cannot bring the same case to a court. If one party concerned does not perform the arbitral award, the other party may apply for enforcement by an IPC at the location of the respondent's residence or the location of the properties.

For arbitral awards rendered by a foreign arbitration institution, Art. 283 of the CPL stipulates that a party should apply for recognition and enforcement directly to an IPC at the location of the residence or the property of the respondent. The court should handle the matter in accordance with the international treaties that China has concluded or participated in, or pursuant to the principle of reciprocity.

The 2017 Judicial Review Provisions have supplemented the CPL with more user-friendly rules. Art. 2 provides that on cases concerning application for the validity of arbitration agreement, the jurisdiction is vested with the IPC or specific people's courts in the place of the arbitration commission agreed in the arbitration agreement, the place where the arbitration agreement is signed, the place of residence of the applicant, or the place of residence of the respondent. Art. 2 applies to both domestic and foreign-related cases. In implementing the Judicial Review Provisions, some cities have assigned one court to deal with both

---

71 最高人民法院关于为自由贸易试验区建设提供司法保障的意见 (Opinions on Providing Judicial Guarantee for the Construction of Pilot Free Trade Zones) (Issued by the SPC on 30 December 2016, effective on promulgation).
72 Xuefeng Ren, '《最高人民法院关于审理仲裁司法审查案件若干问题的规定》解读' (Unscramble the SPC's Provisions on Several Issues Concerning the Trial of Arbitration Judicial Review), 《人民法治》 (*People's Rule of Law*), No. 3 (2018), pp. 16–20, at 17.
73 Arbitration Law Amendment – Draft for Comments (2021), Arts. 91–93.

domestic and foreign-related arbitration judicial review. For instance, in Beijing, since 2018 the No. 4 IPC has the jurisdiction to handle cases concerning application for the validity of arbitration agreements, setting aside arbitral awards, and recognition and enforcement of foreign arbitral awards, as well as awards rendered in Hong Kong, Macao and Taiwan.[74]

In addition, Art. 3 provides that in a case where there is a link between a foreign arbitral award and a case handled by a people's court, if both the residence and properties of parties to whom the enforcement is made are not in mainland China, and an applicant applies for recognition of the foreign arbitral award, the court handling the case has the jurisdiction. If such a court is a basic people's court, the case should be submitted to the IPC which is the direct higher level of the basic people's court. If the concurrent case is handled by an HPC or the SPC, they can decide to handle the case by themselves or appoint an IPC to review. Art. 3 also provides that when a foreign arbitral award and a case handled by a domestic arbitration commission is linked, and both the residence and properties of the respondent are not in mainland China, and an applicant applies for recognition of the foreign arbitral award, the IPC in the place of the arbitration commission which handled the concurrent case has the jurisdiction. To prevent potential overlapping of courts' jurisdiction, Art. 4 states that if an applicant applied to two or more courts, the court that first filed the case has jurisdiction.

It should be noted that the CICCs have a special role in directly handling arbitration-related cases. After an arbitral award is rendered, an application may be made directly to a CICC for setting aside or enforcing the arbitral award.[75]

With regard to the applicable law on the validity of an arbitration agreement, Art. 19 of the AL confirms the principle of independence of the validity of the arbitration clause, namely that an amendment, rescission, termination or invalidity of a contract does not affect the validity of arbitration agreement. Based on Art. 19 of the AL, Chinese courts have followed the principle that if parties agreed on the governing law, they must express this clearly. The governing law for the contract is not necessarily the governing law for the arbitration clause in the contract. The 2017 Judicial Review Provisions further confirmed this principle and added also new rules that are in favour of the validity of the arbitration agreement.[76] For instance, in the absence of the parties' choice concerning the governing law, the law of the place of the arbitration commission or the law of the place of the arbitration seat applies. In case of different results, a court should choose the law which confirms the validity of the arbitration agreement. Under

---

74 北京市高级人民法院关于北京市第四中级人民法院案件管辖的规定 (Provisions on the Jurisdiction of Beijing No. 4 Intermediate People's Court) (Issued by Beijing High People's Court on 5 February 2018, effective on 7 February 2018).

75 General Office of the SPC Notice on the Inclusion of the First Group of Arbitration and Mediation Institutions in the 'One-Stop' Diversified International Commercial Disputes Resolution Mechanisms (2018).

76 Provisions of the SPC on Several Issues Concerning the Trial of Arbitration Judicial Review (2017), Arts. 13–16.

the circumstance that both the arbitration commission and the arbitration seat are not mentioned in an arbitration agreement, but according to the arbitration rules stated in the arbitration agreement, the arbitration commission or arbitration seat may be deduced, the law of the place where the arbitration commission or arbitration seat is located shall be applied. In addition, according to Art. 12 of the SPC's *Interpretations on Several Issues Concerning 'Law on the Choice of Law for Foreign-Related Civil Relations' (I)*,[77] if the parties have not chosen the governing law, and there is no agreement on the arbitration commission or the seat of arbitration, or the agreement is unclear, a court may determine the validity of the arbitration agreement in accordance with the PRC laws. In sum, Chinese courts are guided by three steps in deciding the governing law on the validity of an arbitration agreement: (1) choice of law by the parties; (2) laws of the place of arbitration commission or seat of arbitration; and (3) laws of the place of the court, i.e., the PRC laws.[78]

6.6.3 Procedure for setting aside and resisting enforcement

China has developed an internal reporting system (内请制度) concerning cancellation or non-enforcement of foreign-related and foreign arbitral awards since 1995.[79] Namely, if an IPC is of the view that an arbitration agreement is invalid, or an arbitral award is not to be executed, it shall submit its decision to the high people's court for review. If the HPC agrees with the IPC's opinion, it shall report the case to the SPC. The SPC's opinion is the final decision to be followed by the IPC. The internal reporting system is considered as a safety valve to prevent local judicial protectionism and to guarantee maximum consistency in judicial review. It also demonstrates that China takes a judicial review of arbitral awards seriously and cautiously.

The 2017 SPC Reporting Provisions[80] has further amplified the internal reporting system into a report and verification system (报核制度). First, prior to the 2017 Reporting Provisions, the internal reporting system applied only to foreign-related and foreign arbitral awards. The 2017 Reporting Provisions expand it to apply to domestic arbitral awards as well. However, an IPC only needs to get approval from an HPC for domestic awards, unless the case has one of the two following circumstances: (1) the domicile of the parties in the

---

77 最高人民法院关于适用《中华人民共和国涉外民事关系法律适用法》若干问题的解释 （一）(Interpretations of the SPC on Several Issues Concerning 'Law on the Choice of Law for Foreign-Related Civil Relations' (I)) (Issued on 28 December 2012, revised on 29 December 2020, effective on 1 January 2021).

78 Xuefeng Ren, *supra* note 72, at 19.

79 最高人民法院关于人民法院处理与涉外仲裁及外国仲裁事项有关问题的通知 (Notice of the SPC on Some Issues Concerning Court's Handling of Foreign-Related Arbitration and Arbitration in Foreign Countries) (Issued by the SPC on 28 August 1995, effective on promulgation).

80 Provisions of the SPC on Issues of Reporting and Verification of Arbitration Judicial Review (2017).

case is across different provincial administrative regions; or (2) the grounds for the intended non-enforcement is a concern of public interest. Under these two circumstances, approval by the SPC is required.[81] To extend the internal reporting system to domestic arbitration is also relevant to foreign investors in China. Under a strict interpretation of Chinese law, for foreign-invested Chinese legal entities such as Sino-foreign joint ventures or wholly foreign-owned enterprises (WFOEs), arbitration between them or between a foreign-invested enterprise and a Chinese company may not be considered foreign-related cases. Consequently, they may not be able to benefit from the internal reporting system. Relevant to this, two well-known cases can be mentioned. One is the case of Beijing *Chaolai Xinsheng*'s application for the recognition of the arbitral award rendered by the Korean Commercial Arbitration Court. As the two parties in this case are WFOEs in China, the SPC decided that the case is not foreign related, thus the arbitration agreement is not valid.[82] However, in the case of *Siemens International Trade (Shanghai) Co., Ltd. v. Shanghai Golden Landmark Co., Ltd.* both parties are WFOEs. The No. 1 Shanghai IPC ruled to recognize and enforce the arbitral award rendered by Singapore International Arbitration Centre. One of the reasons given by the Court is that both parties are registered in Shanghai PFTZ.[83]

In addition, to improve the unified judicial review standard, a centralized judicial review approach is further strengthened. The 2017 Centralized Notice clarifies that the trial chamber of each court in charge of adjudicating foreign-related commercial cases shall be the specialized trial chamber to handle arbitration judicial review cases. All arbitration-related cases should be handled by such a specialized trial chamber.[84] In 2000, the SPC established the No. 4 Civil Trial Division to be in charge of foreign-related commercial cases. Following this, all HPCs and some IPCs have set up similar divisions. As there are around 400 IPCs in China, not all of them are involved in handling foreign-related commercial cases. To be

---

81 Ibid, Arts. 2 and 3.
82 最高人民法院关于北京朝来新生体育休闲有限公司申请承认大韩商事仲裁院作出的第12113-0011号、第12112-0012号仲裁裁决案件请示的复函 (SPC's Reply to the Request for Instructions on Beijing Chaolai Xinsheng Sports and Leisure Co., Ltd.'s Application for Recognition of Arbitral Awards No. 12113-0011 and No. 12112-0012 Issued by the Korean Commercial Arbitration Court) (Issued by the SPC on 18 December 2013), https://www.uncitral.org/docs/clout/CHN/CHN_181213_FT_1609.pdf, last accessed on 29 July 2021.
83 最高法院发布的第二批涉"一带一路"建设典型案例之四：西门子国际贸易（上海）有限公司与上海黄金置地有限公司申请承认和执行外国仲裁裁决案 (No. 4 of Second Group of Model Cases Involving Construction of the 'Belt and Road' Published by the Supreme People's Court: *Siemens International Trade (Shanghai) Co., Ltd. v. Shanghai Golden Landmark Co., Ltd.* – Case Concerning Application for Recognition and Enforcement of a Foreign Arbitral Award), *ChinaLawInfo*, https://www.pkulaw.com/en_case/a25051f3312b07f3f4dfc5b826df173fa0b3957d76e32bc2bdfb.html, last accessed on 22 July 2021.
84 Notice of the SPC on Some Issues Concerning Centralized Administration of Arbitration Judicial Review (2017), para. 1.

practical, the HPCs usually instruct some IPCs directly under their jurisdiction to deal with such cases. The Centralized Notice further requires that each such court should establish a centralized management platform for data and information on arbitration judicial review cases, and strengthen information management and data analysis of such cases in order to effectively guarantee the correctness of the application of laws and uniformity of adjudication standards.

The most common criticism of the internal reporting system is its lack of transparency to the parties involved. The parties usually are not aware of whether their cases are under review. A slight improvement is Art. 5 of the Centralized Notice, which provides that if, after receiving the application for review from a lower-level court, a higher-level court considers that the facts related to the case are unclear, it may inquire the parties concerned or return the case to the lower-level court to supplement and ascertain the facts before reporting again. Only at this stage may the parties involved know that their case is being reviewed.

6.6.4 Standards for setting aside and resisting enforcement

Art. 70 of the AL provides setting aside by both parties. Art. 71 of the AL provides resisting enforcement by a respondent. Both Articles refer to the CPL with regard to standards. Art. 274 of the CPL stipulates that a court will not enforce a foreign-related arbitral award, if a respondent provides evidence to prove the award falls under any one of the four circumstances:

(1) The contract between the parties does not contain an arbitration clause or the parties have not reached any written arbitration agreement after a dispute arose.
(2) The respondent is not notified to appoint an arbitrator or of the arbitration procedure, or fails to present an opinion not due to the fault of the respondent.
(3) The composition of the arbitral tribunal or the arbitration procedure is not in compliance with arbitration rules.
(4) The matters arbitrated are beyond the scope of arbitration agreement or the arbitral institution has no power to arbitrate.

Moreover, Art. 274 ends with a general exception clause: if a court is of the opinion that enforcement of an arbitral award is contrary to social public interest, the court shall rule not to enforce the award. This exception clause is similar to the public policy argument that is referred to as 'escape device' in international commercial arbitration.[85]

Obviously, the aforementioned four circumstances concern procedural issues; the exception on public interests is the only grounds that provide courts with

---

85 Gary Born, *International Commercial Arbitration*, 3rd edn. (Alphen aan den Rijn: Kluwer Law International, 2020).

discretionary power. Existing Chinese laws do not provide the meaning and criteria to decide what constitutes public interest. Traditionally, judicial practice generally refers to violation of the mandatory principles of laws, violation of good social custom, or threatening state and social public safety.[86] The new trend is that the SPC has confirmed in various cases that 'a violation of mandatory Chinese law does not warrant non-enforcement of an arbitral award on the ground of public policy'.[87]

The judicial discretionary power on public interest can be rather tricky in concrete cases.[88] For instance, an arbitral award rendered by CIETAC in the 1990s supported two American claimants who signed an agreement with China Women Travel Service (respondent) to perform in China, but the show was stopped by the Ministry of Culture in China for the reason that hard rock song performance diverges from Chinese culture. When the claimants applied for the enforcement of the arbitral award to the No. 1 IPC in Beijing, the Court refused to enforce the award with the argument that the award was contrary to Chinese public policy. In 1997, the SPC issued a reply to support the IPC's decision.[89] This case was viewed as one of the 'bizarre rulings' made in earlier times of arbitration judicial review.[90] Nowadays it is hardly conceivable that the SPC will use public policy to annul such an arbitral award.

As to whether economic interest is equivalent to public interest, local courts and the SPC may have different opinions. In the well-known case of *Dongfeng Garments Factory v. Henan Garments Import & Export Co.*, the CIETAC arbitral award ordered significant damages to be paid to the plaintiffs in April 1992. As the defendant refused to pay, the plaintiff brought the case of enforcement to the Zhengzhou IPC. The IPC rejected the application with the reasoning that

> according to the State policy, law and regulations, the enforcement of the award would seriously harm the economic and public interest of the State

---

86 For a general understanding of public interest and public policy in Chinese legal order, see Yongping Xiao and Zhengxin Huo, 'Order Public in China's Private International Law', *The American Journal of Comparative Law*, Vol. 53 No. 3 (2005), pp. 653–677.

87 Teresa Cheng S.C. and Joe Liu, 'Enforcement of Foreign Awards in Mainland China: Current Practices and Future Trends', *Journal of International Arbitration*, Vol. 31 Issue 5 (2014), pp. 651–673, at 672.

88 Jiong Liu, Minli Tang and Huijie Wu, '中国法院认定外国仲裁裁决违反中国公共政策之标准及实例分析' (Standards and Examples of Chinese Courts on Deciding Violation of Chinese Public Policy in Foreign Arbitral Awards), *AllBright*, 9 February 2018, https://www.allbrightlaw.com/CN/10475/b1e51fcd893a059a.aspx, last accessed on 29 July 2021.

89 最高人民法院关于北京市第一中级人民法院不予执行美国制作公司和汤姆·胡莱特公司诉中国妇女旅行社演出合同纠纷仲裁裁决请示的批复 他(1997)35号 (Reply of the SPC to Beijing No. 1 Intermediate People's Court on the Non-Enforcement of Arbitral Award Concerning a Performance Contract Dispute in the Case of *American Production Co. and Tom Wright Hu Co. v. China Women Travel Service*, Ta (1997) No. 35), *ChinaLawInfo*, https://www.pkulaw.com/chl/8194b91c57e997e6bdfb.html, last accessed on 9 July 2021.

90 Teresa Cheng S.C. and Joe Liu, *supra* note 87, at 655.

and adversely affect the foreign trade order of the State. To compel the defendant to pay damages for its breach would disadvantage social and public interests.

However, the SPC reversed the IPC's opinion by upholding plainly that 'it was incorrect for the Zhengzhou Municipal Intermediate People's Court to refuse to enforce the arbitral award on grounds that enforcement would seriously harm the economic interests of the state.'[91] In a recent case of application for cancellation of a domestic arbitral award by a local government agency, the court took the view that social public interest cannot be simply defined as equivalent to negative impacts on state economic interest.[92]

It is fair to discern that the judicial stand on public interest may evolve over time. For instance, the first Bitcoin arbitration case, arbitrated in Shenzhen by SCIA (2018), with the award of recognizing the use of Bitcoin in a transaction was eventually set aside by Shenzhen IPC (2021) on the grounds of being contrary to public interest.[93] Comparing the Bitcoin case handled by the No. 1 IPC in Shanghai (2019), the Court recognized Bitcoin as a virtual asset and decided to render compensation.[94] A liberal or restrictive interpretation of public interest can be influenced by government policy at a particular time, which unavoidably causes uncertainty for the parties involved.

6.6.5 Enforcement of foreign-related arbitral awards and foreign arbitral awards

According to the 2018 International Arbitration Survey conducted by the Queen Mary University of London, 64% of the survey participants noted that the enforceability of awards was perceived as the most valuable characteristic of

---

91 Ellen Reinstein, 'Finding a Happy Ending for Foreign Investors: The Enforcement of Arbitration Awards in the People's Republic of China', *Indiana International Law & Comparative Law Review*, Vol. 16 Issue 1 (2005), pp. 37–72, at 59–60. Yongping Xiao and Zhengxin Huo, *supra* note 86, at 668–669.

92 安徽安庆宜秀经济开发区管理委员会、安庆大桥建设投资有限公司与安庆市迎春房地产开发有限公司申请撤销仲裁裁决特别程序民事裁定书 (2019)皖08民特4号 (Application of Revocation of Arbitral Award in the Case of *Anhui Anqing Yixiu Economic Development Zone Management Committee and Anqing Bridge Construction and Investment Co., Ltd. v. Anqing Yingchun Real Estate Co., Ltd.*, (2019) Wan 08 Min Te No. 4), *ChinaLawInfo*, https://www.pkulaw.com/pfnl/a6bdb3332ec0adc43f683464ee987f10b3f3d69a821 6a284bdfb.html, last accessed on 9 July 2021.

93 '反转！2018年深圳"认可"比特币财产属性的仲裁案的判决被撤销，因违反社会公共利益' (Plot Twist! Arbitral Award Confirming the Property Rights of Bitcoins in Shenzhen in 2018 Revoked by Court), *NetEase*, 14 January 2021, https://www.163.com/dy/article/ G0AFJ16D0514832I.html, last accessed on 9 July 2021.

94 Guodong Du and Qiang Liu, 'Chinese Court Confirms Bitcoin as Virtual Commodity', *China Justice Observer*, 8 May 2021, https://www.chinajusticeobserver.com/a/chinese -court-confirms-bitcoin-as-virtual-commodity, last accessed on 9 July 2021.

international arbitration.[95] However, it is impossible to provide reliable facts on the enforcement of foreign-related and foreign arbitral awards due to the general lack of statistics available from official or scholarly sources. A few empirical studies with obviously limited scale may shed some light for scholars and practitioners alike who are eager to get some insight.

Chinese research showed that from 2013 to 2015, the rate of setting aside domestic arbitral awards by the Chinese local courts was 15.77%, while for foreign-related awards for which the internal reporting system applied, the rate was merely 5.33%. For non-enforcement, the rate for domestic awards was 4.67%, while for foreign awards it was 0.14%.[96] According to the SPC source, in 2019 courts in China handled a total of 11,029 applications concerning revocation of arbitral awards. These courts eventually set aside or partially set aside arbitral awards in 637 cases, thus the rate of cancellation was approximately 5.8%. Among the 32 cases for the application of recognition and enforcement of foreign arbitral awards, only one case was reported that the court supported the defendant's challenge to such recognition and enforcement.[97] The earlier empirical study by Randall Peerenboom of 89 CIETAC and foreign arbitral award enforcement cases showed that 52% of the foreign awards and 47% of the CIETAC awards were enforced.[98] Obviously, the divergence of the surveys casts doubts on the accuracy of the facts.

In view of the shortage of available systematic statistical data, some spotlight that a general perception is that the enforceability of awards in China has improved as a result of the internal reporting system pioneered by the SPC since 1995. A more recent case analysis signals that 'Chinese judges are getting more experienced and sophisticated in dealing with enforcement applications. They are able to articulate their views and reasoning, and come to sensible and logical conclusions in cases involving complex issues'.[99] However, a different perspective is that 'many foreign investors and commentators report that enforcement of foreign awards in China is often difficult or impossible'.[100] Contrary to this, one supposition is that 'China has managed to build a legal system more effective than

95 Queen Mary University of London, *2018 International Arbitration Survey: The Evolution of International Arbitration*, http://www.arbitration.qmul.ac.uk/media/arbitration/docs/2018-International-Arbitration-Survey---The-Evolution-of-International-Arbitration-(2).PDF, last accessed on 9 July 2021, p. 9. For an in-depth study on enforcement of commercial arbitral awards, see Clarisse von Wunschheim, *Enforcement of Commercial Arbitral Awards in China* (Hong Kong: Sweet & Maxwell, 2014).
96 Jingzhou Tao and Mariana Zhong, 'China's 2017 Reform of Its Arbitration-Related Court Review Mechanism with a Focus on Improving Chinese Courts' Prior-Reporting System', *Journal of International Arbitration*, Vol. 35 No. 3 (2018), pp. 371–378, at 374.
97 SPC, *supra* note 59.
98 Randall Peerenboom, 'Seek Truth from Facts: An Empirical Study of Enforcement of Arbitral Awards in the PRC', *The American Journal of Comparative Law*, Vol. 49 Issue 2 (2001), pp. 249–327, at 252, 254.
99 Teresa Cheng S.C. and Joe Liu, *supra* note 87, at 652, 671.
100 Ellen Reinstein, *supra* note 91, at 51.

is generally believed among most U.S. commentators'.[101] As the SPC has taken new initiatives to improve arbitration judicial review on many aspects, including making the procedure and enforcement more transparent, it is desirable that the SPC will be able to provide accurate and detailed data concerning enforcement of foreign-related and foreign arbitral awards on an annual basis, which can then contribute to a better understanding of the reality.

6.7 Conclusion

At present, the AL promulgated in 1994 is definitely outdated and insufficient for application in arbitration practice, especially where foreign-related arbitration is concerned. The legal vacuum has been largely filled by innovative measures of the leading arbitration institutions and progressive judicial interpretations of the SPC. Consequently, foreign-related commercial arbitration has advanced with the adaptation to more international standards and practice.

Apart from strengthening the internationalization of domestic arbitration institutions internally, leading arbitration commissions have implemented a 'going out' policy by setting up branches abroad or arbitrating abroad to expand China's effect. At the same time, foreign arbitration institutions are 'invited in' to conduct arbitration in designated cities in China. This is considered both convenient for the business community and conducive to raising the professionalism of Chinese arbitration by energetic competition. The current Chinese judiciary, led by the SPC, is keen to create the image of an arbitration-friendly judicial system to facilitate recognition and enforcement of foreign-related and foreign arbitral awards. This has been particularly evident since 2013, as courts are requested to bring their functions in line with China's Belt and Road strategy.

Having said that, to build arbitration credibility and international competitiveness involving all actors in commercial arbitration, whether they are arbitrators, arbitration commissions, courts, and, in the case of China, particularly governments at central and local levels, is a process that may prove to be long and to require collective efforts. The ongoing amendment of the 1994 AL is a touchstone to test how far the Chinese government is prepared to liberalize the arbitration market to accommodate growing expectations for an efficient and effective dispute resolution mechanism and increasing international competition.

---

101 Roger P. Alford, Julian G. Ku and Bei Xiao, 'Perceptions and Reality: The Enforcement of Foreign Arbitral Awards in China', *Pacific Basin Law Journal*, Vol. 33 Issue 1 (2016), pp. 1–26, at 26.

7 Dispute settlement

Investor–state arbitration

7.1 China as a respondent

China's international investment agreements (IIAs) provide investor–state arbitration (ISA) to protect foreign investors' treaty-based rights from infringement by Chinese government agencies. Between 1982, the date of the conclusion of the first bilateral investment treaty (BIT) between China and Sweden, and December 2020 China concluded 138 BITs and 14 free trade agreements (FTAs) with investment chapters.[1] Although the majority of Chinese IIAs provide foreign investors access to ISA against the host states,[2] it is a rather new phenomenon that foreign investors have brought claims against China.

Up to August 2021, there has been a total of eight known ISA cases in which China is the respondent (see Table 7.1).

Some observations can be drawn from the aforementioned ISA cases. First, in recent years the growing number of ISA cases against China is impressive, and demonstrates an intensified utilization of the ISA mechanism by foreign investors to protect their property rights in China. Since the first case, *Ekran Berhad v. China*, lodged in 2011, in the last decade another seven cases were initiated, and in particular, 2020 alone witnessed three cases being filed. The paucity of claims against China before 2017 may be attributed to several causes. In the first place, it

---

1 MOFCOM, 'Department of Treaty and Law, Bilateral Investment Treaty', http://tfs.mofcom .gov.cn/article/Nocategory/201111/20111107819474.shtml, last accessed on 26 April 2021. MOFCOM, 'China FTA Network', http://fta.mofcom.gov.cn/english/fta_qianshu .shtml, last accessed on 26 April 2021.

2 Among the 138 BITs, 130 provide an ISA mechanism, exceptions are BITs between China with Sweden (1982) (renegotiated), Germany (1983) (renegotiated), France (1984) (renegotiated), Finland (1984) (renegotiated), Norway (1984), Italy (1985), Thailand (1985) and Denmark (1985). Among 14 FTAs with investment chapters, 9 provide an ISDS mechanism, with the exception of Regional Comprehensive Economic Partnership (2020), Georgia (2017), Switzerland (2013), Iceland (2013) and Costa Rica (2010). For a comprehensive understanding of China's BIT regime, see Yuwen Li and Cheng Bian, 'China's Stance on Investor-State Dispute Settlement: Evolution, Challenges, and Reform Options', *Netherlands International Law Journal*, Vol. 67 Issue 3 (2020), pp. 503–551. See also Wenhua Shan and Jinyuan Su (eds.), *China and International Investment Law Twenty Years of ICSID Membership* (Leiden: Brill/Nijhoff, 2015).

DOI: 10.4324/9781003168805-8

Table 7.1 China as a respondent in ISA

Year of initiation	Case	Investor's nationality	BIT	Subject matter	Arbitration institution	Outcome
2021	*Eugenio Montenero v. China*	Swiss	China–Switzerland BIT (2009)	Data not available	Data not available	Pending
2020	*AsiaPhos v. China*	Singaporean	China–Singapore (1985)	Sichuan local government's refusal to renew investor's exploitation permit to phosphate mines as the site falls within a newly established natural reserve park	ICSID (UNCITRAL Rules)	Pending
2020	*Goh Chin Soon v. China* (ICSID Case No. ARB/20/34)	Singaporean	China–Singapore (1985)	Qingdao local government's unlawful seizing of investor's real estate development projects, worth over 1.5 billion USD	ICSID	Pending
2020	*Macro Trading Co., Ltd. v. China* (ICSID Case No. ARB/20/22)	Japanese	China–Japan (1988)	Dispute in the construction sector	ICSID	Pending
2019	*Jason Yu Song v. China* (PCA Case 2019-39)	British	China–UK (1986)	Data not available	PCA	Pending

(*Continued*)

Table 7.1 Continued

Year of initiation	Case	Investor's nationality	BIT	Subject matter	Arbitration institution	Outcome
2017	*Hela Schwarz GmbH v. China* (ICSID Case No. ARB/17/19)	German	China–Germany (2003)	Jinan local government's seizure and demolition of investor's production facilities and factories (food processing company) without inadequate compensation, as a part of an 'urban redevelopment project'	ICSID	Pending
2014	*Ansung Housing Co., Ltd. v. China* (ICSID Case No. ARB/14/25)	Korean	China–Korea (2007)	Jiangsu local government's refusal to grant additional land use rights to the investor to complete its project already under construction of a large-scale golf course and resort	ICSID	In favour of state (claim time-barred)
2011	*Ekran Berhad v. China* (ICSID Case No. ARB/11/15)	Malaysian	China–Malaysia (1988)	Hainan local government's revocation of 70-year land use rights previously granted to the investor due to the investor's failure to develop a real estate project as planned according to local legislation	ICSID	Settled

Source: IAReporter, 'Case profiles, Respondents-People's Republic of China', https://www-iareporter-com.eur.idm.oclc.org/arbitration-cases/?fwp_respondents=peoples-republic-of-china, last accessed on 26 April 2021.

was long thought that foreign investors were reluctant to bring ISA against China for fear of antagonising the Chinese government, which could ruin the possibility of doing any business in China in the future.[3] Further, China used to grant foreign investors 'super-national treatment', which makes any claims on breaches of 'national treatment' or 'fair and equitable treatment' in a BIT against China very unlikely.[4] Some also argue that China wanted to protect its 'friendly and fair' image to foreign investors by engaging profusely with foreign investors in dispute prevention and avoidance so as to keep itself clear as a respondent in ISA.[5] The sudden increase of cases against China after 2017 is somewhat indecipherable. One presumption is that the ongoing investor–state dispute settlement (ISDS) reform may bring much uncertainty and unpredictability to the current arbitration mechanism, hence foreign investors wish to bring new claims against China under the existing ISA mechanism which they are familiar with and accustomed to. This presumption is also in line with the global trend. The ISA caseload witnessed a sharp increase at the global level: in the 6 years from 2015 to 2020 a total of 417 cases were initiated, whilst in the previous 28 years from 1987 to 2014 a total of 644 cases were filed.[6] Approximately 39% of the total 1,061 ISA cases worldwide were filed from 2015 to 2020.

Second, based on publicly known information, all cases against China involve local governments' specific measures that are challenged by investors as expropriation, and not a single case concerns the central government's general legislative amendments that may equal to regulatory expropriation. Regulatory expropriation, or indirect expropriation, entails the host states' laws or policies adopted for a public purpose, most commonly environmental or public health protection, that are not targeted specifically at an investment project, but nonetheless may negatively affect the economic interest or anticipated profitability of a foreign investor.[7] In five cases where details are disclosed to the public, the disputes all derived from the local government's expropriatory measures over the investor's property rights. In *Ekran Berhad v. China* and *Ansung Housing v. China*, the disputes arose out of the local government's revocation or refusal

3 Leon E. Trakman, Qiao Liu and Lei Chen, 'Investor-State Arbitration in China: A Comparative Perspective', in Lei Chen and André Janssen (eds.), *Dispute Resolution in China, Europe and World* (Cham: Springer, 2020), pp. 231–261, at 234.

4 Leon E. Trakman, 'Geopolitics, China, and Investor-State Arbitration', in Lisa Toohey, Colin B. Picker and Jonathan Greenacre (eds.), *China in the International Economic Order: New Directions and Changing Paradigms* (Cambridge: CUP, 2015), pp. 268–292, at 280.

5 Ibid, at 280.

6 The number of cases filed was 86 in 2015, 77 in 2016, 80 in 2017, 85 in 2018, 58 in 2019 and 31 in 2020. UNCTAD, 'Investment Policy Hub, Investment Dispute Settlement Navigator', https://investmentpolicy.unctad.org/investment-dispute-settlement, last accessed on 28 April 2021.

7 For a detailed discussion on regulatory expropriation, see Andrew Newcombe, 'The Boundaries of Regulatory Expropriation in International Law', *ICSID Review*, Vol. 20 Issue 1 (2005), pp. 1–57. Aniruddha Rajput, *Regulatory Freedom and Indirect Expropriation in Investment Arbitration* (Alphen aan den Rijn: Wolters Kluwer, 2018).

of land use rights to the investor which were necessary to continue or complete the investment. In *Hela Schwarz v. China* and *Goh Chin Soon v. China*, the disputes involved the local government's expropriation of production facilities or real estate construction. And in the case of *AsiaPhos v. China*, the dispute concerned the local government's refusal to renew the investor's exploitation license of a mine site. Therefore, China as a respondent has never been challenged for regulatory expropriation.

Third, based on publicly known information to date, at least four cases concern disputes over land use rights. In China, land ownership belongs to either the state (urban land) or a collective organization (rural land), only land use rights are transferable on the market. Foreign investment projects usually commence with the obtainment of land use rights, as construction, production or operation of the business are dependent on establishing a site. Depending on the various ways in which foreign investors obtain land use rights, disputes usually arise between the foreign investor and the local government, such as in an assignment, or between a foreign investor and a prior holder of land use rights, such as in a transfer; each of these scenarios entails particular legal risks.[8] All four ISA cases against China involving land use rights disputes are those between the investor and the local government. In *Ekran Berhad v. China* and *Ansung Housing v. China*, both cases were directly caused by land use rights disputes, the former concerned the local government's revocation of previously promised land use rights to investors, and the latter involved the local government's refusal to grant additional land use rights to investors to complete the whole project as planned. In the case of *Hela Schwarz GmbH v. China*, the Jinan Municipal government allegedly both expropriated the land use rights for the duration of 50 years and demolished all existing facilities built upon said lands as part of an urban renovation project, with undervalued compensation remitted to the investor.[9] In *Goh Chin Soon v. China*, the dispute allegedly arose out of the Qingdao Municipal government's expropriation of the Singaporean investor's real estate development project worth 1.5 billion USD.[10] The details are still unknown, but it is likely that the *Goh Chin Soon v. China* case involves the confiscation of the investor's land use rights of the real estate project as well.

The *Regulation on the Expropriation of Buildings on State-Owned Land and Compensation* promulgated in 2011 and its accompanying judicial interpretation

---

8 An assignment means the land use right is directly obtained from government land administration departments in ways such as auction, bidding or agreement. A transfer means the land use right is purchased from another land use right holder on the secondary land market. For a detailed discussion on different ways for foreign investors to obtain land use rights in China and the different legal risks entailed, see Shoushuang Li, *The Legal Environment and Risks for Foreign Investment in China* (Berlin: Springer, 2007), pp. 175–193.

9 *Hela Schwarz GmbH v. China*, ICSID Case No. ARB/17/19, Procedural Order No. 2, Decision on the Claimant's Request for Provisional Measures, 10 August 2018, paras. 35–36.

10 Lisa Bohmer, 'Singaporean Real Estate Developer Launches Treaty-Based Arbitration against China', *IAReporter*, 17 September 2020, https://www-iareporter-com.eur.idm.oclc .org/articles/singaporean-real-estate-developer-launches-treaty-based-arbitration-against -china/, last accessed on 28 April 2021.

stipulate that the decision to expropriate properties and the land use rights attached to them can be legally made by government at the county level or above, and the owner can challenge the expropriation decision or the amount of compensation by initiating either an administrative review or an administrative litigation.[11] In the event that the owner does not initiate any legal proceedings against the expropriation decision, and in the meantime refuses to relocate in the given time, the local government must first obtain a ruling from a competent court for compulsory enforcement of said expropriation decision.[12] This means that local governments must have a court ruling in order to vacate a property to be expropriated, and can no longer use forceful means such as violence or threat, as was sometimes the case in the past.

7.2 Interpretation of 'the amount of compensation for expropriation'

Chinese BITs can be classified into three generations.[13] The first-generation Chinese BITs were concluded from 1982 to 1999, accounting for 64% of the whole Chinese BIT regime (88 out of 138 BITs).[14] First-generation Chinese BITs contain a restricted ISDS clause, namely only 'disputes concerning the amount of compensation for expropriation' can be brought to arbitration. The rationale behind such a restricted ISDS clause is that the Chinese government wished to retain the adjudicative power at domestic courts in resolving disputes with foreign investors, rather than at an international venue which the Chinese government had little control over.[15] Second-generation Chinese BITs were concluded from 1997 to 2011, and account for 33% of the whole Chinese BIT regime (46 out of 138 BITs).[16] The scope of admissibility to ISA in second-generation BITs is expanded to 'legal disputes', or 'disputes in connection with an investment', or

---

11 国有土地上房屋征收与补偿条例 (Regulation on the Expropriation and Compensation of Buildings on State-Owned Land) (Promulgated by the State Council on 21 January 2011, effective on promulgation), Arts. 4, 14, 26.

12 Ibid, Art. 28. 最高人民法院关于办理申请人民法院强制执行国有土地上房屋征收补偿决定案件若干问题的规定 (Provisions of the SPC on Several Issues Concerning Cases for Application to the People's Courts for Compulsory Enforcement of Decisions on Expropriation and Compensation of Buildings on State-Owned Land) (Issued on 26 March 2012, effective on 10 April 2012).

13 Yuwen Li and Cheng Bian, *supra* note 2, at 504–505.

14 Ibid, at 507.

15 Manjiao Chi and Xi Wang, 'The Evolution of ISA Clauses in Chinese IIAs and Its Practical Implications: The Admissibility of Disputes for Investor-State Arbitration', *Journal of World Investment & Trade*, Vol. 16 Issue 5 (2015), pp. 869–898, at 873–874.

16 Yuwen Li and Cheng Bian, *supra* note 2, at 507. The evolution of Chinese BITs does not follow a strict chronological order. For instance, the China–South Africa BIT was concluded in 1997, which belongs to the second-generation. However, BITs concluded after the China–South Africa BIT with Yemen (1998), Cabo Verde (1998), Ethiopia (1998), Qatar (1999) and Bahrain (1999) go back to the first generation.

a combination of 'legal disputes in connection with an investment'.[17] This treaty-making shift is mainly due to China's changing attitude to adapt its BIT regime to prevailing international treaty-making practice and standards, and China's endeavour to integrate into the international investment law and governance.[18] Third-generation Chinese BITs began to appear from 2007, covering disputes where an investor or its investment has incurred loss or damage arising from breaches of treaty provisions that are explicitly referenced.[19] Four BITs include such an ISDS clause and thus belong to the third generation.[20] It is believed that this shift in third-generation Chinese BITs from previous generations is a result of the emulation of the United States Model BITs that are more comprehensive and elaborate, compared to the first and second generations of Chinese BITs that follow a traditionally succinct European style of BIT-making.[21]

Arbitration jurisprudence regarding first-generation Chinese BITs turns out to be the most problematic for its lack of consistency or predictability. In addition to eight cases where China is a respondent (see Table 7.1), there are now eight known cases where the investor is a Chinese national (including Hong Kong and Macao).[22] In these 16 cases, 11 cases involve first-generation Chinese BITs (see

17 Ibid.
18 Stephan W. Schill, 'Tearing Down the Great Wall: The New Generation Investment Treaties of the People's Republic of China', *Cardozo Journal of International and Comparative Law*, Vol. 15 Issue 1 (2007), pp. 73–118, at 113–114.
19 For instance, Art. 20.1 of the China–Canada BIT (2012) stipulates that an investor may submit a claim to arbitration when the investor or its investment has incurred loss or damage by reason of, or arising out of breaches of obligations under Arts. 2 to 7(2), 9, 10 to 13, 14 (4) or 16 of the BIT.
20 Art. 13.1 of the China–Mexico BIT (2008); Art. 20.1 of the China–Canada BIT (2012); Art. 13.2 of the China–Tanzania BIT (2013); and Art. 9 of the China–Cuba BIT (2007).
21 Manjiao Chi, 'From Europeanization toward Americanization: The Shift of China's Dichotomic Investment Treaty-Making Strategy', *Canadian Foreign Policy Journal*, Vol. 23 Issue 2 (2017), pp. 158–170. Axel Berger, 'Investment Rules in Chinese PTIAs: A Partial 'NAFTA-ization' Reintegration', in Rainer Hofmann, Stephan Schill and Christian Tams (eds.), *Preferential Trade and Investment Agreements: From Recalibration to Reintegration* (Baden-Baden: Nomos, 2013), pp. 297–333.
22 These eight cases are *Fengzhen Min v. Republic of Korea*, ICSID Case No. ARB/20/26 (2020); *Wang Jing et al. v. Republic of Ukraine*, administering institution unknown (2020); *Jetion Solar Co. Ltd and Wuxi T-Hertz Co. Ltd. v. Greece*, UNCITRAL Rules (2019), administering institution unknown, discontinued; *Beijing Urban Construction Group Co. Ltd. v. Republic of Yemen*, ICSID Case No. ARB/14/30 (2014); *Sanum Investments Limited v. Lao People's Democratic Republic*, UNCITRAL, PCA Case No. 2013–13 (2013); *Ping An Life Insurance Company of China, Limited and Ping An Insurance (Group) Company of China, Limited v. Kingdom of* Belgium, ICSID Case No. ARB/12/29 (2012); *China Heilongjiang International Economic & Technical Cooperative Corp. et al. v. Mongolia*, PCA Case No. 2010–20 (2010); and *Tza Yap Shum v. Republic of Peru*, ICSID Case No. ARB/07/6 (2007). Data retrieved from UNCTAD, 'Investment Dispute Settlement Navigator, China, Cases as Home State of Claimant', https://investmentpolicy.unctad.org/investment-dispute-settlement/country/42/china, last accessed on 15 August 2021.

Table 7.2), and 5 involve second-generation BITs.[23] Of these 11 cases involving first-generation BITs, 5 cases were decided (including 2 settled cases), 1 case was discontinued, and 5 are still pending (see Table 7.2). In the 5 decided cases, 4 of them rendered Decisions on Jurisdiction,[24] where different tribunals and national courts interpreted 'amount of compensation for expropriation', the term that determines whether the tribunals had jurisdiction over the case, and resulted in opposite outcomes (see Table 7.2).

Two schools of interpretation of 'amount of compensation for expropriation' have been adopted in adjudication. The broad interpretation includes both the liability of expropriation (whether an expropriatory act has taken place) and the quantification of compensation (the monetary amount to be compensated) as admissible disputes to arbitration, while the narrow interpretation only admits the quantification of compensation. By the broad interpretation, the investor is able to resort to arbitration directly, without the need to bring a case to a national court or administrative review of the host state as a prerequisite. Conversely, by the narrow interpretation the investor must first have obtained a confirmation from the host state on the acts of expropriation, and only after that can the investor bring the matter of quantification of compensation to arbitration.[25] If the BIT in issue also contains a fork-in-the-road provision, a narrow interpretation of 'the amount of compensation for expropriation' would result in the invalidation of ISA *ipso jure*, because once the investor chooses to submit the dispute to domestic courts first, it loses its eligibility to resort to ISA later.[26]

In the four cases that decided on jurisdiction, all Tribunals claimed to adhere to Art. 31 of the Vienna Convention on the Law of Treaties (VCLT) in terms

---

23 These five cases are *Fengzhen Min v. Republic of Korea*, ICSID Case No. ARB/20/26 (2020); *Eugenio Montenero v. China*, administering institution unknown (2021); *Ping An Life Insurance Company, Limited and Ping An Insurance (Group) Company, Limited v. Belgium*, ICSID Case No. ARB/12/29; *Ansung Housing Co. Ltd. v. China*, ICSID Case No. ARB/14/25; and *Hela Schwarz GmbH v. China*, ICSID Case No. ARB/17/19 .

24 In *Sanum v. Laos*, *China Heilongjiang et al. v. Mongolia* and *Tza Yap Shum v. Peru*, the Tribunals first rendered Decisions on Jurisdiction, and then Awards. In *Beijing Urban Construction Group Co. Ltd. v. Yemen*, the Tribunal only rendered Decision on Jurisdiction, and then the case was settled between the parties. In *Ekran Berhad v. China*, the case was settled before a tribunal was established.

25 Norah Gallagher and Wenhua Shan, *Chinese Investment Treaties: Policies and Practice* (Oxford: OUP, 2009), p. 316.

26 For example, in *Tza Yap Shum v. Peru*, the Tribunal opines that because the China–Peru BIT includes a first-generation ISDS clause and a fork-in-the-road provision, it is implied that once an investor has chosen to submit a dispute on expropriation to a domestic court, the investor 'may not, under any circumstance, make use of ICSID arbitration to settle a dispute involving the amount of compensation for expropriation'. *Tza Yap Shum v. Republic of Peru*, ICSID Case No ARB/07/6, Decision on Jurisdiction and Competence, 19 June 2009, para. 159. The same opinion was given in *Siemens A.G. v. The Argentine Republic*, ICSID Case No. ARB/02/8, Decision on Jurisdiction, 3 August 2004. August Reinisch, 'How Narrow Are Narrow Dispute Settlement Clauses in Investment Treaties?' *Journal of International Dispute Settlement*, Vol. 2 No. 1 (2011), pp. 115–174, at 129, 135, 167.

Table 7.2 Interpretation of 'the amount of compensation for expropriation' in first-generation Chinese BITs

Case	Year of initiation	BIT	Claimant nationality	Respondent	Status	Position in interpretation	Outcome
Wang Jing et al. v. Republic of Ukraine	2020	China–Ukraine (1992)	Chinese	Ukraine	Pending	–	–
AsiaPhos v. China	2020	China–Singapore (1985)	Singaporean	China	Pending	–	–
Goh Chin Soon v. China	2020	China–Singapore (1985)	Singaporean	China	Pending	–	–
Macro Trading Co., Ltd. v. China	2020	China–Japan (1988)	Japanese	China	Pending	–	–
Jason Yu Song v. China	2019	China–UK (1986)	British	China	Pending	–	–
Jetion Solar Co. Ltd and Wuxi T-Hertz Co., Ltd. v. Greece	2019	China–Greece (1992)	Chinese	Greece	Discontinued	–	–
Beijing Urban Construction Group Co., Ltd. v. Yemen	2014	China–Yemen (1998)	Chinese	Yemen	Concluded	Broad	Jurisdiction confirmed Settled

Sanum v. Laos	2013	China–Laos (1993)	Macao	Laos	Concluded	Tribunal: broad National court of the seat of arbitration (SGHC): narrow Appeal court (SGCA): broad	In favour of State
Ekran Berhad v. China	2011	China–Malaysia (1988)	Malaysian	China	Settled	–	Settled before the establishment of a tribunal
China Heilongjiang et al. v. Mongolia	2010	China–Mongolia (1991)	Chinese	Mongolia	Concluded	Tribunal: narrow National court of the seat of arbitration (SDNY): confirmed the validity of the Award on the ground of arbitrability[a]	In favour of state (jurisdiction declined)
Tza Yap Shum v. Peru	2007	China–Peru (1994)	Hong Kong	Peru	Concluded	Broad	In favour of investor

[a] In 2017, the claimants filed a petition to the US District Court for the Southern District of New York (SDNY), where the arbitration was seated, to annul the Award. The Court ruled in 2019, rejecting the claimants' petition and confirming the validity of the Award. The Court 'finds that the parties clearly and unmistakably agreed to place the question of arbitrability before the tribunal', and did not express any opinions on the Tribunal's interpretation of 'amount of compensation for expropriation'. See *Beijing Shougang Mining Investment Company, Ltd. et al. v. Mongolia*, No. 1:2017cv07436 – Document 21 (S.D.N.Y. 2019), p. 1.

of their interpretative techniques, namely to interpret treaty provisions 'in good faith in accordance with the ordinary meaning to be given to the terms of the treaty in their context and in the light of its object and purpose', but emphasized different aspects and came to divergent conclusions.[27] In *Tza Yap Shum v. Peru*, *Sanum v. Laos*, and *BUCG v. Yemen*, the Tribunals supported a broad interpretation and confirmed their jurisdiction over the dispute, whereas in *China Heilongjiang v. Mongolia*, the Tribunal adopted a narrow interpretation and decided its lack of jurisdiction.[28] The inconsistency of outcomes in these cases is further exacerbated by domestic courts where the respondents sought to annul the Decision on Jurisdiction or the Award at the seat of arbitration. In *Sanum v. Laos*, the Singapore High Court (SGHC) endorsed a narrow interpretation which was later overturned by the Singapore Court of Appeal (SGCA) in support of a broad interpretation and confirmed the jurisdiction of the Tribunal. Meanwhile, in *China Heilongjiang et al. v. Mongolia*, the New York Southern District Court confirmed the Tribunal's lack of jurisdiction on the ground of arbitrability.[29]

Because of the fact that interpretation given by any arbitral tribunals or national courts does not have a binding precedential effect for pending or future cases, first-generation Chinese BITs cannot 'guarantee a formalistic, formulaic or recitative interpretation'.[30] This creates uncertainty and a great potential for more inconsistent outcomes in future arbitration cases when first-generation Chinese BITs are at issue, *inter alia*, in the five pending cases where China is a respondent.

When China ratified Convention on the Settlement of Investment Disputes between States and Nationals of Other States (ICSID Convention) in 1993, following a Notification to Art. 25(4) of the ICSID Convention, China would only be subject to the ICSID jurisdiction disputes over compensation resulting from expropriation and nationalization.[31] This Notification complies with first-generation Chinese BITs with a limited arbitration clause but would appear to be in contradiction with second and third generations of Chinese BITs with an expanded arbitration clause. One explanation is that 'a notification under Art. 25(4) does not amount to a reservation to the Convention', and therefore, 'notifications under Art. 25(4) are for purposes of information only, ... do not have any direct legal consequences', and 'do not bind the Contracting State making the notification'.[32] Others argue that China's Notification in the ICSID Convention does not affect the validity of second and third generations of Chinese BITs

---

27 For a detailed discussion, see Yuwen Li and Cheng Bian, *supra* note 2, at 509–513.
28 Ibid, at 513.
29 Ibid, at 513.
30 Wei Shen, 'The Good, the Bad or the Ugly? A Critique of the Decision on Jurisdiction and Competence in *Tza Yap Shum v. The Republic of Peru*', *Chinese Journal of International Law*, Vol. 10 Issue 1 (2011), pp. 55–95, at 94.
31 ICSID, 'China – Notifications Concerning a Class or Classes of Disputes Which the Contracting State Would or Would Not Consider Submitting to the Jurisdiction of the Centre (Art. 25(4))', 7 January 1993, https://icsid.worldbank.org/about/member-states/database-of-member-states/member-state-details?state=ST30, last accessed on 10 May 2021.
32 Christoph H. Schreuer *et al.*, *The ICSID Convention: A Commentary*, 2nd edn. (Cambridge: CUP, 2009), pp. 343–344.

because all second- and third-generation Chinese BITs were concluded after 1997 and should prevail over this Notification made in 1993 according to Art. 30 VCLT.[33] Indeed, four out of five ISA cases involving second-generation Chinese BITs are nonetheless administered by ICSID (and one unknown).[34]

7.3 Exhaustion of local remedies

The exhaustion of the local remedy clause in IIAs refers to a requirement that investors must first resort to and ultimately exhaust all local remedies in the host state for a given period in order to then be able to initiate an ISA proceeding.[35] Local remedies may refer to an administrative review proceeding according to local laws of the host state, or a judicial proceeding at a domestic court, or both administrative and judicial proceedings.[36]

Only a small proportion of Chinese BITs require the mandatory exhaustion of local remedies as a prerequisite to ISA. According to an empirical study, 15 Chinese IIAs (including BITs and FTAs with investment chapters) include a compulsory clause that requires investors to seek administrative reconsideration or administrative review for three to six months before they are entitled to file a claim to ISA.[37] Notably, these 15 IIAs only require the exhaustion of administrative review of the host state before resorting to ISA, but do not include judicial proceedings at a domestic court.[38]

In terms of judicial local remedies at a domestic court, no Chinese IIAs require the exhaustion of domestic litigation as a pre-ISA condition. Instead, domestic courts are offered as an alternative to ISA for dispute resolution, at the free

33 Art. 30 VCLT provides that between the same parties of two treaties, when two treaties on the same subject matter do not accord with each other, the more recent one should prevail. Peter Turner, 'Investor-State Arbitration', in Michael J Moser (ed.), *Managing Business Disputes in Today's China – Duelling with Dragons* (Alphen aan den Rijn: Kluwer Law International, 2007), pp. 233–258, at 234.

34 *Supra* note 23.

35 M. Sornarajah, *The International Law on Foreign Investment*, 4th edn. (Cambridge: CUP, 2017), pp. 257–258.

36 Martin Dietrich Brauch, 'Exhaustion of Local Remedies in International Investment Law', *International Institute for Sustainable Development Best Practices Series*, January 2017, https://www.iisd.org/system/files/publications/best-practices-exhaustion-local-remedies -law-investment-en.pdf, last accessed on 10 May 2021, p. 2.

37 Chinese BITs use the terms 'administrative review' and 'administrative reconsideration' interchangeably. The two terms are deemed equivalent and refer to the same administrative procedure in Chinese law. Manjiao Chi and Zongyao Li, 'Administrative Review Provisions in Chinese Investment Treaties: "Gilding the Lily"?' *Journal of International Dispute Settlement*, Vol. 12 Issue 1 (2021), pp. 125–150, at 129.

38 For example, Art. 9.3 of the China-Côte d'Ivoire BIT (2002) stipulates that 'if dispute cannot be settled amicably through negotiations, any legal dispute between an investor … and the other Contracting Party in connection with an investment … shall exhaust the domestic administrative review procedure specified by the laws and regulations of that Contracting Party, before the submission of the dispute aforementioned to an arbitration procedure'.

choice of the investor. For example, Art. 10.1 of the China–Poland BIT (1988) stipulates:

> If an investor challenges the amount of compensation for the expropriated investment assets, he may file complaint with the competent authority of the Contracting Party taking the expropriatory measures. If it is not solved within one year after the complaint is filed, the competent court of the Contracting Party taking the expropriatory measures *or* (emphasis added) an *ad hoc* international arbitral tribunal shall, upon the request of the investor, review the amount of compensation.

It is clear from the wording that a 'complaint with the competent authority of the Contracting Party taking the expropriatory measures' is a mandatory prerequisite prior to ISA. Subsequently, an investor may resort to either a domestic court or investment arbitration to resolve a dispute over the amount of compensation. The term 'or' also suggests that the two alternatives are exclusive to each other, as the investor cannot pursue both options parallelly for the same subject matter.

China's administrative review procedure is deemed neither 'independent' nor 'neutral', remains 'largely unclear' procedurally, is 'insufficiently transparent', and 'lacks finality and practical effectiveness'.[39] And there is a general distrust of the independence and impartiality of the Chinese administrative litigation system, and formidability in challenging the local government at a local court.[40] As a result, local remedies may become less appealing for foreign investors in resolving their investment disputes against a local government in China compared to recourse to ISA.

Foreign investors who choose to resort to local remedies in China to resolve their investment disputes may encounter unsatisfactory results. For example, in *Hela Schwarz GmbH v. China*, the BIT in question, namely the China–Germany BIT (2003), has neither an exhaustion of local remedies clause nor a fork-in-the-road clause. The alleged expropriatory act of the Jinan municipal government took place in 2014, when it issued a Housing Expropriation Decision to seize the land use rights and the buildings above where the German investor's food processing factories were located.[41] The investor first filed for an administrative reconsideration of the Shandong Provincial Government to challenge the Expropriation Decision, which was rejected in 2016.[42] The investor then brought an administrative lawsuit against the Jinan municipal government to the Jinan Intermediate People's Court, where the Court ruled to dismiss all claims of the

---

39 Manjiao Chi and Zongyao Li, *supra* note 37, at 134.
40 For understanding the administrative litigation system in China, see Yuwen Li, *The Judicial System and Reform in Post-Mao China: Stumbling Towards Justice* (Farnham: Ashgate, 2014), pp. 165–197.
41 *Hela Schwarz GmbH v. China*, ICSID Case No. ARB/17/19, Procedural Order No. 2, Decision on the Claimant's Request for Provisional Measures, 10 August 2018, para. 36.
42 Ibid, para. 37.

investor.[43] The investor even appealed to the Shandong High People's Court, and the Court sustained the rulings rendered in the first-instance trial.[44] The investor then filed for arbitration with ICSID in 2017 after all domestic remedies had failed.[45] In this case, the German investor has essentially exhausted all available local remedies before its recourse to arbitration, albeit there is no such mandatory requirement in the BIT. Failure in acquiring sufficient compensation at the domestic level has led to the frustrated German investor to seek treaty-based protection in ISA.

7.4 Selection of arbitration institutions

The line between institutional and *ad hoc* arbitration is getting increasingly blurry. Typically, ISA is either institutional arbitration when the proceeding is being administered by an arbitration institution according to the arbitration rules of that institution or *ad hoc* arbitration when the proceeding is administered according to the United Nations Commission on International Trade Law (UNCITRAL) Arbitration Rules.[46] An *ad hoc* arbitration can be facilitated with the service provided by a few frequently used international arbitration institutions such as the Permanent Court of Arbitration (PCA), the International Court of Arbitration of International Chamber of Commerce (ICC), the London Court of International Arbitration (LCIA), the Arbitration Institute of the Stockholm Chamber of Commerce (SCC).[47]

Ad hoc arbitration is the most referred venue of arbitration in Chinese BITs. Out of 138 Chinese BITs, 99 of them provide the option of *ad hoc* arbitration, and 53 of them provide ICSID Arbitration as an option.[48] In contrast, the most frequently selected venue of arbitration in China-related ISA practice is the ICSID. Among eight ISA cases in which China is a respondent, six are ICSID cases, one is administered at the PCA, and one is unknown.[49] In eight cases involving Chinese claimants, four are ICSID cases, two are administered at the PCA, and two are unknown.[50]

In recent years three Chinese arbitration institutions have expanded their jurisdiction to treaty-based investor–state arbitration. In 2016, the Shenzhen Court of

---

43 Ibid, para. 38.
44 Ibid, para. 38.
45 Ibid, para. 41.
46 Chin Leng Lim, Jean Ho and Martins Paparinskis, *International Investment Law and Arbitration: Commentary, Awards and Other Materials* (Cambridge: CUP, 2018), pp. 106–111.
47 In practice, 685 out of 1104 ISA cases worldwide from 1987 to 2020 were administered by ICSID. The second most popular venue of arbitration is the PCA (179 cases). And 75 cases were conducted without any administering institution, taking the third place. UNCTAD, 'Investment Policy Hub, Investment Dispute Settlement Navigator, Institutions', https:// investmentpolicy.unctad.org/investment-dispute-settlement, last accessed on 14 May 2021.
48 Yuwen Li and Cheng Bian, *supra* note 2, at 535–548.
49 See Table 7.1.
50 *Supra* note 22.

International Arbitration (SCIA) amended its existing arbitration rules to expand its jurisdiction to ISA.[51] In 2017, the China International Economic and Trade Arbitration Commission (CIETAC) adopted its standalone investor–state arbitration rules.[52] The Beijing Arbitration Commission (BAC) has followed suit and adopted its standalone investor–state arbitration rules in 2019.[53] These institutional innovations are understood as China's attempt 'to amplify its voice in the international discourse' and 'to break the monopoly of existing Western-initiated institutions'.[54]

Chinese arbitration institutions' enthusiasm and ambition in building the institutional capacity to manage investor–state arbitration is supported by the central government policy to magnify China's impact in international dispute settlement. However, sizable legislative and international obstacles may hinder their practicability.[55] As discussed in Chapter 6 of this book, the current AL does not equip Chinese arbitration institutions with the competence to administer ISA cases either as institutional or *ad hoc* arbitration.[56] Despite the recent legitimization of *ad hoc* arbitration in the Pilot Free Trade Zones (PFTZs), it is strictly confined to commercial arbitration.[57]

To circumvent the legal impediments under the current AL, the three Chinese arbitration institutions 'have designed creative provisions in their ISA rules' to locate their seat of arbitration to outside of mainland China.[58] Both the CIETAC and the SCIA arbitration rules provide that Hong Kong should be the default seat of ISA,[59] and the BAC goes even further to allow an investor–state arbitral tribunal to decide a preferred seat of arbitration.[60] Even Chinese arbitration institutions could admit ISA cases in Hong Kong or at a foreign jurisdiction that allows ISA,

---

51 SCIA, Arbitration Rules (2016), Arts. 2.2. and 3.
52 CIETAC, International Investment Arbitration Rules (For Trial Implementation) (2017).
53 BAC, Rules for International Investment Arbitration (2019).
54 Huiping Chen, 'Reforming ISDS: A Chinese Perspective', in Yuwen Li, Tong Qi and Cheng Bian (eds.), *China, the EU and International Investment Law: Reforming Investor-State Dispute Settlement* (London: Routledge, 2019), pp. 100–111, at 104.
55 For an in-depth and critical analysis of China's arbitration institutions' engagement in ISA market, see Manjiao Chi, 'The ISDS Adventure of Chinese Arbitration Institutions: Towards a Dead End or a Bright Future?', *Asia Pacific Law Review*, Vol. 28 Issue 2 (2020), pp. 279–296.
56 仲裁法 (Arbitration Law of China) (Promulgated by the NPC on 31 August 1994, effective on 1 September 1995, revised in 2009 and 2017), Arts. 2 and 16.
57 In 2016, the SPC issued Opinions on Providing Judicial Guarantee for the Building of Pilot Free Trade Zones, which acknowledge the legality of *ad hoc* commercial arbitration in the PFTZs under certain circumstances. 最高人民法院关于为自由贸易试验区建设提供司法保障的意见 (Issued on 30 December 2016, effective on promulgation), Art. 9(3). The first and only *ad hoc* arbitration rules in China are the Ad Hoc Arbitration Rules in Hengqin Pilot Free Trade Zones (Zhuhai). 横琴自由贸易试验区临时仲裁规则 (Adopted by Zhuhai Arbitration Commission on 18 March 2017, effective on 15 April 2017).
58 Manjiao Chi, *supra* note 55.
59 CIETAC, International Investment Arbitration Rules (For Trial Implementation) (2017), Art. 74. SCIA, Guidelines for the Administration of Arbitration Under the UNCITRAL Arbitration Rules (2019), Art. 3.
60 BAC, Rules for International Investment Arbitration (2019), Art. 26.

the competence of these arbitration institutions can still be challenged. Assuming that China will remove those legal impediments when introducing the new AL, practical barriers remain. Considering the established reputation of ICSID and PCA, and the high demand for independence and neutrality of arbitration institutions and arbitrators, Chinese arbitration institutions face formidable stumbling blocks to gain international trust. However, as international business is turning to the East, one can expect that the ISA will also follow. In order to create an ISA-friendly jurisdiction, the Chinese government needs to revise its AL to create a broad arbitration-friendly regime, and Chinese arbitration institutions need to improve their reputation and credibility, and all these may take time and demand a substantial change of actors involved within arbitration and judiciary circles and beyond.

7.5 Enforcement of arbitral awards

Up to now there has been no arbitral award rendered in favour of a foreign investor against China, enforcement therefore has not yet been a pressing issue. However, in theory, enforcement of ISA awards can be problematic in China.

China acceded to the ICSID Convention in 1993, hence it is obliged to recognize and enforce ICSID awards in accordance with Arts. 53 to 55 of the ICSID Convention. These articles declare that ICSID awards are binding on the parties and cannot be brought to any appeal or to any other remedy at the domestic level. Art. 54(2) provides that a State party should designate a competent court or other authority for recognition and enforcement of ICSID awards. Because there is not any specific domestic legislation to clarify the recognition and enforcement of ICSID awards in China, and the Chinese law is not at all clear on the applicability of international treaties in the domestic legal system, i.e., whether a Chinese court can directly apply the ICSID Convention to enforce an arbitral award thereof, enforcement of ICSID awards in China remains uncertain.[61]

For non-ICSID ISA awards, the Convention on the Recognition and Enforcement of Foreign Arbitral Awards (New York Convention) in principle could be relevant to their recognition and enforcement. However, by accession to the New York Convention in 1987, China made a commercial reservation to the application of the Convention, namely that only foreign arbitral awards of disputes arising from contractual or noncontractual commercial legal relationships can be recognized or enforced in China.[62] Moreover, in 1987, the Supreme

---

61 Julian G. Ku, 'Enforcement of ICSID Awards in the People's Republic of China', *Contemporary Asia Arbitration Journal*, Vol. 6 Issue 1 (2013), pp. 31–48.
62 The reservation stipulates: 'The People's Republic of China will apply the Convention only to differences arising out of legal relationships, whether contractual or not, which are considered as commercial under the national law of the People's Republic of China'. New York Arbitration Convention on the Recognition and Enforcement of Foreign Arbitral Awards, 10 June 1958, Contracting State, Declarations and Reservations, China, https://www.newyorkconvention.org/countries, last accessed on 10 May 2021.

People's Court (SPC) issued the *Circular on Implementing the Convention on the Recognition and Enforcement of Foreign Arbitral Awards*, which further defines commercial disputes to exclude those between a foreign investor and a state.[63] With this explicit exclusion of applicability of the New York Convention in China regarding foreign ISA awards, it remains unclear whether and how non-ICSID awards can be recognized or enforced in China.

As a result, under China's current domestic legal system, there is a 'lacuna' with regard to recognition and enforcement of ISA awards.[64] The existing Chinese legislation does not provide any legal source for the enforcement of investor–state arbitral awards. If an award is rendered against China ordering compensation to an aggrieved investor, a number of outstanding issues can be raised. It is unknown which court or authority should be competent or responsible to handle the matter. Also, which level of the government will remunerate remains in question. Is it the liability of the central government, or will the local government that imposed the concrete measures indemnify, or will it be a shared responsibility of both? In addition, CIETAC, SCIA, and BAC arbitration rules on ISA indicate the intention of these institutions not only to adjudicate investor–state disputes in China but also to be able to have their ISA awards enforced and executed in China. But to recognize and enforce ISA awards rendered by Chinese arbitration institutions is just as problematic as an ISA award rendered by an international arbitration institution. Although so far China has never been obliged to pay any compensation to foreign investors, this may occur in light of the six pending ISA cases against China. In that event, how recognition and enforcement of ISA awards in China can be carried out continues to be a perplexity.

Another significant obstacle to execute an ISA award in China against state assets is sovereign immunity. Sovereign immunity is a recognized principle of customary international law, which includes the absolute doctrine and the restrictive doctrine.[65] Absolute sovereign immunity means that 'one state is not subject to the jurisdiction of another state' and enjoys 'absolute rule of immunity' from the national judiciary and enforcement.[66] Restrictive sovereign immunity acknowledges a series of specific exceptions, in which a state's conduct is non-immune and subject to the jurisdiction of another state, such as a state's commercial activities or a state's implied consent as a waiver.[67] Chinese

---

63 最高人民法院关于执行我国加入的《承认及执行外国仲裁裁决公约》的通知 (Circular on Implementing the Convention on the Recognition and Enforcement of Foreign Arbitral Awards) (Issued by the SPC on 10 April 1987, effective on promulgation), Art. 2.

64 Chad Catterwell and Brenda Horrigan, 'China', in Julien Fouret and Eversheds Sutherland (eds.), *Enforcement of Investment Treaty Arbitration Awards: A Global Guide*, 2nd edn. (Surrey: Global Law and Business, 2021), pp. 255–282, at 270.

65 For a comprehensive understanding of sovereign immunity, see Hazel Fox and Philippa Webb, *The Law of State Immunity*, 3rd edn. (Oxford: OUP, 2015). Malcolm N. Shaw, *International Law*, 8th edn. (Cambridge: CUP, 2017), pp. 523–588.

66 Hazel Fox and Philippa Webb, *supra* note 65, pp. 26–32.

67 Ibid, pp. 32–37.

domestic law in general doesn't address the matter of sovereign immunity, with the only exception being the *Law on Immunity of Assets of Foreign Central Banks from Judicial Compulsory Measures in China*.[68] In one commercial arbitration case, namely *Democratic Republic of the Congo v. FG Hemisphere LLC*, the NPC had the opportunity to express its affirmation on absolute sovereign immunity against the enforcement of state assets.[69] In this case a private company, Energoinvest, entered into contracts with the Democratic Republic of the Congo to finance the construction of a hydroelectric project. When Congo defaulted on its payment, Energoinvest initiated two commercial arbitration proceedings against the country at the ICC. In 2003, two awards were rendered in favour of Energoinvest, which later sold its entire benefits granted by the awards to another private company named FG Hemisphere. FG sought to enforce the awards against Congo's state assets located in Hong Kong, while Congo cited sovereignty immunity as a defence to refuse enforcement. Because the Hong Kong Court of Final Appeal held that state immunity was a matter of foreign affairs, and its interpretation was a competence of the NPC Standing Committee, the Court referred to the NPC to determine the matter. The NPC's reply has explicitly confirmed that 'the position on state immunity adopted by China is ... absolute immunity', and that state properties should be exempt from enforcement even if the state acts in a commercial function.[70] A recent study points out that 'it is almost impossible for ISA awards to be enforced' in China 'in light of China's adherence to absolute immunity ... unless China shifts to restrictive immunity'.[71]

---

68 This Law grants foreign central banks' assets the immunity from judicial enforcement within the Chinese territory. 中华人民共和国外国中央银行财产司法强制措施豁免法 (Law on Immunity of Assets of Foreign Central Banks from Judicial Compulsory Measures in China) (Promulgated by the NPC on 25 October 2005, effective on promulgation). Julian G. Ku, *supra* note 61, at 43.

69 *Democratic Republic of Congo and others v. FG Hemisphere Associates LLC*, [2009] 1 HKLRD 410 (Court of First Instance); [2010] 2 HKLRD 66 (Court of Appeal); and FACV 5-7/2010 (Court of Final Appeal).

70 'The Explanations on the Draft Interpretation of Paragraph 1, Article 12 and Article 19 of the Basic Law of the Hong Kong Special Administrative Region of the People's Republic of China by the Standing Committee of the National People's Congress', at the 22nd Session of the Standing Committee of the Eleventh National People's Congress on 24 August 2011, https://gia.info.gov.hk/general/201108/30/P201108300217_0217_83274.pdf, last accessed on 18 May 2021, p. 7.

71 Manjiao Chi, *supra* note 55. For a detailed discussion on China's position on sovereign immunity in ISA, see Manjiao Chi, 'The Impeding Effects of the Immunity Plea on International Arbitration: China's Position Revisited', *Asian International Arbitration Journal*, Vol. 12 Issue 1 (2016), pp. 21–39.

7.6 China's position on ISDS reform

China's position on ISDS reform has become gradually unequivocal when China submitted its reform proposal to the UNCITRAL Working Group III in 2019.[72] In China's view, the structural problems of the current ISDS regime include a lack of 'an institutionalized and reasonable mechanism for correcting errors', difficulty for 'arbitration tribunals in different cases to guarantee the stability and predictability of the awards', arbitrators' questionable professionalism and independence and the problem of double hatting, conflicts of interests in third-party funding, and lengthy and costly processes.[73] Hence, China recognizes the need to 'improve the rules for selection and disqualification of arbitrators to increase transparency and reasonableness', to actively promote conciliation as an alternative resolution measure, to include pre-arbitration consultation procedures, and to stipulate transparency rules for third-party funding.[74]

With regard to institutional reform, China advocates the establishment of a permanent appeal mechanism in addition to a reformed and improved investor–state arbitration at the first instance, which is shared by other countries such as Morocco, Chile, Israel, Japan and Ecuador.[75] The appeal mechanism would enable the disputing parties to seek error-correction, strengthen the legal predictability of ISA, establish limitations for the conduct of judges, and 'foster further standardization and clarification of procedures'.[76] Without delving into the detailed designs of the appeal mechanism, for example, how the adjudicators of the appeal would be selected, China is in the position that 'the right of parties to appoint arbitrators at the first-instance stage of investment arbitration ... should be retained in any reform process', because the disputing parties should control the composition of the tribunal, the suitability of the arbitrators and the expertise required for a particular case.[77]

China's position in ISDS reform is viewed by scholars as a middle ground: on the one hand, China acknowledges the structural deficiencies of the current ISA mechanism and prefers to reform the system in ways that go much beyond simple patchwork and is hence more systemic, *inter alia*, a permanent multilateral appeal. On the other hand, China still shies away from officially endorsing the Multilateral Investment Court (MIC) that is adamantly proposed by the

72 UNCITRAL Working Group III, 'Possible Reform of Investor-State Dispute Settlement (ISDS): Submission from the Government of China, A/CN.9/WG.III/WP.177', 19 July 2019, https://undocs.org/en/A/CN.9/WG.III/WP.177, last accessed on 10 May 2021.

73 Ibid, pp. 2–3.

74 Ibid, pp. 4–5.

75 Yuwen Li, 'The Notion and Development of International Investment Court', in Julien Chaisse, Leïla Choukroune and Sufian Jusoh (eds.), *Handbook of International Investment Law and Policy* (Singapore: Springer, 2021), pp. 1685–1704.

76 UNCITRAL Working Group III, *supra* note 72, p. 4.

77 Ibid.

European Union (EU), and prefers to retain the parties' rights to appoint arbitrators.[78] The EU intends to garner China's as well as other developing countries' support and endorsement for the MIC by adopting a mandate in its ongoing and future IIA negotiations which proposes to replace the current ISA regime with an Investment Court System starting at the bilateral level.[79] For those who were expecting a debut of an unprecedented 'EU–China Investment Court System' akin to its EU–Canada counterpart in the Comprehensive Economic and Trade Agreement, the much-anticipated conclusion of the EU–China Comprehensive Agreement on Investment (CAI) in December 2020 comes as dismay, as the Agreement at its current form has not yet included a chapter on ISDS.[80] It still remains to be seen whether and when China is willing to endorse the establishment of an MIC in the future.

7.7 Conclusion

China's IIA-making and its ISA practice are characterized by a dichotomy. On the one hand, as a capital-importing country, China wishes to protect its defensive interest as a host state. Chinese IIAs, and especially the early ones that include a first-generation ISDS provision, are intended to restrict foreign investors' access to ISA and retain the judicial prerogative at home in resolving investment disputes with foreign investors. China seeks to avoid being a respondent in ISA, and in the event that a case against China arises, China prioritizes the possibility of settlement with the claimant in order to avoid a potentially defeated award. On the other hand, as a capital-exporting country, China is also mindful of protecting its proactive interest as the home country of Chinese investors abroad. This is substantiated by China's vigorous engagement in international investment law, *inter alia*, concluding new-generation IIAs with important trading partners such as the CAI and the Regional Comprehensive Economic Partnership, expanding Chinese arbitration institutions' jurisdiction to ISA, and activism in ISDS reform in the context of the UNCITRAL Working Group III.

While recognizing certain perennial flaws in the existing ISDS system, China advocates for reform directed towards more transparency, consistency, predictability and the possibility of appeal as quality control. Foreign investors in China, at least for the time being, can expect that ISA is still a favoured option in

---

78 Ming Du and Wei Shen, 'The Future of Investor-State Dispute Settlement: Exploring China's Changing Attitude', in Julien Chaisse, Leïla Choukroune and Sufian Jusoh (eds.), *Handbook of International Investment Law and Policy* (Singapore: Springer, 2021), pp. 2483–2506. Yuwen Li and Cheng Bian, *supra* note 2, at 531.

79 Yuwen Li, *supra* note 75.

80 Section VI, Sub-section 2, Art. 3 of the EU–China CAI stipulates that the parties 'shall endeavour to complete such negotiations within 2 years of the signature of the present agreement' on 'state-of-the-art provisions in the field of investment dispute settlement, taking into account progress on structural reform of investment dispute settlement in the context of the UNCITRAL'.

protecting their treaty-based rights and interests. Nevertheless, China's position in ISDS may evolve in unpredictable ways affected by both internal and external circumstances. Foreign investors in China are well advised to advert to the ongoing ISDS reform in general, as well as to China's position in particular in designing their dispute settlement strategy.

Index

2015 Draft Foreign Investment Law 25, 98, 108–109, 119

Ad hoc arbitration: in foreign-related arbitration 153, 173; in investor-state arbitration 194–196
Administrative Licensing Law 143, 149
American Chamber of Commerce in China 25, 50, 122, 137
Anhui Longlide Packaging and Printing Co., Ltd. v. BP Agnati S.R.L. 162–164
Anti-Foreign Sanctions Law 8, 30, 52, 54, 57, 104, 106, 107; Countermeasure List 30, 32, 51, 52, 54, 57, 106
Anti-Monopoly Law 22, 79, 82, 108; anti-monopoly review 32, 77, 79, 82, 92–93, 101, 138, 146
Anti-Unfair Competition Law 128, 149
Arbitration Law 151–154, 156–158, 160, 162–165, 169–171, 173, 174, 177, 181, 196–197; 2021 Draft Amendment 153, 158, 167, 171, 173, 196; SPC Judicial Interpretation 154, 163
Arbitration-related judicial review 154, 171–172; governing law 174–175; jurisdiction 173–174; public interest as exception for enforcement 177–179; report and verification system 175–177; scope 172–173; standards for setting aside 177

Beijing Arbitration Commission (BAC) 155–157, 159, 169, 196, 198
Beijing Cottonfield v. Muji 128–129
Beijing Joint Declaration 159
Belt and Road Initiative 49, 153, 154, 159, 167, 181

Branches of a foreign company 34–35
Brentwood Industries Inc. v. Guangdong Fa-anlong Mechanical Equipment Manufacture Co., Ltd. 166–167
Business license of legal persons 83

Cangzhou Donghong Packing Materials Co., Ltd. v. DMT Ltd. 161–162
Carlyle–Xugong takeover 94, 117
case-by-case approval 5, 6, 15, 17, 18, 23–25, 35, 40, 46–49, 55, 56, 70, 72, 80, 87, 100, 101, 131, 139, 140, 145
Catalogue of Industries Guiding Foreign Investment 5, 6, 20–21, 23, 32, 46–49, 62, 72, 99, 139
Central National Security Commission (CNSC) 102–103
China–Hong Kong Closer Economic Partnership Arrangement (CEPA) 59
China International Commercial Courts (CICC) 169–170, 174
China International Economic and Trade Arbitration Commission (CIETAC) 152–158, 160, 169, 178, 180, 196, 198
China National Intellectual Property Administration (CNIPA) 121, 123, 124; Patent Office 121, 123; Trademark Office 121, 125, 126
China Securities Regulatory Commission (CSRC) 33, 47, 84–88, 94, 98
China-US bilateral investment treaty (BIT) 23–24, 59
Chinese Africa Joint Arbitration Centres 159
Chinese bilateral investment treaties (BITs): exhaustion of local remedies 193–195; selection of arbitration

institution 195–197; three
generations of Chinese BITs 187–188
Civil Procedure Law 151–152, 154,
161, 166, 169–173, 177
Coca-Cola–Huiyuan takeover 93
commercial secrets 147–149
Committee on Foreign Investment of
the United States (CFIUS) 90–91,
112, 114, 118, 119
Communist Party of China (CPC) 16,
19, 102, 107
Companies limited by shares 33–35, 44
Company Law 17, 24, 33–35, 43–44,
48, 75, 146
complaint system 38, 42–43
Comprehensive Agreement on
Investment (CAI) 59, 201
Contract Law 17, 20, 97, 99
Convention on the Recognition and
Enforcement of Foreign Arbitral
Awards (New York Convention)
13, 152, 161, 166, 197; China's
reservation 158, 197, 198
Convention on the Settlement of
Investment Disputes between States
and Nationals of Other States (ICSID
Convention) 13, 192, 197
Copyright Law 12, 120, 134, 135
Corporate governance of foreign-
invested enterprises (FIEs) 17, 24,
43–44, 48
Corruption Perceptions Index 1
counterfeiting and piracy 129–131,
136, 150
Covid-19 pandemic 1, 7, 27, 104
Criminal Code 149

*Daesung Industrial Gases Co., Ltd., et
al. v. Praxair (China) Investment Co.,
Ltd.* 164–165
deglobalization 7
*Democratic Republic of the Congo v. FG
Hemisphere LLC* 199
Deng Xiaoping's Southern Tour 19
dual-track system 5, 9, 20, 43

enforcement of arbitral awards:
foreign-related and foreign
commercial arbitral awards
179–181; investor-state arbitral
awards 197–199; sovereign immunity
198–199
environmental impact assessment 53, 55
European Union 8, 13, 26, 91, 116, 201

European Union Chamber of Commerce
in China 25, 51, 71, 92, 122
Export Control Law 8, 9, 28–29,
103–105, 107
expropriation: relating to investor-state
arbitration 185–187; relating to the
Foreign Investment Law 41, 67–68;
relating to the interpretation of the
amount of compensation 187–193

financial sector 6, 62, 67, 111; banking
sector 47, 56–57, 62–65, 69, 97
fixed-asset investment project approval
32, 52, 55, 78, 81, 101
Forced transfer of technology (FTT)
6, 40, 150; accusations of FTT in
China 136–142; effectiveness and
ineffectiveness of the FIL in curbing
FTT 145–147; paradoxical narrative
of FTT 142–145
Foreign direct investment (FDI):
China's allure for FDI 3–4; China's
FDI inflow 1–2, 74; a policy mix of
incentive and control 21, 44
foreign exchange control 18, 20–22, 33,
41–42
foreign-invested enterprise (FIE):
contractual joint venture (CJV) 5,
17, 19, 20, 33, 43, 44, 46; equity
joint venture (EJV) 5, 16, 21, 33,
43, 44, 46, 67; wholly foreign-owned
enterprise (WFOE) 2, 4, 5, 17, 21,
33, 43, 44, 46, 76, 95, 96, 100, 176
foreign-invested start-up investment
company 35–36, 77
Foreign Investment Law (FIL): Article
2 (definition of foreign investment)
10, 75; Article 4 (pre-establishment
national treatment with a negative
list approach) 38, 48, 81; Article
5 (protection of foreign investors'
legitimate rights and interests)
41; Article 9 (equal application of
supportive national policies) 65;
Article 15 (standard setting) 66;
Article 16 (government procurement)
66; Article 20 (expropriation) 41, 67;
Article 21 (free transfer of investment
assets) 41; Article 22 (intellectual
property rights protection, prohibition
of forced transfer of technology) 42,
136, 143, 145, 147, 150; Article
23 (prohibition on divulgation of
commercial secrets) 42, 148, 150;

Article 26 (complaint system) 27, 42–43; Article 28 (negative list for foreign investment) 38, 54, 65; Article 30 (licensing) 66; Article 31 (corporate governance of FIEs) 43–44; Article 34 (information reporting) 27, 39, 40; Article 35 (national security review) 11, 27, 39, 54, 104, 109, 118, 146; Article 39 (legal liability of divulgation of commercial secrets) 149, 150; Article 42 (five-year grace period) 43

Foreign Investment Law (FIL) Implementing Regulation: Article 6 (equal treatment in business operation) 65; Article 12 (equal application in state preferential policies) 65; Article 13 (equal participation in standard setting) 66; Article 14 (equal application in compulsory national standards) 66; Article 15 (equal application in government procurement) 66; Article 21 (expropriation) 67; Article 23 (intellectual property right protection) 136; Article 24 (Prohibition of forced transfer of technology) 145; Article 25 (commercial secrets) 148; Article 40 (national security review) 39

Foreign mergers and acquisitions (M&A): approval for listed target companies 83–89; approval for non-listed target companies 77–83; flow 73–74; foreign complaints 90–100

General Agreement on Tariffs and Trade (GATT) 20

Global Innovation Index 1, 121

greenfield investment 5, 14, 52–54, 73–75, 80, 81, 100, 101, 104, 108, 110, 116

Hela Schwarz GmbH v. China 67–68, 184, 186, 194–195

Holistic national security outlook 102–103, 106–107, 110

Hong Kong International Arbitration Centre (HKIAC) 159

Huawei 7, 8, 27–29

Inbound and outbound M&As 90

indirect investment 41, 75, 100, 104, 110, 116

information reporting system 6, 24, 25, 27, 33, 38–41, 48, 72

Intellectual Property Court 12, 132

Internationalization of Chinese arbitration institutions 154–160

Internet Court 132–133

investment FIE 35–36, 77

investor-state arbitration: China as a respondent 182–187; China's position on ISDS reform 200–201; Chinese investors as claimants 188

IP infringement 121, 122, 130, 133, 135

IP litigation 132–133; judicial bias 133–134; low damages awarded 134

a lack of level playing field 50, 68, 83, 89–91

lack of reciprocity 38, 48–50, 56, 91, 101

land use right 5, 18, 47, 53, 55; in investor-State arbitration 67, 184, 186–187, 194

Lax law enforcement 6, 26, 122, 130–131, 133, 136, 150

Lego v. Lepin 135

Lilly Company v. Watson Pharmaceuticals (Changzhou) Co., Ltd. 134–135

limited liability companies 33–35, 44

local content requirement 19, 21

local protectionism 32, 41, 72, 83, 132, 133, 175

low quality of patents 123–124

Made in China 2025 49–51, 70, 144–145

Michael Jordan v. Qiaodan 126–127

Ministry of Commerce (MOFCOM) 22–24, 29, 32, 36, 39, 40, 42, 47, 52, 60, 62, 73, 76, 78, 80, 84, 87, 88, 93, 94, 98, 101, 104, 107–109, 112–113, 117, 146, 147

Multilateral Investment Court (MIC) 200–201

National Copyright Administration 121

National Development and Reform Commission (NDRC) 11, 24, 32, 39, 47, 52, 55, 60, 62, 78, 81, 107, 109, 112–113, 115, 118, 146, 147

National Enterprise Credit Information Publicity System 39, 40

National Security Law 103, 106, 107, 110

National security review: evolution 107–109; national security concept 110; outcome 114–115; in the

PFTZs 108–109; recommended improvement 115–119; review procedure 113–114; sectors subject to review 111–112; transactions subject to review 110–111; Working Mechanism 112–113

Negative List for Foreign Investment 10, 26, 32–34, 37, 38, 48, 51, 52, 54, 56, 57, 60–65, 71, 72, 77, 78, 80, 81, 101, 131, 139, 146

Negative List for Foreign Investment in Hainan Free Trade Port (HFTP) 26, 62

Negative List for Foreign Investment in the Pilot Free Trade Zones (PFTZs) 26, 52, 59–61, 78

Negative List for Market Access 33, 52, 54, 56–57, 60, 62, 66, 72, 78, 81, 139, 146, 150

Ningbo Beilun Licheng Lubricating Oil Co., Ltd. v. Formal Venture Corp. 165–166

Notice on Further Facilitating Cross-Border Trade and Investment (Order No. 28) 37, 77

Online Enterprise Registration System 39, 40, 83

Organisation for Economic Co-operation and Development (OECD) 22, 83; Guidelines for Recipient Country Investment Policies relating to National Security 116–118; Regulatory Restrictive Index 6–7

partnership enterprise 33, 34, 36, 43, 48, 146

Patent Law 12, 120, 134

People's Bank of China (PBoC) 33, 56

Pilot Free Trade Zone (PFTZ) 24, 52, 59–62, 78, 80, 108, 196; Hainan Free Trade Port (HFTP) 26, 61–62; LinGang New Area in Shanghai PFTZ 167–168; Shanghai PFTZ 24, 47, 167, 176

post-establishment national/ equal treatment: in government procurement 66; lack of enforceability 68–71; in national preferential policies 65; in sectoral approval and licencing 66–67; in standard setting 66

pre-establishment national treatment with a negative list approach 6, 10, 14, 23, 24, 38, 48–51, 55, 58–59, 71, 80, 81, 145

Preferential treatment to foreign-invested enterprises (FIEs) 5, 18, 32

Provisions on Mergers and Acquisitions of Domestic Enterprises by Foreign Investors (Order No. 10) 15, 23, 76, 78, 80–81, 101, 108

Qualified Foreign Institutional Investor (QFII) 84–87, 101

Qualified Foreign Limited Partner (QFLP) private equity investment fund 35, 36, 77

Red-chip enterprise 98

reform and opening up 1, 5, 16, 19, 44

Regional Comprehensive Economic Partnership (RCEP) 59, 182, 201

Registration of establishment of legal persons 47, 52, 54–55, 79, 83

representative office 34–35

Rules on Counteracting Unjustified Extra-Territorial Application of Foreign Legislation and Measures (Blocking Rules) 8, 29–30, 57, 104–107

selective/targeted law enforcement 11, 71, 92–94, 101

Shanghai International Arbitration Center (SHIAC) 155, 159, 169

Shenzhen Court of International Arbitration (SCIA) 155, 157–159, 169, 179, 196, 198

socialist market economy 19, 45

special economic Zone (SEZ) 5, 18–20, 31

standard essential patent (SEP) 138, 141, 146

State Administration for Market Regulation (SAMR) 24, 33, 35, 39, 40, 79, 82, 83, 121, 141, 146

State Administration of Foreign Exchange (SAFE) 22, 33, 37, 40, 41, 77, 85, 86

state-led economy 50, 68, 71

State-Owned Assets Supervision and Administration Commission (SASAC) 33, 47, 78, 81–82, 94, 118, 139

State-owned enterprise (SOE) 14, 19, 22, 32, 33, 45, 62, 68–73, 82, 92–94, 139, 148

Stock Connect 84, 88–89, 101
strategic foreign investor 84, 87–88, 101
Supreme People's Court (SPC) 31,
 98, 99, 120, 127, 132, 134, 135,
 151, 154, 158, 162–166, 169–172,
 174–176, 178–181, 198

Tesla 4, 125
three primary foreign investment laws
 17, 25, 33, 43, 46, 48, 72, 146
trademark squatting 124–129, 136, 150
Trump administration 5, 29, 45

United Nations Commission
 on International Trade
 Law (UNCITRAL): Arbitration
 Rules 157, 183, 188, 195; Model
 Law on International Commercial
 Arbitration 153; Working Group III
 200, 201
United Nations Conference
 on Trade and Development
 (UNCTAD) 58, 74
United States Trade Representative
 (USTR) 301 Investigation 57, 137,
 139, 142–143, 147
Unreliable Entity List 8, 27–28, 32, 51,
 52, 54, 57, 104–105, 107
US-China Business Council 65, 137

US-China Tech War 7
US-China Trade War 5, 7, 25, 38, 45,
 51, 104, 138; Phase I Agreement 6,
 62, 143
US Department of Commerce 7, 8, 27

Variable interest entity (VIE): Alibaba
 96–97; benefits 97; compliance and
 regulatory problems 97–98; judicial
 cases 98–100; legality 98; purpose 96;
 structure 94–95
Vienna Convention on the Law of
 Treaties (VCLT) 189, 192, 193

World Intellectual Property
 Organization (WIPO) 1, 121; WIPO
 Arbitration and Mediation Shanghai
 Service 168
World Trade Organization (WTO) 21,
 22, 56, 70, 71, 137, 138

Xin Bai Lun v. New Barlun 127–128

Yonghui-Zhongbai acquisition 118–119

zoning approval 47, 53, 55
*Zublin International GmbH v. Wuxi
 Woke General Engineering Rubber
 Co., Ltd.* 160–161

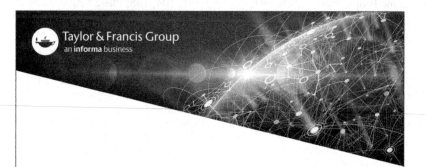

Printed in the United States
by Baker & Taylor Publisher Services